Milly Pierce

A Slave Turned Slave-Owner in Pre-Civil War Virginia

by

CeCe Bullard

Library of Congress Cataloging-in-Publication Data

Milly Pierce: A Slave Turned Slave-Owner in Pre-Civil War Virginia,

CeCe Bullard

Summary: This is the true story of Milly Pierce, an enslaved woman who won her freedom and found that the only way she could survive was to herself become a slaveholder in pre-Civil War Virginia.

E-ISBN: 978-1530178599

Published by Miniver Press, LLC, McLean Virginia
Copyright 2016 Kristie Miller
Interior Design by Janet McNulty

All rights reserved under International and Pan-American Copyright Conventions. By payment of the required fees, you have been granted the non-exclusive, non-transferable right to access and read the text of this print or e-book. No part of this text may be reproduced, transmitted, down-loaded, decompiled, reverse engineered, or stored in or introduced into any information storage and retrieval system, in any form or by any means, whether electronic or mechanical, now known or hereinafter invented, without the express written permission of Nell Minow. For information regarding permission, write to editor@miniverpress.com

First edition June 2016

Injustice, poverty, slavery, ignorance—these may be cured by reform or revolution. But men do not live by fighting evils. They live by positive goals, individual and collective, a vast variety of them, seldom predictable, at time incompatible.

Isaiah Berlin

…history is that impossible thing, the attempt to give an account, with incomplete knowledge, of actions themselves undertaken with incomplete knowledge. So that it teaches us no short-cuts to salvation, no recipe for a new world, only the dogged and patient art of making do.

Graham Swift, Waterland

CONTENTS

I. FREE NEGROES: A MOST PECULIAR SITUATION	1
II MILLY PIERCE: A FOOTHOLD AMONG THE FREE	11
III LYDIA PIERCE COUSINS: THE MIDDLE GROUND	103
IV JOHN PIERCE, JR.: WHITE AMBITION	135
V AN ENDURING LEGACY	205
NOTES	211
SELECTED BIBLIOGRAPHY	235

I.

FREE NEGROES: A MOST PECULIAR SITUATION

A slave, she was born the chattel of a white man. At twenty-five, already the mother of five, she became a "free Negroe." In a society built upon the absolute distinction between black and white, slave and master, Milly Pierce in 1795 found herself adrift in a shadow land.

FREE BLACKS: NEITHER SLAVER NOR MASTER

Slavery has been called "the peculiar institution," but Milly Pierce's legal and social position as a free black was even more peculiar. In ante-bellum Virginia, center stage was occupied by a powerful but small white majority and a powerless but burgeoning black minority, locked in a fateful embrace. In the wing, a few free blacks hovered uncertainly. They had no voice, and no well-defined role, yet their lives hung in the balance, every twist and turn in the drama affecting their fate. Ultimately, their very existence was a choral commentary on the horrors of slavery, and too close for comfort to the protagonists, they were, unwillingly, drawn into the impeding tragedy.

Like all people consigned to a social and legal limbo, free blacks haunted the imaginations and consciences of their oppressors. Just as feminists today inflame the antagonism of the political and religious right and rally the faithful to the cause of "family values," free blacks aroused in those who persecuted them an unsavory mixture of fear, racism and regret—and, perversely, energized the supporters of slavery. As early as 1691, Virginia's ruling class wanted free blacks—perceived as a danger to the "peace of the colony"—out of sight and out of mind. The assembly first forbade masters to liberate their slaves unless they paid for their transport out of the colony. Then, in 1723, they summarily banned private manumission. Driven by loathing and guilt, the white oppressors circled, determined to maintain and rationalize their position of superiority, while the oppressed tumbled helplessly in a vortex of suspicion and fear.[1]

FREE BLACKS: THE GREAT AMERICAN ANOMALY

If they could not bring themselves to effect a final solution to the free black problem, if they shied away from severing forever the word free from black, white Virginians still could not accept the idea that a black might be treated as an equal. Slavery was the great American paradox; free Negroes were the great American anomaly. Mistrusted as a class and marginalized as individuals, free African Americans were almost a part of the American dream, yet remained always apart—on the fringes of freedom.

Free blacks in Virginia never enjoyed all of the rights assumed as natural and inalienable by the white citizenry. When the House of Burgesses abolished private manumissions of slaves in 1723, it also, at the urging of Virginia's Governor, denied

---

[1] William W. Hening, comp., *The Statues at Large; Being a Compilation of All the Laws of Virginia*. 13 vols., (Richmond, New York, Philadelphia, 1800-1823), III. p. 87 [1691 law] *ibid.*, IV, p. 133-4 [1723 law]

Milly Pierce

free blacks "the great Privilege of a Freeman"—the right to vote. The Governor believed it imperative that the law must "make the Free Negroes sensible that a distinction ought to be made between their offspring and the Descendents of an Englishman with whom they were never to be accounted Equal." [2]

Almost free but never equal to whites, less valuable and therefore more vulnerable than slaves, Virginia's free blacks were convenient scapegoats, their fate inextricably entangled in the web of rationalization and paranoia that surrounded the institution of slavery. The more agitated white Virginians became about slavery, both as a moral question and a peril to the stability of the state, the more vigorous became their attacks on the freedoms of emancipated blacks.

Often described as shiftless troublemakers, free blacks were suspected of fomenting slave insurrections, although there is little evidence to support this accusation. Any direct threat they posed to the status quo was more imagined than real. Milly Pierce was, however, truly subversive, although in ways that the white slave-owner could never afford to admit: her very existence and especially her economic success undermined the carefully cultivated rationale that slavery was a benevolent institution for a benighted people.

---

[2]Hening, *op. cit.* IV, pp. 133-134 [1723 loss of vote]; Donald R. Wright, *African Americans in the Colonial Period: From African Origins through the American Revolution* (Arlington Heights, Ill., 1990), p. 123 [Hugh Drysdale quote]

CeCe Bullard

WHITE AMBIVALENCE

Why did a society, structured on a simple but absolute divide between whites who were by birth entitled to freedom and blacks who were "by Nature" suited only to slavery, tolerate a third, ambiguous class of people who were neither white nor slaves? From the first, free blacks were a tiny splinter that festered in the consciences and inflamed the fears of white slave-owners. Deeply ambivalent about the institution of slavery and even more conflicted about the humanity of individual blacks, white Virginians agonized endlessly over what to do about an even more troubling and troublesome class—free Negroes. At best, they were a nuisance; at worst, a nightmare. Yet, against all logic and self-interest, the white master race always stopped short of enslaving or eliminating them.

Why? Because ultimately, despite their convoluted rhetoric to the contrary, white southerners could not deny the humanity of free blacks. Because, somewhere deep in the recesses of their consciences, white slave-owners knew that slavery was an abomination. Because, having recently fought for their own freedom from oppression, Americans valued liberty above all. And, because, Milly Pierce and many others in this troubling class, despite their dark skin, were their faithful servants, their peaceable neighbors—and their children.

Milly Pierce

FREE BLACKS AND THE LAW: AN EVER TIGHTENING VISE

The desire to control, if not eliminate, this most disturbing class of people generated a disproportionate amount of legislation and public debate in Virginia. As a consequence of this preoccupation, the public record provides an adequate, if impersonal, outline of the free black experience in Virginia, albeit solely from the white point of view. The laws regarding free blacks began to appear just after the middle of the seventeenth century when, having pushed the terms of white indentured servitude to the limit, the colonists settled upon enslaved blacks as the solution to their labor problems. Greed had outrun principle, and henceforth Virginians would rely on black slaves to produce Virginia's "gold"—tobacco. Faced with a flood of imported slaves, the colonial assembly began to create the laws that would constitute Virginia's slave code.[3]

As the colonists laid the legal foundations for institutionalized slavery, they simultaneously sought to define and limit the free black class. The first law regarding free blacks was both a simple clarification and an acknowledgment, if indirect, that there was a distinct group of people who were both black and free. The law, passed in 1662, stated that the child of an Englishman and a Negro woman would be recognized as a slave or as a free person depending upon the status of the mother.

---

[3]Edmund S. Morgan, *American Slavery, American Freedom: The Ordeal of Colonial Virginia* (New York, 1975) offers an excellent discussion of the American paradox and the evolution of slavery in colonial Virginia.

The General Assembly's recognition of free blacks did not necessarily entail a guarantee of their freedom—much less equality. Instead, it proved to be an incitement to suppression, and an act of 1668, directed specifically at free black women, signaled the bedrock of resistance to full equality for free blacks that would endure until the Civil War. Denied many of the rights accorded white citizens, free blacks were never relieved of all of the responsibilities that accompanied those rights, a situation succinctly spelled out in the 1668 law:

> It is declared by this general assembly that Negro women, though permitted to enjoy their freedom, yet ought not in all respects be admitted to a full fruition of the exemptions and impunities of the English, and are still liable to payment of taxes. [4]

Milly Pierce and her sisters, unlike white women, would never enjoy one of the few legal benefits accorded their sex—freedom from taxation.

MILLY PIERCE: CASTING A LONG SHADOW

The official record makes the status of the free black class and the attitudes of whites quite clear. To capture the life experience of an individual free black, however, is another matter. Those few individuals who do emerge as more than a name in a document must be regarded as exceptional. Only a few free African Americans enjoyed enough economic success to have their holdings, either real or personal,

---

[4]Hening, *op cit.*, II, p. 167 [1662 law—mother status of child]; *ibid.*, II, p. 267 [1668 law free black women to pay tax]

Milly Pierce

recorded regularly in the county tax ledgers. An even smaller number appear in the reports of the Overseers of the Poor as laborers to be bound out as punishment for minor crimes or to pay off their debts. A very few free blacks can be identified in various court proceedings, both civil and criminal. Virtually nothing, however, is recorded about the vast majority of ante-bellum free blacks who led lives of minimal self-sufficiency or quiet desperation.

Among the exceptional cases in which it is possible to create a coherent and revealing picture of an individual life is Milly Pierce of Goochland County in Piedmont Virginia. As with the histories of many private persons, black or white, Milly's story must be stitched together from the barest of facts and basted with occasional surmise. There are no letters or diaries or newspaper clippings to fill the interstices or to animate the facts with lively detail. Yet, the simple outline of Milly's life captures the character and courage of a woman who succeeded in the face of seemingly insurmountable obstacles. If she were entirely typical of her class, we would know even less about her than we do, but she did walk the same common ground on the same narrow path as her peers. She simply cast a longer, bolder shadow than many. [5]

---

[5] In later years, Milly is sometimes referred to as Mildred, but, early on and most often, she is called Milly. Her surname varies in spelling occasionally, sometimes spelled Pearce rather than Pierce.

CeCe Bullard

A MIRROR OF HER TIME AND PLACE

Milly's life is the backbone of this story, but not the whole story. Her life was framed by the two defining moments in this nation's history. Milly walked away from slavery and secured a comfortable life for herself and her family, despite growing hostility and limitations on her freedom, during the same period in which the country moved from the idealism of the war for independence to the disillusion of the Civil War. A beneficiary of the revolutionary faith in freedom, she was a precursor of the war for her race's liberation. Black, female and on her own, Milly embodies in many ways the long, complex and convoluted quest for freedom that continues to characterize the odyssey of American minorities.

Milly's life mirrored the national landscape; but it was also deeply rooted in a particular time and place. Life in a sparsely populated, rural county such as Goochland was a tightly woven tapestry of constantly intersecting lives. What renders Milly's story especially rich and rewarding is not merely the single thread of her life, but also the several stories of her extended family and neighbors which both weave through and lead beyond her own. Collectively, these stories both reinforce the central, peculiar realities of all free black lives and highlight the myriad ways in which individuals either transcended or succumbed to the pressure of unremitting prejudice.

During her eighty years, Milly, like every free person of color, was subjected to increasingly restrictive and sometimes punitive laws designed to limit the freedoms of the not-quite-free black population and to restrict its growth. As the prevailing degree of white paranoia rose, Virginia's legislators tightened the vise. In the course of

Milly Pierce

Milly's life, she lost the right to travel freely, the right to worship as she chose, the right to assemble, the right to an education, and the right to trial by jury. By the time the opening shot of the Civil War echoed across Charleston harbor, free blacks had lost many of their basic rights; their freedom, although severely compromised, was almost all they had left to lose.

While the strictures of the law forced many free blacks to abandon their homes or suffer re-enslavement, others, overwhelmed by unaccustomed challenges and responsibilities, saw freedom slip through their fingers and were reduced to involuntary servitude. A few, like Milly, held their ground (both literally and figuratively) and made the most of their precious, if fragile and imperfect, freedom.

A BLACK WOMAN OF EXCEPTIONAL CHARACTER

Survival for free blacks was, perhaps above all, a question of character. Eventually, slaveowners were allowed to manumit only those slaves who demonstrated "extraordinary merit and general good character and conduct." Character, however, was much more than a question of statutory law for free blacks in ante-bellum Virginia. To negotiate a maze of crippling and entrapping laws, a free black must have possessed iron will and extreme patience. To win the acceptance of the white community, a free black must have been constantly working, honest and responsible. To face a hostile world bent upon her destruction, a free black must have drawn on deep reserves of courage. Simply to be tolerated, a free black had to be above reproach—a standard far from foreign to today's African Americans.

CeCe Bullard

Milly shouldered not only the burden of her color, but also of her gender. To be both black and female was to live in double jeopardy. When Thomas Jefferson declared "all men are created equal" he really meant all white males. A woman's economic survival, regardless of her color, most often depended on a good marriage, yet marriage marked the end of her legal and economic independence. Milly Pierce remained by choice unmarried and in control of her own destiny, and she took full advantage of those few rights granted her. She availed herself of the right to work for wages and the right to own property and achieved economic security for herself and her family. She did precisely what the white patriarchy wished to believe was beyond the capabilities of a woman and a former slave.

Milly Pierce did not merely survive white oppression, she made a place for herself in the white power structure—and prospered. Milly Pierce was truly a "free woman of colour" rather than a freed slave. Somehow she turned a critical corner when given her freedom: she did not accept her freedom meekly as a gift from her white master; she claimed that freedom as her own natural condition. Faced with a freedom that was fraught with both promise and fear, Milly Pierce proceeded to piece together her own peculiar life—a life that actually bridged the great divide between black slave and white master—and make it work.

II

MILLY PIERCE: A FOOTHOLD AMONG THE FREE

At 80, her back may have been bent, her legs may have been bowed, but Milly Pierce's spirit was strong and serene. Rocking quietly on her porch, just across the green from the Courthouse—her domain—she may have nodded as Judge Clopton tipped his hat on his way to court, a measure of the respect she had reaped during her long life. Perhaps on market days, she avoided the porch, and her perfect view of the slaves being led to the auction block. Had she happened to glimpse them, she might have been forced to acknowledge that "There, but for the grace of God..."

Born a slave, Milly Pierce would become a free woman of property. By 1805, Milly owned 23 acres in Goochland County, Virginia, which she leased profitably to a white farmer, Samuel Johnson. Milly's "reputed" husband, John Pierce, was property, a slave owned by a local doctor, James Brydin. Milly and John Pierce's son, John Pierce, Jr., then about 12, would become a prosperous dealer in property, both real and, ironically, human. [6]

This extraordinary family saga centers, however, on Milly—an unmarried black woman, member of a despised class and matriarch of a large family—a center

---

[6] Goochland County Deed Book (GDB) 19, pp. 365-6 [Milly's lease to Samuel Johnson]. Milly was apparently illiterate. She always signed with an "X." GDB 18, p. 679 ["reputed" husband owned by Brydin]; Goochland County Register of Free Negroes (GFN) # 128 John Pierce, Jr. registered in 1814 at 21.

that, against all odds, held. Given the circumstances of her birth, the prospect of a long and prosperous life as a free woman was, at best, remote. Like most of her race, Milly seemed destined to a life of despotism and drudgery as just one more cog in the slave-driven economy that sustained southern society.

She began life as just plain Milly, a slave without a surname, the property of Tucker Woodson. Member of a prominent Goochland family, Woodson lived at "Brightly," a comfortable 600 acre plantation along the James River, just south of Goochland Courthouse. Of Quaker stock, Woodson, perhaps as a matter of conscience and most probably as an act of gratitude for services rendered, emancipated Milly and her children—Jude, Lucy, and Ledy—in his will. When the will was proved September 21, 1795, "Mary Pollock and Margaret Payne made oath that the testator declared on the 18th day of May 1895 that the children (Jack and Sukey) of Milly the Negro woman in the testator's will named, and born since the execution thereof, should likewise be free at his death as well also as her further increase..." [7]

Virginia's Quakers had worked diligently for many years to legalize private manumission by deed or will, an early colonial prerogative that had been revoked in

---

[7] Tucker Woodson was a descendant of John Woodson (died 1715) who, rather than being "a typical Friend farmer" was a large landowner in the Richmond area, including several thousand acres in what would become Goochland Jay Worrall, Jr., *The Friendly Virginians: America's First Quakers* (Athens, Ga., 1994), p. 85. Tucker Woodson may no longer have been a practicing Quaker. His son Samuel, forced to chose between his faith and fighting in the Revolution, chose the latter—Worral, *op. cit.*, p. 219, and in 1778 John Woodson (3) was a member of the vestry when Beaverdam Episcopal Church in Goochland was founded (Helene B. Agee, *Facets of Goochland County Historical Society Magazine* vol. 9, no. 2, pp. 32-35. GLT 1793 [Woodson 600 acres]; GDB 16, pp. 484-5 [Tucker Woodson's will]

Milly Pierce

1723. When in 1782, their efforts were rewarded by the legislature, many Friends promptly responded and emancipated their slaves. On October 21, 1782, Thomas Pleasants, Jr. was one of several Goochland Quakers who arrived at the county Courthouse to record deeds of manumission. The sentiments expressed by Pleasants when he freed his forty-four slaves may reflect the spirit in which Tucker Woodson penned the will that liberated Milly and her children, the last of his slaves: "being fully persuaded that freedom is the natural right of all Mankind and that it is my duty to do unto others as I would desire to be done by in the like situation…I do hereby set free all and every [one of my slaves who] are to enjoy the benefit of freedom in as full and simple manner as if they had been born to free parents." [8]

Quaker idealism may well have inspired Tucker Woodson's decision to emancipate Milly and her children in his will. Pragmatism too quite probably figured in his decision. Wills rather than deeds of manumission were, for good reason, the most popular instrument of emancipation. The slaveowner, having enjoyed full benefit of his slaves' labor during his lifetime, could still die with a clear conscience, having finally done the right thing. [9]

---

[8] Hening, *op. cit.*, IV p. 132 [1723 law revokes private manumission]; Worrall, *op. cit.*, pp. 225-7 [Quakers and the private manumission law of 1782]; Hening, *op. cit.*, VI, pp. 39-40 [Law of 1782—reinstates manumission]; GDB 13, p. 246 [Thomas Pleasants, Jr., deed of manumission]. Also manumitting their slaves that day were Mary Youngblood and Benjamin Watkins. The language of the deeds is identical suggesting its origin in the Quaker Meeting.

[9] John H. Russell, *The Free Negro in Virginia 1619-1865* (Baltimore 1913), pp. 84-86 [Emancipation by will]

CeCe Bullard

A FREE WOMAN OF PROPERTY

Possessed of her freedom and five children to feed and clothe, Milly, then 25 years old, must have regarded the future with anticipation and trepidation in almost equal measure. Whatever fears she may have felt as she surveyed the uncharted territory before her, Milly apparently approached her new life with the courage and determination that were to be hallmarks of her character. With no more than a toehold on the ill-defined middle ground between slavery and freedom—the domain of all free blacks—Milly never missed a step as she worked her way toward the economic security that would make her freedom not merely a legal technicality but an enduring reality.

In less than eight years of freedom, Milly managed to save 138 pounds with which she purchased 23 acres of land on Beaverdam Creek, just a quarter of a mile southeast of Goochland Courthouse. No small feat for a young, newly emancipated slave who was, by then, the mother of nine. Her walk from her master's house to the Courthouse to obtain her deed was short, but it was a momentous step in her life. On a personal and social level, Milly's modest acquisition rivaled Thomas Jefferson's recent Louisiana Purchase in importance. [10]

Milly was the first free black woman, and one of the first three free blacks, to purchase land in Goochland county. A landmark in the progress of free blacks in Goochland, her acquisition of real property had symbolic as well as economic

---

[10] GDB 18, p. 679 [Payne to Pierce deed]

significance. With her purchase, Milly distanced herself not only from slaves, but from the majority of her own class. Slaves were denied the right to own property, and few free blacks could afford it. [11]

For a woman, black or white, to purchase property was in itself a rarity. Milly was one of just twenty-two free black women to own land in Goochland prior to the Civil War, and, like the majority of nineteenth century women, most had acquired their property through inheritance. Of Goochland's female free black landowners, at least thirteen had inherited their land. In the first decade of the century, only Elizabeth Grantham, a free mulatto and mid-wife, owned more property than Milly, but Grantham had inherited her 47 acres from her husband, David, and held it only as custodian for her son, James Mealy, the ultimate heir. [12]

---

[11] Goochland Land Tax (GLT), 1804. In this year, and others, the tax collector did not note which of the tax payers was a free black; but none of those listed can be identified as a free black, except Milly. Before 1804, only Roger Cooper and David Grantham can be identified as free black landowners.

[12] GLT 1797 to 1860 [Free black female landowners]. Other women who owned land in Goochland prior to 1860 were Bridget Allen (inheritance), Sally Banks (inheritance), Martha Brooks (inheritance), Mary Cook (inheritance), Evelina Copland (inheritance), Louisa Copland (inheritance), Lydia Pierce Cousins (inheritance and purchase), Chloe Cousins (inheritance), Margaret Cousins, Polly, Cousins, Susanna Cousins (inheritance), Paulina Fox, Sally Fulcher, Polly Fulcher (inheritance), Elizabeth Grantham (inheritance), Milly James (owned jointly with Timothy Pleasants), Charlotte Lynch (inheritance), Salina Lynch, Jane Pierce (inheritance and purchase), Mary Pierce (inheritance and purchase), and Rissa (no surname). Lebsock, *op. cit.*, p. 164 [women and property]; GOB 19. P. 64 [David Grantham's Will] Grantham is also spelled Grantum in the Goochland records. The Mealys remain in Goochland today, owners of the Mealy Funeral Home and prominent members of the community.

Milly's land was solely hers to do with as she pleased, and an enterprising, even ambitious woman, she soon turned her property into a moneymaking proposition. In 1805, she placed her mark on a lease to Samuel Johnson who agreed to pay her an annual rent of $33.67 for ten years. The lease is a thoughtful and careful document. Milly did not hesitate to spell out certain restrictions on Johnson's tenancy and to reserve for herself and her family the right to erect a dwelling on the land and to maintain a garden there. Milly's lease is not a document dictated by a black woman who found bargaining with a white man intimidating, rather it is the work of a property owner confident in the assertion of her prerogatives. [13]

MAKING A LIVING, BUILDING A NEST EGG

Milly's rise from slave to free landowner was pivotal to the Pierce family's progress toward the independence that only economic security can provide, but how, in a mere ten years, had a former slave become a woman of property with a guaranteed income?

A likely source of at least some of Milly's money was the Woodson family. It would seem entirely out of character for Tucker Woodson to have emancipated Milly and her children without making some provision for their future. In the spring of 1793, three years prior to his death, Woodson carefully put his house in order, entrusting all of his real estate to his oldest son, Samuel, and making detailed arrangements for his

---

[13] GDB 19, pp. 365-6. [Pierce to Johnson lease]. Milly, apparently illiterate, signed with an "x."

Milly Pierce

declining years. In an Article of Agreement between father and son, Samuel Woodson promised to pay Tucker 50 pounds per annum, to furnish him with a good riding horse, saddle and bridle and to accommodate the elderly Tucker and his younger son Tarleton "with decent board as two of the family." Most probably, Milly and her children, who remained Tucker's property until his death in 1795, also moved to Samuel's home, "Snowden." Following Tucker Woodson's death and her emancipation, Milly may well have remained there and worked alongside her daughter Lydia whom Samuel Woodson acknowledged as a valued servant in his will. No longer a slave, Milly may have received not only her room and board but a modest allowance. [14]

The restrictive language in a later deed to Milly points to another possible source of income. The unusual and very specific wording of this deed suggests that Milly may have run a "House of Entertainment" or ordinary, although no record of a license for such an establishment can be found—nor can any citations for operating such without a license. Suzanne Lebsock's investigations of the free women of Petersburg indicate that even for single white women, "occupational choices were few" and "the more disreputable the business, it seems, the more women were to be found in it." Among the less than respectable businesses commonly run by women were houses of entertainment—private homes where food and spirits were sold. Milly was specifically forbidden to operate such an establishment on the optimal property

---

[14] GDB 19, pp. 70-71 [Tucker Woodson's agreement with Samuel Woodson]; GDB 20, p. 530 [Samuel Woodson's will identifies Lydia as his servant]

adjacent to the Courthouse, which she purchased in 1825. This restriction, not found in other deeds, certainly raises questions about how Milly had made money in the past. [15]

Whatever the source of the purchase money, in 1803 Milly, who only eight years previously had been Tucker Woodson's slave, became his son Samuel's next door neighbor.

A WAGE-EARNING SLAVE

Milly may well have worked for the Woodsons and even quietly supplemented her income with a house of entertainment, but there is another likely source of her nest egg, or at least a portion of it—her husband, John Pierce. Milly was not, in fact, entirely alone as she began her life as a free woman. The deed which transferred the 23 acres on Beaverdam Creek from John C. Payne and Mary Barns Payne described her as "Milley [sic] Pierce, the reputed wife of Pierce, a mulatto man the property of Doctr. James Brydin." [16]

Although slaves could not legally marry, John and Milly Pierce appear to have been much more than "reputed" husband and wife. As one traces their names

---

[15] GDB 24, p. 355 and GDB 26, p. 168 [Deeds reference House of Entertainment]. The first deed is to John Pierce and the second to Milly Pierce. Both make reference to the prohibition against a House of Private Entertainment. Suzanne Lebsock, *The Free Women of Petersburg: Status and Culture in a Southern Town, 1784-1860* (New York, 1984) pp. 98, 147, 177-178 [Quote, p. 178] Lebsock's Chapter on Free Women of Color is an excellent discussion of Milly's situation in general, although with an urban slant.

[16] GDB 18, p. 679 [Payne to Pierce, "reputed wife"]

Milly Pierce

through the records of Goochland County, the threads of their lives are intimately entwined from well before Milly's emancipation in 1795 until John's death in the late 1820s. She and John Pierce appear to have been husband and wife in every sense but the legal. The Clerk of Court's decision to describe Milly in terms of her relationship to John Pierce not only affirms the importance and general recognition of that relationship, it may, also, suggest how Milly was able to accumulate the 138 pounds she paid for her property.

John was the only slave owned by Dr. James Brydin who lived at Goochland Courthouse. His master had neither wife nor children, however, and presumably made few demands on his servant. What Dr. Brydin apparently needed most were not John's direct services, but rather the cash that could be generated by allowing John to take outside jobs. [17]

Plagued by cash-flow problems, Dr. Brydin frequently resorted to legal action to collect his fees. Brydin's first lawsuit for services rendered was filed in 1797 against one Peter Berry. The Court awarded Brydin three pounds, six shilling plus 5% interest from December 19, 1795. To satisfy the judgment, the Sheriff was ordered to sell certain of Berry's possessions: eleven bushels of corn, a feather bed, bolster and quilt and one barrel. Although poorer for it, Berry at least survived Dr. Brydin's attentions. On several occasions, Brydin filed suit against his patients' estates, leading

---

[17] Dr. Brydin never paid tax on more than one slave and that slave is first identified as John Pierce in Milly's 1803 deed. Goochland Order Book (GOB) 25, p. 376—A plat of the two acres condemned for the Courthouse in 1823 indicates "Brydin's old house" was very close to the southeast corner of the old Courthouse. United States Census 1810, Goochland County (USCG) indicates that Dr. Brydin had no family.

to some doubt about the efficacy of the good Doctor's ministrations. Outcomes aside, the Doctor consistently prevailed in court, although he frequently settled for less than the full amount. [18]

Even when he served at the pleasure of the county court, Brydin somehow came up with the short end of the stick. In 1804, he was allocated ten dollars from the county levy for attending the castration of Leak's Jack, a slave convicted of "attempting to commit a rape in and upon the body of Nancy Lacy a free white woman." Humphrey Parrish, who performed the castration, was paid $50; Dr. John F. Swann, who was also in attendance, received $23.34. [19]

If the Doctor had difficulty making a living from his profession, he had a ready means of alleviating his financial situation in the person of John Pierce. Although Virginia law forbade slaves to work for wages, Eugene Genovese has observed that, "Many slaves were permitted to hire themselves out under circumstances that allowed them to pay rent to their master, provide for their own sustenance and still save something…" Prior to 1803, there is no indication of how John Pierce might have earned money for both Dr. Brydin and himself, but in that

---

[18] Brydin's suits for payment of his fees begin in 1797 with the suit against Peter Berry (GOB 20, p. 480). In the eight suits recorded through 1800, four of the defendants were deceased.

[19] GOB 23, p. 547 [Trial of Leake's Jack]; GOB 24, p. 287 [Brydin paid from County Levy for attending castration]

Milly Pierce

year, the Goochland levy includes the first of many notations of payments to John Pierce for services at the Courthouse. [20]

A slave, John Pierce was not, at first, paid directly. Instead, the 1803 levy shows payments of $13.34 and $2.00 were made to Joseph Payne, Sheriff, on behalf of John Pierce for "keeping the Courthouse;" $55.70 was paid to John Smith "for John Peirce [sic]" for "finding [taking care of] criminals in jail." Similar payments were made on John's account to county clerk William Miller for "sundry claims," keeping the Courthouse, and criminal prosecutions in 1804, 1805 and 1806. In this last year, John is, for the first time, referred to as the "jailor," [sic] a position he would hold until 1827. The court's official recognition of a slave as the county's jailer is remarkable; the notation that the payments were made to Miller because Pierce was "blk."—overlooking his legal status as a slave—is curious. [21]

By 1807, however, the court was apparently no longer concerned by either John's color or his status, and he was directly paid an annual salary of $35.00 for keeping the jail and fueling the courthouse stove. In addition to his salary, John routinely submitted accounts for services related to criminal prosecutions and for odd jobs. In 1807, for instance, he received not only his salary but also $3.50 for "nine

---

[20]Hening, *op. cit.*, II. P. 59 [1781 law forbidding slaves to earn wages]; Eugene D. Genovese, "the Slave States of North America," *Neither Slave Nor Free: The Freedmen of African Descent in the Slave Societies of the New World* (Baltimore, 1972), p. 267.

[21]GOB 23, p. 622 (Payne and Smith paid for Pierce); GOB 25, p. 334 [The County Levy includes a payment of $22.68 to "John Pierce, Sr. jailor" [sic] for a claim in connection with criminal prosecutions "to be paid Wm Miller [clerk of Court] blk," this last referring to Pierce.

panes of glass and putting same in the windows of Goochland Courthouse," and in 1808, he earned an additional $15 for erecting a stove in the Courthouse. [22]

How had a slave obtained a paid position of such responsibility? There is no obvious explanation. Possibly, John's job was another instance of the Woodson's patronage of the Pierces; perhaps it was a gesture of good will toward their nearby and seemingly needy neighbor, Dr. Brydin. From 1796 to 1803, the county paid Samuel Woodson for "keeping the Courthouse." It is unlikely that Woodson actually performed these services himself, and must more likely that he received these payments on behalf of a slave or servant. Samuel Woodson was, almost certainly, acquainted with John Pierce through Milly, and conceivably he had arranged with Brydin for John to do the work. The 1803 payments made in John's name may well have been little more than official recognition of an existing situation. Certainly, this scenario makes sense in light of the 138 pounds in cash Milly paid in 1803 for her 23 acres. However thrifty Milly may have been, it seems unlikely that a house servant with nine children could have saved such a sum. [23]

If the Pierces benefited from John's paid employment, so too did Dr. Brydin who would have been relieved of supporting his slave. Presumably, whatever John had left after paying for his own keep was his to do with as he wished. As a slave he could

---

[22] GOB 26, p. 82 [Pierce is paid $35 for keeping jail and stove, an amount he continued to receive annually until 1816 when it increased to $50. Also paid for glass.]; GOB 26, p. 546 [John paid for stove]

[23] GOB 21, p. 33, p. 321; GOB 22, p. 107, p. 406; GOB 23, p. 27 [Samuel Woodson paid for "keeping the Courthouse"]

not purchase property, but there was nothing to prevent him from contributing to Milly's nest egg.

A SLAVE JAILER AND HIS POOR WHITE PRISONER

Even if allowing a slave to hold employment was not unheard of, Goochland's leaders' decision to entrust their jail to the care of a slave seems extraordinary—especially when his duties extended to guarding and tending white prisoners.

Among the most troublesome white criminals consigned to John Pierce's care was one Richard Layne. On June 18, 1810, Richard Layne was brought before the court and charged with the felony of "stealing from the plantation of Joseph Shelton…a quantity of corn supposed to be about ½ bushel."

Although Layne pleaded "not guilty," the Court believed otherwise, and he was "remanded to jail where to remain until thence discharged by due course of law" or until bond was posted. Prior to his next court date in August, Layne was released on his own recognizance when six upstanding citizens came forward as his securities. Layne, however, failed to appear as ordered, and each of his bondsmen was required to pay the court $20.[24]

Richard Layne was eventually apprehended when, in 1811, he was charged with a second crime: "feloniously killing and carrying away one hog," also the

---

[24]GOB 27, pp. 430-431 [Richard Layne charged with stealing corn]; GOB 28, p. 455 [Layne fails to appear]

property of the unfortunate Joseph Shelton. Although initially unable to make bail, Layne, now charged with two felonies, was eventually released on bond. The elusive Layne, however, failed to appear in court at scheduled hearings in 1811, 1812, 1813, 1814, 1815 and 1816. Finally, in May of 1816, "with the consent of the Court a nolleprosequay was entered by the commonwealth's attorney." [25]

In early 1818, however, Layne was captured, convicted, and, once again, remanded to the county jail. He did not remain there for long. On April 12, the Goochland Court was summoned for the "trial of Peyton, a Negro man slave, the property of Thomas Miller…charged with feloniously breaking the jail of said county and releasing from thence Richard Layne, a criminal charged with grand larceny." Peyton, however, was acquitted, and Layne recaptured. Apparently held harmless in the criminal's escape from the dilapidated jail, a source of constant complaint from the Sheriff, John Pierce was paid significant sums ($134 total) in both 1818 and 1819 "on account of Richard Layne" for "finding" the felon in jail. [26]

Layne's incarceration must have made his family's difficult situation even more difficult. When he first embarked on his career of crime, Richard Layne was the father of five children under the age of ten and owned no land or taxable personal property. Working as a farm hand, he must have been hard-pressed to support a family of seven, and his thefts of the corn and the hog may well have been desperate attempts

---

[25] GOB 28, p. 292 [Layne charged with stealing hog]; GOB 29, p. 450 [Layne nolleprosequey]

[26] Goochland Court Minute Book 1811-16, p. 438 [Trial of Peyton]; GOB 28, pp. 264 and 287, GOB 30, p. 28 [Payments to John Pierce on account of Layne]

to keep starvation at bay. By 1820, the Layne family's situation must have been even more dire, the sheriff having been ordered in 1811 to seize whatever personal property Layne possessed while Layne was on the lam. The Layne family was apparently reduced to reliance on charity, the county, despite its pursuit and prosecution of Layne, actually stepping in at one point to pay for the education of two of the Layne children.[27]

When first confined to the Goochland jail, what must this poor white man, scrambling to survive, have thought about his jailer, a relatively prosperous and gainfully employed slave? And when in 1818, he was returned to jail and deprived, albeit temporarily, of his freedom, what was his reaction upon finding that same jailer a free man?

THE LIMITS OF FREEDOM: FREE BLACK APPRENTICESHIP

John may have enjoyed a rarified status for slave and a better life than his white prisoner, but he was still a slave. Milly was a woman of property, relatively rare in itself, but in the eyes of the law she was just another unmarried, free black female. Even as she was making her way up the economic ladder and enjoying the fruits of her

---

[27] USCG 1810 [Layne family size]; GPPT and GLT, 1810 and 1820 [Layne owned no taxable property, employed in agriculture]; GOB 28, p. 622 [Sheriff to seize Layne chattels]; Legislative Manuscripts, Goochland ms. A7110 [Mayo petition: Layne children's education to be paid by county]; Layne's legal troubles did not end here. In 1830, he was tried and found not guilty of stealing "a parcel of undressed leather" (GOB 31, p. 506).

freedom, Milly was summarily reminded that, although she might own more property than many whites, she would never be their equal—nor was she fully free.

In 1804, less than a year after her first land purchase, Milly's eleven-year-old son John was "bound out to Samuel Johnson by the Overseers of the Poor according to law." Although freed along with his mother by Tucker Woodson's will, John was subject to a 1691 law requiring free mulatto bastards to be bound out to a responsible white person, males until they reached the age of 21 and females, the age of 18. According to the original apprenticeship law, masters were expected to educate their charges in the Christian religion and to teach them reading, writing and arithmetic. In 1800, however, the legislature, wary of education as an instrument of sedition, eliminated the educational requirements. [28]

By the time John Pierce, Jr. was apprenticed, not only was education no longer a part of the bargain, but, like John, many free black children were not placed with skilled craftsmen, but instead bound out in virtual slavery as farm workers. John Pierce apparently fared better than most. Not only did his mother have a relationship, presumably amicable, with Samuel Johnson who leased her land in the following year, the Johnsons may have adhered to the spirit of the original apprenticeship laws and

---

[28]GOB 24, p. 205 [John Pierce bound to Samuel Johnson]; Hening, *op. cit.*, XII, pp. 27-28 [apprenticeships moved from wardens to overseers; requirements]; Samuel Shepherd, ed., *The Statutes at Large in Virginia*, 3 vols., (Richmond, 1835), vol. 2, p. 124 [education dropped]

Milly Pierce

educated their young charge. Although both of his parents were illiterate, John Pierce, Jr. as an adult was both literate and possessed of some skill as a businessman. [29]

John's apprenticeship may originally have consisted of working his mother's land, but if so, the arrangement was temporary. Samuel Johnson died in 1807 and, upon the request of his widow, Milly was compelled to purchase the balance of the lease for $45 and lost her annual rental income as well. What became of John's "apprenticeship" is unknown.[30]

A FREE BLACK SLAVEOWNER

If the termination of Johnson's lease was a financial setback for Milly, there is no evidence to that effect. In fact, her economic situation continued to improve. In 1809 Milly purchased a horse or mule, and by 1810, her household included not only eleven free persons, but two slaves as well. Considering the size of her family and the work required to cultivate her farm, Milly obviously could have used some help, and from this time on, she owned from one to four slaves. In retrospect, it may seem extraordinary that a former slave should purchase slaves of her own. In fact, it was not uncommon, at least not among the more affluent members of the free black caste. [31]

---

[29] Ira Berlin, *Slaves Without Masters: The Free Negro in the Antebellum South* (New York, 1974), pp. 226-7 [conditions of apprentices]; See p. xxx this ms regarding John's literacy and business skills.

[30] GDB 19, p. 631 [Ann Johnson terminates Milly's lease]

[31] Goochland Personal Property Tax (GPPT) 1809 Milly is listed here for the first time and paid tax on one horse or mule; USCG 1810 [Milly's

In 1810, twelve of Goochland's 77 free black households included at least one slave, although at that time no free black owned more than two slaves. In two instances, the slaves were actually family members. Philip Dean owned his wife; Edward Gwyn, his wife and daughter. On the surface, owning a spouse or a child is shocking. In reality, the purchase of a family member was a sign of great affection and enormous sacrifice. After 1806, Virginia law mandated that newly emancipated blacks be sold back into slavery by the Overseers of the Poor if they did not vacate the Commonwealth within twelve months. Somehow Philip Dean and Edward Gwyn managed to save the considerable sums needed to purchase their wives. What they could not do was give them their freedom. Had they done so, they would have faced the prospect of either having to leave the state or seeing their wives offered for sale at a public auction. [32]

Milly's slaves were not family members, nor were those owned by Miles, Edward and Jacob Cowper, members of a long-established free black family whose patriarch was Cupid Cowper. Nor is there any evidence that, like some Quakers, these

---

household]; GPPT 1809-1851 Milly paid taxes on 1 to 4 slaves; John H. Russell, "Colored Freemen as Slave Owners in Virginia," *Journal of Negro History*, vol. 1, June 1916, no. 3, pp. 233-243; Philip J. Schwarz, "Emancipators, Protectors, and Anomalies: Free Black Slaveowners in Virginia." *The Virginia Magazine of History and Biography*, vol. 95, no. 3 (July 1987), pp. 317-338.

[32] USCG 1810 and GPPT 1810 [households owning slaves. The two records do not entirely agree, the 12 slave-owners appear in one or the other and sometimes both]; Shepherd, *op. cit.,* vol. 3, p. 252 [1806 law]; for more about this law, see pp. xxx of this ms. Eventually, both Dean and Gwyn did emancipate their families and secured permission for them to remain in Goochland. USCG 1820 all members of the Gwynn, also spelled Guinn, household are free; USCG 1830 Philip Dean's wife is listed as free.

free black slaveowners purchased bondsmen with the intention of providing a better and quasi-free life for their nominal slaves. Rather, like the majority of white slaveowners, they had purchased slaves as laborers or servants. [33]

Southern culture offered no real alternative to the use of slave labor for those free blacks who, like Milly, could afford house servants or field hands. No white person would work for a black, and free blacks seem to have been almost as reluctant to work for their own kind. For a free black who needed additional hands, there were essentially two choices: to purchase slaves or rent them, a more expensive option in the long run. Not only was there no real alternative to slave labor, but as perverse as it may seem, slavery, the economic foundation of southern society, was so deeply ingrained in the culture that purchasing black labor would have been more routine than aberrant for an affluent free black. [34]

BLACK BOATMEN ON THE JAMES RIVER

Milly's acquisition of two slaves was not the only notable purchase by a Pierce during this period. In 1811, John Pierce registered a boat "for navigation of the James above the falls of Richmond." Such a purchase was highly unusual, illegal in

---

[33] USCG 1810. All of the Cowpers (later Cooper) like Milly, had free black families. Miles and Edward Cooper owned one slave each; Jacob, two. Berlin, *op. cit.*, pp. 143-144 [quasi-free slaves]

[34] Schwarz, *op. cit.*, p. 325 [free black slave owning]

fact, for a slave. But, then, John Pierce's status as Goochland's jailer and even his use of a surname were also outside the norm. [35]

Plying the James with cargo had become a viable occupation when, in 1808, the James River Company had succeeded in making 220 miles of the river from Richmond through Goochland and westward navigable for commercial traffic. Batteaux, long, narrow boats, designed to carry twelve hogsheads of tobacco, were poled along the river regularly, carrying produce downstream to Richmond and supplies from the city on the return trip. [36]

Free blacks dominated the boating trade on the James River and elsewhere. As reported by a contemporary observer of the river scene, "The boatsmen were, for the larger number, the servants of the planters or freed men. Running the river, as it was called, had not a high name for any of the cardinal virtues." Apparently, boatmen had a reputation for succumbing to "the temptation to visit the hen roosts and to inquire into the condition of the pigsty," yet, at their regular stopping places, they were known "to make friends of all conditions and were a laughing, humorous set, liked by everybody except the young fishing boys" who complained that the boatmen's poles scared away the fish. Evidently, the boatmen working the James enlivened the local scene considerably, and "some of these fellows, indeed, had reputations for cunning

---

[35] GOB 28, p. 69 [John registers a boat]

[36] Wayland Fuller Dunaway, *History of the James River and Kanawha Canal Company*, (New York, 1922), p. 87 [Canal to Maidens]; Anthony R.D. Perrins, "The James River and Kanawha Canal in Goochland," *Goochland County Historical Society Magazine*, vol. 13, 1981, p. 35 [description of bateaux]

Milly Pierce

exploits which were the talk of the great house and the Negro cabin on both sides of the James, from Richmond for 100 miles." [37]

Almost thirty of Goochland's free black men were, over the years, identified as boatmen in the County records, although John Pierce, still a slave, was the first to purchase his own boat. The Pierces were a family given to firsts. [38]

MOST LIKELY TO BE FREE

Good fortune in the form of the Woodson family continued to benefit Milly and her family. On May 12, 1810, Samuel Woodson added the following codicil to his will:

> I give unto Lydia Pierce, a daughter of Milly Pierce, one half acre of my land…and I direct my executors at the expense of my estate to cause a dwelling house thereon to be built of twenty pounds value in consideration of her faithful services in my family.

---

[37] Berlin, *op. cit.,* pp. 218-219 [free blacks and boat trade]; Perrins, *ibid.* [description of boatmen on the James]

[38] Other free black boatmen found in the orders books, personal property records and census were: Peyton Cooper, John Coplan, Samuel Howell, Charles Gray, Caesar Giles, Philip Cousins (John's grandson), Samuel Cousins, James Frenti, IshamFuzmore, Jordan Giles, Henry Logan, Jeremiah Mayo, Peyton Mayo, Richard Morse (Moss), Henry Smith, Isaac Smith, Moses Brooks, James Cousins, Robert Crump, James Henley, William Howell, Henry Logan, John Logan, Robert J. Logan, John Lynch, Billy Martin, Thomas Moss, John Sims, John Snead, and Matthew Snead.

Unlike his father, Samuel Woodson, who had forsaken the Friends to fight in the Revolution, did not liberate his slaves in his will. He did, however, recognize Lydia's special place in his family. His estate, bequeathed to his wife Elizabeth Payne Woodson, included fourteen slaves: "old Jenny" valued at $25, two younger women, three children and eight young men in their prime, presumably field hands, who were valued at over $400 each. Although Lydia Pierce was already free, Woodson's special consideration for a valued house servant reflects the preferences that characterized the selective emancipations practiced by many southern slaveowners. [39]

As the nineteenth century progressed, the wholesale manumissions that followed the Revolution—reflecting the new nation's fervent belief in freedom for all—gave way to very specific, preferential emancipations, leading to a distinct demographic divergence between the slave and free black populations. Both Lydia and Milly Pierce—mulatto, female and house servants—were among those who were most likely to be given their freedom. As women, they were less threatening than black men and more likely to work closely with their owners. As house servants, they shared the daily lives of their white owners and often enjoyed an intimacy that approached that of a family member. Indeed, affection and appreciation apparently outweighed prudence with some slaveowners, for emancipating a woman was an almost surefire way to swell the number of free blacks. The mother's status, even if the father were a slave,

---

[39] GDB 20, p. 530 [Samuel Woodson's will]; Worrall, *op. cit.*, p. 219 [Samuel served in Revolution]; GDB 20, p. 631 [Samuel Woodson's inventory]; Berlin, *op. cit.*, pp. 150-152 [selective emancipations].

determined the status of her children. Even so, women were more frequently freed than men. [40]

Color, too, was a factor in determining who was most apt to be freed, and both Milly and Lydia—who was described as "bright yellow"—were mulatto. Paradoxically, many slaveowners preferred mulatto house servants, although their very existence signaled illicit relationships and the mixing of the races so abhorrent to many whites. In 1850, almost 30% of southern free blacks were of mixed ancestry, and only 14% of slaves. By 1860, 40.5% of free blacks were of mixed ancestry as opposed to 14.3% of slaves. Although Goochland's free black population remained predominantly black and male, as manumissions became increasingly selective in the course of the nineteenth century, these preferences among white slaveowners skewed the composition of the free black class toward women and mulattos in many areas. Even in Goochland, the most prominent and successful free black families were mulatto. By 1850, of the county's 42 free black landowners, the ten who owned 50 acres or more were all mulatto. [41]

---

[40]Berlin, *op. cit.*, pp. 151-152 [women emancipated]

[41]Berlin, *op. cit.*, pp. 56-57 and 150-152; E. Franklin Frazier, *The Negro Family in the United States* (New York, 1948), pp. 145-146 [mulatto's status]; John H. Russell, *The Free Negro in Virginia 1619-1865* (Baltimore, 1913), pp. 127-128 [mulattos]; Benjamin Quarles, *The Negro in the Making of America* (New York, 1987), p. 84; Berlin, *op. cit.*, p. 178 [1860 census figures]; Designations about skin color in the Goochland records are imprecise and inconsistent. Of the 42 free blacks who paid taxes on real estate in 1850, 8 were black; 6 were brown; 5 were "of colour;" 3 cannot be determined; and 20 were mulatto. All ten of those who owned 50 or more acres were mulatto. For more on this subject, see pp. xxx this ms.

CeCe Bullard

MARRIAGE IN THE PIERCE FAMILY AND THE BAPTIST CONNECTION

Lydia's color and her inheritance from Samuel Woodson positioned her to join Goochland's free black elite who were, in fact, more commonly mulatto than black. In Goochland, as elsewhere, light skin conferred a certain status not only in the white community but also within the free black class. So deeply had the prevailing notion of the white oppressors' superiority penetrated all levels of southern society that light skin was valued even by those oppressed because of their own dark skin. In 1812, Lydia further solidified her place in the upper echelons of Goochland's free black society when she married Henry Cousins, a free black cooper and member of a prosperous and propertied family. The couple settled on Lydia's land one quarter of a mile east of the courthouse and close to, if not adjoining, Milly's property. [42]

Lydia Pierce and Henry Cousins were married by Lewis Chaudoin, a white Baptist minister of Huguenot descent, in a ceremony attended by her mother Milly and her father John "a Negro man of Dr. James Brydin's" and witnessed by another free black, Thomas Gilpin. In an 1837 interview with the *Richmond Enquirer*, Chaudoin claimed that in the course of his ministry, he had "joined in matrimony six hundred and twenty-five couples," a number which, according to the Goochland marriage register, must have included most of the county's free black couples. [43]

---

[42] Frazier, *op. cit.*, pp. 300-308 and Berlin, *op. cit.*, pp. 56, 57, 247 [Mulatto elite]; GMR, 1812, p. 353 [Lydia Pierce m. Henry Cousins]; USCG 1850 [Henry Cousins identified as cooper]; for more about the Cousins family see p. xxxx this ms.

[43] GMR, *ibid.* [Chaudoin minister]; Cameron Allen, "Francis (Francois) Chaudoin," *The Virginia Genealogist*, vol. 40, no. 2, (April-June 1996), pp.

Milly Pierce

It was no accident that virtually all of Goochland's free black couples were married by Baptist ministers. In 1785, Virginia's Baptists, like the Quakers and Methodists, had declared slavery an affront to God's will. Baptists welcomed blacks into their congregations, and for many years, black and white often worshipped side by side. By the end of the eighteenth century, thousands of free blacks had joined Baptist churches, and when, in 1806, Goochland Baptist Church held a revival aimed particularly at the black community, more than 100 were baptized. [44]

Several months after Lydia's marriage, Lewis Chaudoin married another free black couple, Lucy Pierce and Daniel Moss. In later years, he also performed the wedding of Susan (Sukey) Pierce and Austin Isaacks, Sally Pierce and Reuben Dungee, Phebe Pierce and Page Carter, and Martha Pierce and Wilson Morris. Lucy, Susan, Sally, Phebe and Martha were almost certainly Milly's daughters, and although never legally their father, John Pierce officially witnessed the weddings of Lydia, Phebe and Martha. [45]

87-92 [Chaudoin family]; James B. Taylor, *Virginia Baptist Ministers*, (Philadelphia, 1859), series 2, pp. 219-21 [quote from Richmond Enquirer]

[44] Garnett Ryland, *The Baptists of Virginia, 1699-1926* (Richmond 1955), pp. 150-55 [Baptists denounce slavery]; Russell, *Free Negro*, pp. 57-58 [Quakers and Methodists and free blacks]; Berlin, *op. cit.*, p. 66 [free blacks join Baptists]; Robert B. Semple, *A History of Baptists in Virginia*, (Polyanthus, Inc., Cottonport, La., 1810, reprint 1970) p. 140 [Goochland revival]

[45] GMR p. 353, Lucy Pierce m. Daniel Moss Oct. 23, 1812; p. 356, Susan Pierce m. Austin Isaacks Mar. 6, 1815; p. 361, Sally Pierce m. Reuben Dungee Jan. 21, 1819; p. 364, Phebe Pierce m. Page Carter Nov. 8 1820; p. 368, Martha Pierce m. Wilson Morris July 21, 1825. John Pierce is listed as the official witness for the weddings of Lydia, Phoebe and Martha.

All of Milly's offspring, who numbered at least twelve, cannot be identified with absolute certainty. Several of her children, however, can be named with reasonable confidence: Lydia (Ledy), born 1787; Lucy, born 1789; Judith (Jude), born 1792; John (Jack), born 1793; Susan (Sukey), born 1795; Sally, born 1797; Isaac, born 1817; Phebe, born 1800; Martha, born 1806; Thomas, born 1811; Mary, born in 1815; and Jane, born1817. In some instances, there is not a definitive, direct link between Milly and her presumed offspring, although there is an accumulation of affirmative evidence. In 1813, however, the tax collector left no doubt about two of her children, John and Judy, naming them as free persons between 16 and 21 living with Milly. In the previous year, only John was listed and then not by name, but merely as a free male between 16 and 21, the standard practice for all free males, black or white, in this age group. Why the change in 1813, and why the enumeration of children over 16 only in the listings of free blacks? [46]

---

[46]The birth dates of Milly's children are approximate as the Goochland Register of Free Negroes indicates ages "about 21," and there are inconsistencies in the ages several of them gave in various censuses. Judith (Ude), Lucy, and Ledy (Lydia) are cited in Tucker Woodson's will. John (Jack) and Susan (Suky) are cited when the will was proven. Sally's wedding was witnessed by Milly's son-in-law Henry Cousins. Isaac Pierce cited his emancipation by Tucker Woodson's will when he registered as free black #241 in 1819 at age 21. Phebe's wedding was witnessed by John Pierce. Martha's wedding was witnessed by John Pierce. Thomas, Jane and Mary were cited by Milly as her three youngest children in her 1850 will. A Rebecca Pierce who registered as free Negro #303 in 1823 at age 16 might also have been Milly's daughter, although there is no more information about her. GPPT 1813 [John and Judy named]

Milly Pierce

PAYING FOR THE WAR OF 1812: A POLL TAX ON FREE BLACKS

The care with which the tax collector recorded all free blacks aged 16 and above in 1813 reflects the Virginia General Assembly's 1812 enactment of a law pertaining to free blacks that can only be described as punitive: every free black over the age of 16 was required to pay a poll tax of $1.50. The "Head" tax was imposed ostensibly to replenish a treasury depleted by the War of 1812. Despite the desperate condition of the state's finances, however, free blacks alone were called upon to finance the war effort. [47]

Over the years, blacks paid, and paid again, for their freedom. Some slaves actually paid for their freedom. Self-purchase was a possibility for a slave of exceptional industry with a benevolent master. Free blacks paid to retain their freedom. Virtual re-enslavement was the penalty for failure to pay the tax collector, yet cash was not easy to come by for a people who survived largely by subsistence farming or hiring themselves out as cheap labor. Somehow most managed, even when subjected to extraordinary taxes. Free blacks not only had to pay routine land and property taxes, but, as in 1813, they were on occasion subject to special and oppressive poll or head taxes, a practice that would continue into this century when the poll tax as a tool of racial suppression was used to limit black access to one of the fundamental rights of all free people—the right to vote. [48]

---

[47] _____. Acts of the General Assemby (Acts). 1812 (Richmond, 1813), p. 20

[48] Russell, *Free Negro*, pp. 62-63, p. 170 [Self Purchase]: Hening, *op. cit.*, XI, 40 [working off taxes]

CeCe Bullard

Ante-bellum free blacks were sitting ducks for the tax collector. The white populace could have risen up in protest at this imposition of new taxes, either by exercising their right to vote or their right to assemble and publicly demonstrate their objections. Free blacks were denied both of these rights. Any expression of dissatisfaction with white governance by free blacks would have been suicidal. Deportation or enslavement were ever present threats. Despite the watchword of the Revolution, theirs was truly taxation without representation.

No doubt the revenue from the poll tax was welcome, but there was a hidden agenda of equal if not greater importance behind the tax that remained in effect until 1816. The poll tax was in reality a diabolic device for reducing the free black population. The hefty tax not only gave free blacks an added incentive to leave the state, it was also an effective mechanism for enslaving those who remained.

Since 1793, the Virginia legislature had been intent on reducing the number of free blacks in the Commonwealth, yet despite its best efforts, this most disturbing population had continued to grow. While Virginia's free blacks numbered only 30,570 in 1810, a mere three percent of the total population, this number represented an increase of 17,804 from 1790. Goochland in 1810 had 10,203 inhabitants of whom slightly more than half were slaves. There were only 509 free blacks in the county, but this figure was more than double the 1790 number. The actual number of free blacks might seem negligible; it was the rate of increase—many times higher than that for either whites or slaves—that alarmed many whites. The legislature had already made an attempt to limit the growth of the free black population when in 1793 it had

Milly Pierce

outlawed free black immigration into the Commonwealth, yet manumissions and births alone had been sufficient to fuel dramatic growth. [49]

Although free blacks posed no real threat to the political or economic stability of the Commonwealth, their very existence undermined the standard justification for enslaving all persons of color—their alleged moral and intellectual inferiority. In the minds of whites, at least, every free black stood as a refutation of slavery as a benevolent institution and a beacon to those still enslaved, beckoning them to claim their freedom.

NOTHING LEFT TO LOSE

As a result of the poll tax, Milly Pierce paid a total of $6.59 in personal property taxes in 1813. Had she been white her tax burden would have been only $2.09. Milly's tax bill reflected $4.50 in poll tax; $1.77 for her three slaves; and 32 cents for her two horses or mules. The disparity between the $1.50 poll tax and the 59 cent rate for slaves indicates the severity of the former. [50]

---

[49] Hening, *ibid.*: _____ Acts (Richmond, 1814), p. 61 [free blacks hired out to pay taxes]; USC Virginia 1790 Free blacks numbered 12,866, whites 442,117, and slaves 292,627. In 1810, whites numbered 551,534 and slaves, 392,518; USCG 1790 Free blacks numbered 257, whites 4130 and slaves 4656; USCG 1810 Whites numbered 4240 and slaves 5454. All 1790 figures are estimates as the original census was burned during the War of 1812. Shepherd, *op. cit.*, vol. 1, p. 239 [1793 law forbade immigration]

[50] GPPT 1813 [Milly's tax burden and tax rates]

Although Milly Pierce was able to meet her rather substantial obligation to the tax collector, her contemporary, Billy Perry, was less fortunate. One of several slaves freed in 1808 by Isaac W. Pleasants, member of the prominent Quaker family, Billy Perry never acquired either a family or property, but managed to survive as an independent "free Negroe" until the imposition of the poll tax. In 1813, he was able to come up with the $1.50 to satisfy the tax collector, but in 1814, his name is included on a list of "persons delinquent in property taxes" for that year. Not surprisingly, of the twenty-eight people on this list, fifteen are "free Negroes," all of whom are delinquent in paying the $1.50 tax on "self." Among the whites on this list, the most common debt is twenty-one cents for a horse or mule, and the largest debt is seventy-nine cents for a slave. Indeed, all tax rates had gone up, but the poll tax remained disproportionately high. [51]

In 1815, the number of free blacks in arrears for the poll tax, now increased to $2.50 but limited to males sixteen and older, had grown to twenty-nine. Included in that number was Billy Perry. Several of the free blacks on the 1815 list of tax delinquents disappear forever from Goochland's public records. George, Henry, Jackson, Gabriel and Lually Royster, emancipated in 1812 by the will of Anderson Royster, all make a single appearance in the Goochland personal property tax ledger in 1815. In the same year, John, Henry, Jackson and Gabriel Royster were certified as delinquent in payment of their poll tax. In 1816, only Lually, now called LuallyCocke,

---

[51] GFN #54 Billy Perry registered at age 31 in 1808 citing his emancipation by Isaac W. Pleasants as the result of a court decree. For more about the court case, see pp. xx this ms; GOB 21, p. 669 [Tax delinquents for 1814]

Milly Pierce

and living as part of the household of white slaveowner John Royster, remained free in Goochland. By taking Lually in, Royster may well have been responding to his brother's final "injunction that the legatees will not see them [his slaves] suffer." As for Lually's brothers, perhaps they left the state. More probably, they were bound over to the Overseers of the Poor to work off their tax debt at the stipulated rate of no less than eight cents a day. [52]

Billy Perry's name, however, appears one last time in the country records. On December 19, 1815, almost exactly two months after his tax delinquency was certified to the court in preparation for the revocation of his freedom, Billy Perry was the subject of an inquest held by William Gray, coroner. Destitute, and no doubt desperate, Billy Perry was found the morning of December 13 on the River Road, having frozen to death during the night. [53]

Unlike Billy Perry, Milly Pierce paid her taxes and prospered. The years of 1815 and 1816 may well have been the best years of her life. Had she paused to take stock, Milly, at forty-five, must have been well satisfied with her situation in life. Three of her daughters had married—and married well—but they were still nearby, and the rest of her children were still at home. John had earned over $100, including a $15 bonus from the surplus levy, in 1815, and they now owned four slaves, nine cattle and two horses or mules. As a further sign of their material success, Milly more than

---

[52]GOB 22, pp. 72-73 [Tax delinquents for 1815]; _____ Acts (Richmond, 1815), p. 8; GDB 20, p. 10 [Anderson Royster's will]; GOB *ibid.*; GPPT 1816 [Lually listed with John Royster; others gone]; _____ Acts (Richmond, 1813), p. 20 [rate for working off taxes]

[53]GOB 22, p. 190 [coroner's request]

doubled her land holdings to 56 ¼ acres when she purchased an additional 34¾ acres on Beaverdam Creek from Benjamin Anderson and wife for $600. This deed, unlike the first, was in the name of Mildred, not Milly, Pierce, a sign perhaps of her increased stature in the community, but was, the clerk noted, delivered to John Pierce. John was no doubt handy, going about his chores at the Courthouse. Beyond that, he was obviously considered reliable; and although still a slave, was recognized as Milly's partner in life, and possibly in this purchase. John and Milly Pierce appear to have moved forward in tandem, a committed, if unmarried couple, whose relationship was, perhaps, more of a partnership than the conventional nineteenth century model of the dominant, paternalistic male and the dependent, domestic female. [54]

THE MEASURE OF FREEDOM: "EXTRAORDINARY MERIT AND GENERAL GOOD CHARACTER"

The importance of the Pierce's financial success pales when compared to the legal and social implications of events in 1816. Although not first chronologically,

---

[54]GPPT 1815. In this year only, the tax collector includes cattle as another revenue generator; GDB 22, p. 51 [Deed from Benjamin Anderson]; 23 acres and 34.75 acres would add up to 57.75 acres. This discrepancy is, in part, explained in GDB 21, p. 682 which records Milly's trade of 2.20 acres to her neighbor William Miller for .90 acres from Miller, reducing her 23 acres to 21.70. This would make her total acreage 56.45, not 56.25. Discrepancies of even an acre or so are not uncommon, however, in Goochland deeds and land taxes. GOB 29, pp. 293, 344, 347, 248. [Payments to John Pierce]; Lebsock, *op. cit.*, pp. 33-35 [19th c. marriages]

Milly Pierce

first in importance was John Pierce's emancipation. On November 20, 1816, county clerk William Miller recorded the following deed of manumission:

> Know all men by these presents that I john Curd of the County of Goochland taking into consideration the extraordinary merit and general good character and conduct of my man slave John Pierce aged about 58 years doth by these presents emancipate and set free said Negro man slave.

Although he appears to have lived virtually free for many years, the county's aging jailer must have long hoped for this moment. At last, the stigma of slavery had been removed, and he now stood on an equal footing with his wife and children. [55]

How John Curd became John Pierce's emancipator is something of a puzzle. Dr. Brydin, John's owner for many years, had died in 1815, and at some point, John Pierce passed into John Curd's possession. Regardless of how he acquired John Pierce, Curd, had he been so inclined, could well have put Pierce to work alongside his 26 other slaves. He might also have offered John for sale, although a 58 year old slave was no longer prime property. Had he been unscrupulous and conscienceless, Curd might have considered a third option. Saddled with an aged slave who was unaccustomed to hard manual labor and possibly unsaleable, some slaveowners would have found emancipation a convenient way to dispose of worn-out and unwanted property, even though such a move was illegal. The manumission law of 1782 had specifically proscribed the practice of dumping aged slaves—partly for humanitarian

---

[55]GDB 22, pp. 292-3 [John's deed of manumission]

reasons, partly to keep them off the public dole. Curd could have had little choice but to keep John Pierce as his personal property and responsibility. Fortunately for both John Curd and John Pierce, the latter was manifestly self-supporting. [56]

While John Curd, a wealthy landowner, could afford to give John Pierce his freedom, John Pierce had probably constituted the bulk of Dr. Brydin's estate. The doctor owned no land and his single slave was his only taxable personal property. Brydin's financial struggles may, in fact, explain how his only slave became John Curd's. John Curd was at the time Goochland's sheriff, and as such, was charged with collecting all debts recognized by the court. It is possible that John Curd had "seised" John Pierce to satisfy Brydin's debtors, for even if the doctor were not in debt at the time of his death, his estate was soon encumbered with at least one significant liability as the result of a lawsuit by none other than Milly Pierce. [57]

A FREE BLACK'S RIGHT TO LEGAL REDRESS

In July of 1816, Milly sued Benjamin Anderson, "administrator of James Brydin deceased debtor." Anderson's attorney first attempted to have a writ of inquiry

---

[56] GOB 29, p. 295 [evidence of Bydin's death; executor named]; GPPT 1815 [John Curd's slaves]; Hening, *op. cit.*, VI pp. 39-40 [1782 no slave dumping]

[57] GOB 29, p. 295 Although the court appointed five men to "appraise the personal estate of Dr. James Brydin," no record of that appraisal can be found. The procedure was pro forma, and possibly there was no possessions to be reported. Brydin never paid personal property taxes on anything except one slave over the age of 16. He is never listed in the land records. GOB 29, p. 454 [John Curd, Sheriff, collector of levy]

Milly Pierce

of damages and an office judgment in favor of Milly set aside. He then "pleaded payment." Upon the objection of Milly and her attorney, a jury of white males was impaneled to hear the case. Originally selected as a member of the jury, Tarlton W. Pleasants was excused so that he might speak to the truth of Milly's case. The jury found for Milly, having determined that:

> the defendant intestate in his life time did assume upon himself in manner and form as the plaintiff has complained and they do assess the plaintiff damages by occasion of the non-performance of that assumption to two hundred and twenty-five dollars with six per centum per annum interest thereon from the 1st day of July 1813 till paid.

To satisfy this judgment, Anderson was ordered to pay damages as described above and Milly's legal fees from the goods and chattels of the Brydin estate which included his only slave, John Pierce. [58]

The nature of the "assumption" or informal contract between Milly and Brydin is never elucidated. Perhaps, if it were known, it might shed light on one of the enduring questions about Milly: why did she not purchase John Pierce? Had she done so before 1806, she could have emancipated him. After that, she could have, at least, ensured that although still a slave he remained with her and their family. In the years before John's emancipation, Milly had purchased land, horses and slaves, suggesting that she could have afforded to buy John from Dr. Brydin, yet she did not. Certainly,

---

[58]GOB 29, p. 440 [Milly's suit against Brydin's estate]

John enjoyed an unusual degree of privilege and freedom for a slave, yet Dr. Brydin, often pressed for cash, might have had no choice but to sell his only tangible asset. [59]

Possibly, John and Milly took a calculated risk, and rather than buying John's freedom chose to invest in the future for their family. It is equally possible that even had Milly, or Milly and John together, chosen to spend everything they could save on John's freedom, it still would not have been enough to purchase it outright. Conceivably, then, the assumption in question might have been an unfulfilled agreement in which Brydin had committed to sell John to Milly on the installment plan.

While the basis of Milly's lawsuit remains unclear, what is clear is that Milly Pierce, a free black woman, was able to obtain justice and to prevail in a lawsuit against a white man in a white court. The trial was her right by law; her triumph may well have been the result of her character and the esteem with which she was regarded by the white community. Character was a critical issue, not only to Milly and John Pierce but to all of their caste. Every free black walked a fine line between freedom and slavery—always by law presumed a slave until proven otherwise, eventually subject to enslavement for various offenses. A good reputation and the respect of the white community were indispensable to the success, even survival, of all free blacks. [60]

---

[59] Shepherd, *op. cit.*, vol. 3, p. 252 [1806 law]

[60] Free blacks were never deprived of the right to seek redress in the courts for civil matters; see Russell, *Free Negro*, pp. 98-99 for a discussion of how this presumption of slavery developed in common law [presumed a slave]

Milly Pierce

THE LAW OF 1806: FREE BUT NOT FREE TO STAY

Character, however, had real legal implications for the free and potentially free. As first determined by the Virginia legislature in 1806, only a slave of "good character" who had demonstrated "extraordinary merit" could be manumitted. Once emancipated, however, a freed slave faced yet another major challenge—obtaining permission to remain in the state. The 1806 law had specified that should a slave be granted freedom and not leave the Commonwealth within twelve months, he or she "shall forfeit all such right [to freedom] and may be apprehended and sold by the overseers of the poor." [61]

John Pierce was, finally, a free man, but there was no guarantee that he would be allowed to remain among family and friends and enjoy the life he had created for himself. Although freedom was a precious commodity, it was tainted by the prospect of forsaking all that was familiar. Banishment from the state was a severe sentence for Virginia's free blacks, many of whom had deep roots in communities where their families had lived for generations. The 1806 law posed a grave threat to the stability of many families with its potential for forcing the newly emancipated to abandon spouses and children either previously freed or still enslaved. Some former slaves, presented with the choice of leaving home or risking re-enslavement, elected to take that risk and

---

[61] Shepherd, *ibid.* [1806 law]

remained illegally. Others actually refused to leave their masters and the only home they had ever known. [62]

Rather cavalierly, the legislature did not concern itself with where an emancipated slave was to go. Anywhere other than Virginia would do, but as neighboring states soon enacted laws prohibiting the immigration of free blacks, the Virginia law became something of a Catch-22. Ohio, a major terminus on the underground railroad for escaped slaves, also became a primary safety valve for Virginia's banished free blacks. [63]

Despite the intent of the law, many petitions by newly freed blacks for continued residence in the state were granted. The philosophical and political arguments for ridding Virginia of a despised class aside, many of the individuals who petitioned the court had been freed for the very reasons that would justify their remaining. They were the most valued servants, the hardest workers and, sometimes, the children of their emancipators. Even so, after 1806, a number of Goochland's young, single free black men appear in the record only once, suggesting that they did, indeed, leave the state once they were free. This diaspora of the young and newly emancipated—in conjunction with the advanced age of many manumitted by will, a

---

[62]Berlin, *op. cit.*, p. 145-147 [manumitted remain illegally]; Russell, *Free Negro*, p. 76 [Some freed slaves would not leave home]

[63]In 1800, North Carolina required free black immigrants to post a 200 pound bond. Kentucky outlawed free black immigration in 1807; Maryland in 1808; Delaware in 1810. (Berlin, *op. cit.*, p. 92); Quarles, *op. cit.*, p. 79 [Ohio open]

gradual decline in the free black birth rate, and the dumping of old and worn-out slaves—led eventually to the aging of the free black population. [64]

TOO MANY FREE BLACKS FOR COMFORT: THE VISE TIGHTENS

What had happened to post-revolutionary emancipation euphoria? In part, those who had greeted American independence with an idealistic commitment to freedom and equality for all, and expressed this idealism by freeing their slaves, had succeeded too well. Following the 1782 legalization of private manumission in Virginia, the commonwealth's free Negro population had exploded. St. George Tucker in his *Dissertation on Slavery* estimated the 1782 free black population to be around 1800, a figure he later revised to 2800. With the legalization of private manumission in the same year, the numbers escalated rapidly, reaching 12,766 in 1790 and 20,124 in 1800. [65]

The numbers are impressive, but in themselves do not explain why Virginia's leaders viewed them with such anxiety. Significantly, the 1806 law requiring the newly manumitted to leave the state within twelve months, unless special permission was granted, was buried within an act of the General Assembly primarily concerned

---

[64]The Goochland Personal Property records list free black male titheables over 21 whether or not they owned personal property. Eight free black males listed first in 1806 do not reappear in the records, and seven first listed in 1807 also disappear; Berlin, *op. cit.*, p. 175 [aging of free black population]

[65]Russell, *Free Negro*, p. 12 [St George Tucker's estimate]; USC Virginia 1790 and 1800

with limiting the importation of slaves into Virginia. With the exception of section 10 of 16, the entire act is devoted to restrictions on bringing slaves into Virginia and the penalties to be imposed on violators. As would prove to be the case over and over again until the Civil War, slaves, not free blacks, were the primary cause of white concern, yet free blacks, incidentally and indirectly involved though they were, bore the brunt of the legislators' anxiety. [66]

The law of 1806, linking freedom to exile, clearly marked the end of the late eighteenth century enthusiasm for emancipation and the beginning of the Virginia legislature's efforts to reduce or even eliminate the free black population, primarily through various deportation schemes. As harsh as it may seem, this piece of legislation was actually a compromise between those who wished to end all private emancipation and those who contended that the door to freedom should be left open.

The debate surrounding the 1806 law was intense and, in the course of their heated rhetoric, Virginia's legislatures laid bare the ugly reality of slavery's divisive and demeaning impact on the Commonwealth's white population. As reported in the *Richmond Argus*, Delegate Thomas Bolling Robertson of Dinwiddie County favored ending emancipation entirely and argued that "those blacks who are free…can organize insurrection. They will no doubt unite with slaves." This was a standard argument against tolerance toward free blacks, but, as Robertson continued, he

---

[66]Shepherd, *ibid.* [Law of 1806] The law forbade anyone from bringing a slave into Virginia for more than a year; the penalty, forfeiture. Bringing slaves into to sell or hire out was prohibited; the penalty, $400 fines on both seller and buyer. The section regarding free blacks was actually a Senate amendment to a House bill regarding the incorporation of slaves.

eventually reached the crux of the matter, "Tell us not of principle. Those principles have been annihilated by the existence of slavery among us." Indeed, as long as Virginia supported slavery, economic self-interest and fear, not principle, would prevail in the formation of public policy.

Not all Virginians had abandoned the principles of liberty and justice for all on which the country had been founded. Delegate George Mason of Greensville County rose to speak in response to Robertson, asking "Can we contravene the bill of rights which declares that 'all men are by nature free'?" Despite Mason's contention that Virginians must preserve their forebears' "love of liberty" and the Negro's hope of eventual freedom, there was, also, a sharp edge of cynicism in his suggestion that "divide and conquer" was an effecting strategy for dealing with Virginia's black population. In his opinion free blacks were "the sureties of the slaves" and "it would be in their interest to give information of insurrections." [67]

A SLAVE INSURRECTION AND FREE BLACKS SUFFER

Slave insurrection preyed upon the minds of Virginia's citizens. If any single event can be said to mark the beginning of a shift in Virginians' attitudes about emancipation as a possible solution to slavery, it would be the panic in the white community over "Gabriel's Rebellion" in 1800. Following hard on the heels of the slave revolt in Haiti, Gabriel Prosser's plan to march on Richmond, a city of 8000,

---

[67] *Richmond Argus*, Tuesday, Jan 17, 1805, pp. 2-3 [Debate on free black law]

with 1100 fellow slaves provoked a profound change in white attitudes towards both slaves and free blacks. Gabriel's plan was thwarted by bad weather, but, betrayed from within, he was executed on October 7, 1800. No free blacks were implicated in Gabriel's plot, but they were, in the minds of many whites, implicitly involved. As Delegate Robertson remarked in justifying the end of private manumissions, "If blacks see all of their color slaves, it will seem to them a disposition of Providence, and they will be content. But, if they see others like themselves free, and enjoying rights they are deprived of, they will repine." Or revolt, he might have added. [68]

The compromise law of 1806, written to encourage emancipated slaves to leave the state, had paradoxically turned manumission into a mechanism for reducing the free black population—either by forcing them to leave the Commonwealth or reducing them once again to slavery. To some extent, it succeeded. The young men who fled Goochland ahead of the law after 1806 had little to lose and, perhaps, a brighter future elsewhere. John Pierce, no longer young, father to a large family and well established in a good job, had everything to lose.

As a consequence of the 1806 law, on the day of John Pierce's emancipation, it was ordered that the magistrate be summoned "on the 1st day of the January Court next to take into consideration the propriety of permitting John Pierce an emancipated slave to remain in this County." Accordingly, on January 20, 1817, the Gentlemen Justices of Goochland County ordered:

---

[68]Douglas R. Egerton, *Gabriel's Rebellion: The Virginia Slave Conspiracies of 1800 and 1802* (Chapel Hill, 1993); *Richmond Argus, ibid.*

Milly Pierce

> ...that on account of the said John Pierce's general good character and extraordinary merit as a slave acting as a jailor [sic] of this Court, keeping and taking care of the Courthouse and public jail for a number of years, that he remain in this County and enjoy the liberties of a free man of color and be entitled to all the benefits and priviledges [sic] he can enjoy..."

While those "benefits and privileges" were not what they would have been for a white man, John Pierce was at least to free to remain in Goochland. [69]

FREEDOM OF ANOTHER KIND: FORGOING THE BONDS OF MARRIAGE

Among the benefits that John Pierce might have enjoyed as a free man was the right to affirm legally his long-time relationship with Milly. The idea of this middle-aged couple celebrating John's freedom—and a salary increase to $50—with a wedding appeals to the imagination. Yet, practicality seems to have prevailed over romantic fantasy. Milly would have sacrificed much and gained nothing by marrying John Pierce. [70]

It was not uncommon for free women of color to remain unmarried, and, as Lebsock has observed, "Nonmarriage among free blacks...was evidently as much a matter of ethics as expenses, for even the propertied showed no consistent tendency to

---

[69] GOB 29, p. 514 [Magistrate summoned for John]; GOB 29, p. 550 [John given permission to stay]

[70] GOB 29, p. 454 [John's raise to $50]

make their conjugal ties legal." Women like Milly were, understandably, reluctant to forego their independence; only as long as a woman remained unmarried was she assured both legal and economic autonomy. Under common law once a woman married, her husband acquired all rights to her property. Beyond this, she sacrificed her right to enter into contracts, to sue in a court of law, to execute a valid will, and to purchase or emancipate slaves. Each of these was a right that Milly, at some point in her life, would exercise, and for a woman not long out of slavery, being bound in marriage may have too closely resembled being bound in servitude. [71]

In 1830, the high-water mark of the free black population in Goochland, 38 of the county's 136 independent free black households were headed by unmarried women. In 1860, the number of households had declined to 129, but of these, 49 were headed by single women. Mutual consent was, of necessity, the basis for slave marriages, and it seems to have prevailed frequently in the free black community as well. In the case of the Pierces, John's freedom had no real impact either on their legal or economic status. Even so, from 1817 through 1822 John Pierce temporarily replaced Milly as the person identified as responsible for the personal property tax, and in 1820 John, not Milly, is listed as the head of their household in the census, a change which may say more about white attitudes and conventions than it does about the Pierces. [72]

---

[71] Lebsock, *op. cit.*, p. 106 [quote], pp. 23, 103-111 [discussion of free black women's legal and economic status]

[72] USCG 1820 free blacks numbered 685; in 1830, 795; in 1840, 653; in 1850, 649; in 1860, 691. The number of women is from the same source.

Milly Pierce

CHARACTER MATTERS: A DEED CONTINGENT ON RESPECTABILITY

John's emancipation may have had little impact on Milly's life, but in 1821, John Pierce proclaimed his freedom and his standing in the community when he became a landowner in his own right. For fifty dollars, he purchased one acre at Goochland Courthouse from Benjamin Anderson, one of a long line of powerful Goochlanders who owned much of the property around the Courthouse. Lydia Pierce's benefactor Samuel Woodson had preceded him, and John S. Fleming and John Thompson, Jr., both of whom figure later in this narrative, would follow him. Until 1823 when the county condemned two acres of his property, Anderson actually owned the land on which the courthouse stood. [73]

In John Pierce's deed, his property is proclaimed his freedom and his standing in the community when he became a landowner in his own right. For fifty dollars, he purchased one acre at Goochland Courthouse from Benjamin Anderson, one of a long line of powerful Goochlanders who owned much of the property around the Courthouse. Lydia Pierce's benefactor Samuel Woodson had preceded him, and John S. Fleming and John Thompson, Jr., both of whom figure later in this narrative, would follow him. Until 1823 when the county condemned two acres of his property, Anderson actually owned the land on which the courthouse stood. [74]

---

[73] GDB 24. p. 355 [John's Deed from Benjamin Anderson]; GDB 25, p. 375 [For $1 Benjamin Anderson sells 2 acres to the county]

[74] GDB 25, p. 161 [plat of Courthouse]; GDB 24, p. 355 [John's deed]

CeCe Bullard

In John Pierce's deed, his property is described as "the same land on which the said John Pierce hath lately built a house for his dwelling house" and was bounded by the fence around the house. An 1821 plat of the Courthouse shows "Pierce's house" just south of the Courthouse grounds and, beyond his house, an area marked "Pierce's garden." The house and land were granted to John Pierce and his wife for their lifetimes, and after their death to any of their children whom they might designate as heirs. To this point, the deed was fairly standard, but what followed were several "special reservations." [75]

Benjamin Anderson maintained a popular tavern on his Courthouse property, and he included a non-compete clause in the deed—perhaps, with good cause, considering suspicions about Milly's past activities. John Pierce or any other person was expressly forbidden to maintain a House of Entertainment or sell spirits on Pierce's property. Anderson was also greatly concerned about "depredations" to the field he owned around Pierce's house. Pierce was required to keep his livestock "well-enclosed," and when Anderson grew grain in the field, Pierce was "to prevent his fowls from doing any injury thereto."

Beyond this, the deed specified that if any of John Pierce's heirs should be "guilty of any dishonorable act unbecoming a respectable citizen and thereby becomes an undesirable neighbor" or if Pierce or his heirs wished to sell the land, Anderson or his heirs would have the right to buy back the land. These highly unusual restrictions make it abundantly clear that, despite considerable evidence of the good and

---

[75] GDB 24, p. 355 [John's deed]

Milly Pierce

responsible character of John Pierce, as a free black he was still not considered entirely trustworthy nor was he dealt with as an equal, even by whites who knew him well. [76]

FAR FROM EQUAL IN THE EYES OF THE LAW

Regardless of Benjamin Anderson's reservations about John Pierce as a neighbor, the county's confidence in its black jailer continued unabated. In 1822, John received not only his salary of $50 from the county, but also a special allocation of $31.75 for "finding John Pleasants a criminal in the jail of this county and for commitment." Indeed, the frequency with which John was paid for claims related to criminal prosecutions suggests that, despite its rural location and pastoral character, Goochland was not entirely peaceful nor crime-free. [77]

John Pleasants, a free black laborer, spent the summer of 1822 in the county jail awaiting trial on charges of rape and robbery. On May 30, his accuser Phebe Harris, a free person of color, testified that Pleasants "did forcefully and against her will ravish her and did also take from her possession one silver dollar." Despite the arguments of the defendant's lawyers, Charles F. Pope and H. H. Harrison, both prominent white attorneys, the gentlemen justices were of the opinions that Pleasants

---

[76]GOB 30, p. 213 [John's 1822 raise to $50]; Superior Court Orders 1809-1822, p. 530 [paid for John Pleasants]. In the course of John's 24 years as jailer, he received at least 13 payments specifically for criminal prosecutions.

[77]GOB 30, p. 217 [Pleasants charged]; _____ Acts 1831-1832, p. 22 [no trial by jury]; Superior Court Orders 1809-1822, p. 510 [Pleasants found not guilty]

was guilty and ordered that he be tried in the Superior Court of Law. While slaves were summarily tried by a panel of the county justices, free blacks were, until 1832, on an equal footing with whites in the courtroom and entitled to a trial by jury. When Pleasants came to trial on September 18, 1822, he was found not guilty by the white male jurors. [78]

John Pleasants' summer in the Goochland jail was still punishment for a man found innocent. Although a report to the court in 1820 described the two-room, timber jail as secure and commended John Pierce for providing "good and sufficient food [and] bed covering," it also noted that there was not heat in winter and that "in very warm weather prisoners must suffer considerably for want of air and from the effluvium that must necessarily arise in such close buildings…" Considering that summertime temperatures in the county often reached 90 degrees with humidity to match, Pleasants must have had a miserable time of it, John Pierce's ministrations not withstanding. [79]

A summer in jail, however uncomfortable, was actually a small price to pay in light of a recent action by the Virginia legislature. In early 1822, the Commonwealth had passed a law which ordered that, in addition to "stripes at the discretion of the jury," any free Negro or mulatto felon would "be adjudged to be sold

---

[78] Agee, *op. cit.*, p. 23 [jail conditions]

[79] _____. Acts 1822-1823, p. 56 [deportation for felony]; _____ Acts 1824, p. 36 [law extended to misdemeanor]; _____, Acts 1827, p. 29 [repeal of this law]; Russell, *Free Negro*, p. 106 [claims 35 persons deported]; _____, Acts of 1827-1828, p. 29 [new felon law]

as a slave, and transported and banished beyond the limits of the United States." In 1824, this punishment was extended to any free Negro or mulatto guilty of "grand larceny to the value of $10 or upwards." Despite deep reservations about free blacks, Virginia's citizenry were offended by the inhumanity of the law, and four years later it was repealed, but not before a number of free blacks had been enslaved and deported. Although not as harsh, the subsequent law was blatantly discriminatory. Free black felons were sentenced to a minimum of five years in the penitentiary; white felons, to two. Although no longer a matter of law, some might argue that little has changed in terms of relative sentencing. [80]

THE PUZZLE OF THE PIERCE'S COURTHOUSE PROPERTY

John's salary as jailer afforded the Pierces a rare and valuable commodity among rural free blacks—a regular cash income. Beyond this, their farm kept the Pierce family supplied with essential foodstuffs, provided produce for barter and may have generated some cash. Revenues from John's boat would have added to their income. Relative to the majority of free blacks and many whites, the Pierces were doing well. Even so, they may not have had much cash to spare with six children under 14, three under 26 and two slaves to feed and clothe. In 1822, John found it necessary to borrow $200 from his son John Pierce, Jr. The loan with interest, secured by John's Courthouse property, was payable on demand. As was customary, John

---

[80]USCG 1820 [Pierce household]; GDB 25, p. 144 [John's deed of trust on land]; GOB 30, p. 157 [John registers boat]

placed his property in trust with the clerk of court. Neither the loan agreement nor the deed of trust offers an explanation of the debt, but conceivably it originated with John's 1821 purchase of another boat "for the navigation of the James River above the great falls at Richmond...marked 'John Pierce Senr. Goochland No. 1.'" Whatever the reason, John's need for ready cash may have had unexpected consequences. [81]

Although the record makes no further mention of John Pierce's debt to his son, in 1825, Milly Pierce purchased the very same property with which John had secured the loan. The only reasonable explanation for this strange turn of events is that John Pierce, Jr. held his farther to the letter of their agreement; his father was unable to pay on demand, and, as stipulated in the deed of trust, the land was offered for sale. That a son would cause his father to lose his home seems implausible, until one considers the character and career of John Pierce, Jr. for who money, above all, seems to have mattered.

If John Pierce, Jr. did, in fact, force the sale of his father's house, it would explain why Milly Pierce paid John S. Fleming sixty dollars for "the two acres of land whereon the dwelling house of the said Mildred is now located which said two acres of land the said Mildred is to have and to hold during the joint life of herself and John Pierce, and the life of the longest lived of them." The discrepancy in acreage between

---

[81]GDB 26, p. 168 [Milly's deed for 2 acres from Fleming] Although the deed clearly states 2 acres and Fleming's property is reduced from 381 to 379 acres, these 2 acres are never included in Milly's holdings and the Land Tax records continue to show John as owning 1 acre

Milly Pierce

John's 1821 deed and Milly's 1825 deed may reflect the Pierces de facto ownership of the garden plot southeast of their home at the Courthouse. [82]

As Milly's deed points out, John Fleming had acquired these two acres as part of a much larger 381 acre parcel purchased for $11,000 from Isaac Curd. The land Fleming purchased from Curd was the same Courthouse tract previously owned by Benjamin Anderson and sold at public auction to satisfy Anderson's debts. Benjamin Anderson had held right of first refusal on John Pierce's property at the Courthouse, a right he may have exercised if William Miller had been forced to sell John's land to satisfy his debt to his son. If this occurred, John's land would have, once again, been a part of the Anderson tract when it was sold to Curd who subsequently sold it to Fleming. [83]

Like Anderson's deed to John Pierce, Fleming's deed to Milly was contingent upon "the express condition that the said Mildred shall not keep a House of Entertainment for others," an act which, in this instance, would simply void the deed. Initially, Fleming specified that upon the deaths of Mildred and John Pierce the land should revert to him at which time he would pay their heirs sixty dollars without

---

[82] GDB 26, p. 285 [Curd to Fleming]; GDB 25, p. 381 [Anderson deed of trust] John S. Fleming and Charles F. Pope authorized to sell Anderson's land to settle his debts; GDB 26, p. 282-283 [Anderson to Curd]

[83] GDB 26, p. 168 [Milly's deed] Fleming's note about his conversation with John is entered immediately following the deed. For more about the transfer of this tract from Fleming to Thompson, see pp. xx this ms. Milly was still living on the Courthouse land at her death in 1850, and her daughters Mary and Jane continued there until 1855, the last year the acre is listed in John Pierce's name.

interest. In an amendment written some two months after the deed, Fleming altered this last stipulation:

I have this day had a conversation with John Pierce and have promised him that when he and his wife Mildred shall die if his children living with him shall wish to reside on the land which his wife now holds a life estate in they may do so as long as it may be agreeable to them, provided they behave in such a way as not to incommode me or the tenants that I may have on the Courthouse farm.

Although Fleming, like Anderson, would eventually lose the land to satisfy his debts, his successor, John Thompson, Jr., a business associate of John Pierce, Jr.'s, appears to have honored Fleming's promise to John Pierce. [84]

While it seems that Milly did in fact buy the same land John had owned previously, the issue is further clouded by the fact that the tax collector continued to carry the property on the books as one acre owned by John Pierce—not two acres owned by Milly Pierce—until 1855. Although confusing, the discrepancy between the deed which lists Milly as the owner and the tax collectors' entries which assign the land to John is probably nothing more than a reflection of the tax man's chauvinism. Harder to explain and compounding the questions surrounding this transaction is the clerk's note next to the deed which indicates that the deed was "executed and delivered to Thomas Pierce [Milly's youngest son] for Milly Pierce, 7 May 1840."

---

[84]GLT 1825-1855 [John Pierce or "John Pierce dec'd." taxed on 1 acre]; GDB 26, p. 168 [note that deed delivered to Thomas Pierce]

Milly Pierce

Why the fifteen year lapse between recording the deed and its execution and delivery? There is no ready explanation. [85]

FREE BLACK REGISTRATION: RESTRICTING THE PRACTICE OF NEGROES GOING AT LARGE

With the matter of their home at the Courthouse settled, Milly and John may have spent the year of 1826 taking stock. Change was in the air. Both Milly and John were getting on in years. Milly was about fifty-six; John about sixty-eight. Most of their children were grown, and as required by law had presented themselves at the Courthouse to be registered as "free Negroes."

In an early expression of the white community's discomfort with the explosive growth of the free black population, the Virginia legislature in 1793 had passed a law forbidding the immigration of free blacks into the Commonwealth. As part of this law, the lawmakers also acted "to restrain the practice of Negroes going at large," denying free blacks their right to unlimited mobility. Henceforth, every free black was required to register with the local court. For 25 cents, he or she could receive a copy of the registration with the seal of the court. Only with such "freedom papers" could a free black move between localities with impunity or obtain employment legally. [86]

---

[85] Shepherd, *op. cit.,* vol. 1, p. 238 [1793 immigration and registration law]

[86] The Goochland Register of Free Negroes was maintained from May 21, 1804 through November 23, 1864. Although the last numbered registration is

Considering that every black was presumed a slave without proof to the contrary and the penalty for being caught without one's freedom papers was imprisonment, a rush to register might seem predictable. In actuality, registration was rather haphazard, enforcement of the law lax, and, as a result, the registers of free Negroes are far from comprehensive. The majority of rural free blacks—self-employed and content to remain where they were known—had no pressing reason to register. There may also have been a real reluctance on the part of many free blacks to have any dealings with the white authorities who were the enforcers of ever more oppressive anti-free black laws. [87]

With little sense of urgency, many free blacks simply waited until they had occasion to travel to the Courthouse to register. Frequently several family members registered at the same time. Over the years, however, registration apparently evolved into a rite of passage for many young free blacks, and a significant number presented themselves for registration when they reached the age of twenty-one. Milly's oldest son John marked his coming of age in 1814 by registering with the clerk as "a free man of color about 5 ft. 8 inches high and abt. 21 yrs. of age of yellow complexion." His brother followed suit in 1819. [88]

2046, the records were misnumbered in the original jumping from 1099 to 2000. The actual number of free blacks who registered was 1145.

[87] Many of these registrations occur in clumps of family names on the same date. Of those who registered, 32% did so around age 21. GFN # 128 John Pierce, Jr. emancipated by the will of Tucker Woodson; GFN # 241 Isaac Pierce "of colour" emancipated by the will of Tucker Woodson.

[88] 47% of those who registered were female. GFN #758 Clarissa Cowigg or Cowig was black and cited her emancipation in 1782 by Thomas Pleasants, Jr. (GDB 13, p. 246)

Milly Pierce

For free women, registration had special importance; their status determined that of their children. Over fifty percent of those who made the trek to the Courthouse to register were mothers determined to ensure that their children were recognized as free. Even so, there seems to have been no particular hurry about registering. Clarissa Cowigg, emancipated in 1782 by Thomas Pleasants, Jr.'s deed of manumission—the first recorded in Goochland—did not go to the trouble to register until 1847 when she was 79 years old. The elderly woman probably made the effort at the urging of her children, anxious to make certain that no questions could be raised about her descendants' right to freedom. [89]

The primary reason to register, however, was to travel safely beyond the borders of the county. Several of Milly's daughters and their husbands moved to other parts of Virginia or left the state entirely. Their departures followed hard on the heels

---

[89] GFN # 249 Sally Dungee; # 265 Phebe Carter; #350 SukeyIsaacks; #352 Martha Morris; and #380 Lucy Moss. A Page Carter is listed in the Richmond Census. In the 1830 Richmond census, only a Phoebe Carter is listed as the head of a household of eight containing no adult male. Presumably Page either left or died. Sally and Reuben Dungee disappear from the County records and the Virginia census following their marriage in 1819 and Sally's 1820 registration. Lucy and Daniel Moss remained in Goochland until around 1827 when they disappear from the Personal Property records and Lucy registered. They do not appear in the 1830 or 1840 Virginia census. Austin and Susan Isaacks were still in Goochland in 1826 when Austin sued John Martin (GOB 21, p. 50). In 1827, however, in another hearing regarding this suit he is described as "a non-resident of the Commonwealth" (GOB 31, p. 131). GMR, p. 368-Martha Pierce m. Wilson Morris, 21 July 1825. A Wilson Morris appears in the 1830, 1840 and 1850 Richmond census, but his wife's name is Nancy. A cooper, he was John Pierce Jr.'s partner in a land deal in Richmond in 1849. When the property was sold in 1851, he and Nancy had moved to Philadelphia (Hustings (Richmond) Deed Book (RDB) 66, p. 305). Possibly he was Martha's widower?

of their registrations. Sally Dungee registered in 1820 at age 23, and both she and Reuben Dungee disappear forever from Goochland records. A year later, at age 21, Phebe Carter registered immediately after her 1825 wedding to Wilson Morris and just before they left Goochland. Susan and Austin Isaacks remained in the county for some time after their marriage, but in 1825 at age 23 Susan registered, and by 1827, the couple had departed the Commonwealth. They may have been accompanied by Susan's sister Lucy who registered the same year at age 38, and with her husband, Daniel Moss, who also apparently left the state. [90]

Unlike their off-spring, neither John nor Milly ever registered. Presumably, they never had occasion to leave Goochland, and, secure in their position in the county and certainly well-known to those in authority, they simply never bothered to do so—even though it would have entailed nothing more than a stroll across the Courthouse Square.

A SHIFT IN PRIORITIES

Not all of Milly and John's children left home, or Goochland. By 1830, Judith—another independent and self-supporting Pierce woman—was living nearby as

---

[90] USCG 1830 Judith Pierce's and Lydia Pierce Cousins' households: GPPT 1821, Isaac is listed as living as a free male over 21 in John Pierce, Jr.'s household and appears to still be there in 1830; USCG 1830 John Pierce, Jr. household: "John Pierce...lived between the Courthouse and Bolling Hall, east of Little and Cheney Creeks." (William Bolling, "The Diary of Colonel William Bolling May 1836," *The Goochland County Historical Society Magazine*, vol. 9, no. 2, p. 31)

Milly Pierce

head of her own household of one. Lydia Pierce Cousins, now the mother of four girls and four boys, was just next door. Isaac, too, had not gone far. He had moved just up the road to live with his brother John who had married and started a family of his own. John now headed a household of 27 which included two free boys under 10, one free male between 24 and 36 (Isaac), two free males between 36 and 55 (John was one), three free girls under 10 and one free female between 24 and 36 (his wife, Eliza) and 18 slaves. John Pierce, Jr. owned no land at this time, but may have rented or leased property just west of the Courthouse in an area where he would, one day, become a large landowner. [91]

Still at home with John and Milly were three males and three females between 11 and 24 years of age, one boy under 10 and one slave. Milly's three youngest children, Thomas, 19, Mary 15, and Jane 13, were almost certainly among those living in Milly and John's household. Who the other four may have been is pure

---

[91] USCG 1830 [composition of Pierce household]; Thomas, Mary and Jane were still living with Milly when she died in 1850. Their ages are based on the registrations as free blacks. GFN # 532 1835 Thomas about 24; GFN # 812 1843 Mary about 28; and GFN #625 1840, Jane about 23. The only information about Rebecca Pierce is her registration as # 303 in 1823 at age 16 in which she is described as "of colour" and born free in Goochland. Madison Pierce registered as #514 in 1833 and was described as about 21, light yellow and born free in Goochland. William Henry Pierce registered in 1840 as #626 and was about 22, bright yellow and born free in Goochland. They were not Milly's as she clearly identified Thomas, Mary and Jane as her three youngest children in her will. Based on their ages, both Madison and William could have been John Pierce, Jr.'s sons. The suspicion about their relationship to John is also raised by the fact that both are listed in the personal property records with John, Jr. in 1855 and 1858, and Madison, at least, was living with John Jr.'s son John Pierce. John Pierce, Jr. m. Eliza Ligon Dec. 8, 1820 in Chesterfield County, Va. (County Marriage Register, p. 160).

speculation, although it is possible three of them were a Rebecca Pierce who would have been 23, James Madison Pierce, about 18, and William Henry Pierce, aged 10 or so. Rebecca may have been Milly's daughter, but Madison, as he was called, and William almost certainly were not. Most likely the two boys were the illegitimate children of John Pierce, Jr. who had not married until 1820 when he began a legitimate family. [92]

As they surveyed their emptying nest and considered their advancing years, Milly and John appear to have decided that a shift in priorities was in order. With their homegrown labor force rapidly diminishing, they reduced the size of their farm. In 1826, Milly sold the 34¾ acres she had purchased from Benjamin Anderson in 1815 to John S. Fleming, Anderson's successor as owner of the Courthouse tract. She would retain the 21 acres remaining from her original 23 for the rest of her life. With less farm work to do, Milly also sold two of her three slaves, and from this time on, she never owned more than one slave. Relying primarily on John's job at the Courthouse and his involvement in the growing commerce on the James River and Kanawha Canal, they could still live comfortably. By 1826, John's base salary had risen to $120 and, with payments for his assistance with criminal prosecutions, his total income from the county that year was $185.30. John also increased his investment in river

---

[92] GLT 1826 Milly's land holdings were reduced to 21 acres in the tax records with a note that 34 ¾ acres had been sold to John S. Fleming, but no deed can be found. Hereafter, she paid tax only on the 21 acres. GPPT 1826 Milly taxed on only 1 slave and 1 horse. GOB 31, p. 58 [John's 1826 salary], p. 84 [$65.50 for "attending…prosecutions"]; GOB 31, p. 245 [John registers second boat.]

commerce with the purchase of another boat which had registered as "John Pierce, No. 2 Goochland County" in 1828. [93]

COMMERCE ON THE JAMES RIVER AND KANAWHA CANAL

The James River and Kanawha Canal extending from Richmond through Goochland and on to the west had first been envisioned by George Washington as a major commercial artery across Virginia to the Ohio River. Although this dream was never realized, it appears that John Pierce found his initial investment in a boat sufficiently rewarding to justify the purchase of another. Indeed, John was no longer the only black canal boat owner in Goochland. In 1821, John Copland, Lydia Pierce Cousins' brother-in-law, had registered a boat "for navigating the James above the great falls of Richmond," as had two other free blacks, Samuel Howell and Charles Gray. Gray, emancipated by Isaac W. Pleasants along with Billy Perry who died of his freedom, had fared rather better as a free man than his friend. [94]

The canal had been much improved in recent years, and by 1825 extended to Maidens Adventure, just south of Goochland Courthouse. In fact, it was a walk of

---

[93] GDB 30, p. 165 [Copland, Howell, and Grey register boats]; GMR, p. 366 Ridley Cousins married ~~married~~ John Copland in 1824. The only Samuel Howells in the Goochland records are free blacks who appear in the Marriage Register, personal property and census records, but none of the right age registered. The free black Howell family was large and moderately successful, owning some property. Charles Gray registered as # 161 in 1815 at age 31 and cited his emancipation by Isaac W. Pleasants.

[94] Dunaway, *op. cit.*, p. 87 [canal improvements]

little more than a mile from John's house to the canal. The James River and Kanawha Canal Company had built a series of twelve locks which connected the river with a basin at Richmond and a nine mile pond at Maiden's Adventure to serve as a feeder for the upper portion of the canal. River transport between Goochland and Richmond was greatly facilitated by these improvements, and no doubt John Pierce took advantage of the increased commerce on the River. [95]

Unfortunately, John would not live to enjoy the heyday of canal transportation in Virginia. It was not until the 1850s that the canal became the main artery of commerce in Virginia, especially central Virginia. The canal reached its height as a revenue producer in 1863 "when its tonnage was 210,032, its gross revenue $293,512,92, and its net revenue $170,368.81." Maximum tonnage was not reached until 1860, but revenues had begun to decline. Ultimately, destruction by Union forces during the Civil War, floods and the arrival of the railroad along the banks of the James spelled the end of the canal. [96]

DEFYING STEREOTYPES: A FREE BLACK CAREER WOMAN

It is appealing to imagine John busily engaged in canal commerce when in 1827 he was relieved of his duties as Goochland's jailer. After 24 years of serving in

---

[95] *Ibid.*, p. 168 [Canal tonnage and revenues]; Agee, *op. cit.*, pp. 74-76 [end of canal]

[96] GOB 31, p. 254 [John omitted from Levy] John served as jailer from 1803 through 1827

Milly Pierce

the county in this position, he might have relished the idea of being his own boss and spending more time on the river. In reality, it is more likely that, approaching 70, he was either no longer up to the task or even dead. In 1830, Milly replaced John as head of the Pierce household census, and in 1833, John's acre at the Courthouse was recorded in the land tax ledger as the property of "John Pierce, dec'd." [97]

The name "Pierce," however, did not disappear from the county levy, only it is Milly Pierce, rather than John, who was paid $70 in 1828 for taking care of and cleaning the courthouse, furnishing water and fuel, making fires and taking care of the public square. Sheriff William Gray was paid $50 for his "public services as jailer" as well as his $75 salary as Sheriff. Without breaking stride, Milly assumed John's duties at the Courthouse. She also began to solidify the Pierce family's position as dependable, even indispensable, retainers to those at the seat of local power. [98]

That Milly was allowed to step into John's role at the Courthouse was one more measure of her exceptional character and the respect she received from Goochland's most powerful white men. She may not have actually performed the work at the Courthouse—after all she had able-bodied children and grandchildren as well as a slave—but it was she who negotiated with and was paid by the county. For a woman, black or white, to step into a man's role was unusual, and although the job

---

[97] GOB 31, p. 254 [Milly in county levy; Sheriff paid as jailer]

[98] Lebsock, *op. cit.*, p. 147 [women's work]

was essentially that of a servant, it pushed the limits of traditional women's work in both responsibility and pay. [99]

From 1828 through 1841 Milly earned $70 a year for tending what was, in fact, a new Goochland Courthouse, a handsome white-columned, red brick Jeffersonian building completed in the summer of 1827. Milly also was paid an additional $4 to $15 for cleaning the courthouse and providing water and wood when the Circuit Superior Court of Law and Chancery was in session. In 1842, her county salary was increased to $75, an amount she continued to receive until her death. Some of the increase may have covered the candles she was now expected to provide. Milly clearly enjoyed the favor of the powers-that-were at the Courthouse. When the Gentlemen Justices settled an 1838 dispute about who was in charge of taking care of the public square, setting aside an order delegating the job to Peter J. Archer, and assigning it instead to Richard C. Vaughan, they also took the opportunity to "affirm that Milly Pierce is in charge of the cleaning and care of the Courthouse and furnishing the Court with fuel, fire and water." [100]

---

[99] GOBs 1828-1841 each year Milly was paid $70; Agee, *op. cit.*, p. 49 [new courthouse]; Circuit Superior Court of Law and Chancery Order Book 1837-1846 and 1847-1863. Milly was paid twice a year in the spring and fall in amounts from $4 to $8 per session; GOB 32, p. 470 [Milly paid $75]; GOB 1836-44 (not numbered), p. 83 [Milly's job affirmed]

[100] GOB 32, p. 160 [Thomas becomes jailer]; *ibid.*, p. 272 [Thomas cares for Underwood]; *ibid.*, p. 501 [Thomas paid for two lunatics in jail]; *ibid.*, p. 226 [Thomas paid $15 for whitewashing]; *ibid.*, p. 406 [Thomas paid for repairing rail]; GOB 1838-1843, p. 156 [Judith paid for straightjacket]; *ibid.*, p. 264 [Henry Cousins paid for ford]

Milly Pierce

SERVING THE WHITE ESTABLISHMENT

Milly was not the only member of her family who enjoyed the good will of the officials at the Courthouse. Among her most enduring legacies to her family were her Courthouse connections. Whenever some service was required at the Courthouse, there was a Pierce ready and willing to perform it.

Milly's youngest son, Thomas, first appears in the county levy in 1832 when he was paid $26.26 for his services as "jailer of the county," a job he filled until 1838. In 1833, he received $10.10 "on account of George Underwood, a lunatic kept in the jail as there was no room in the hospital in Staunton." Lunatics, rather than criminals, seem to have occupied much of Thomas's time. In 1836, he was paid a total of $31.98 for "attending" two lunatics and only $11.01 1/3 for criminals. Unlike his father, Thomas never received a salary but was always paid on a case by case basis. During this period, Thomas was also paid for odd jobs at the Courthouse: $15 for whitewashing the jail and $20 for repairing a railing at the Courthouse. In 1839, his older sister Judith received $2 from the county levy "for making a straight jacket for Wm. Cheatham a lunatic (& who has no property) whilst in the jail of this County..." Milly's son-in-law Henry Cousins, too, benefited from her connections: in 1840, he improved the ford of the creek at the Courthouse for a sum of $15.91. [101]

---

[101] GOB 1838-1843, p. 403 [Milly paid for Sims coffin]; Elisha Sims is occasionally referred to as Elijah and his last name sometimes spelled "Syms." All information on Sims is from the GPPT records. 1788 through 1837 and the USCG 1810, 1820 and 1830. He is presumed to have been alone and possibly a resident of the Poor House because there are no Sims at all in the 1840 Goochland census.

In 1842, Milly's account with the county government included a special allocation of $3 for making a coffin for Elisha Sims. No doubt one of Milly's sons or grandsons performed this task for Sims, an aged free Negro who died apparently on the dole. A free man for at least 54 years, Elisha Sims had over the years moved almost annually from one white-owned farm to another to find work as a ditcher or a planter, unskilled and menial jobs. Even so, he and his wife had raised two daughters and a son, and periodically owned a horse or mule. Despite an industrious life, Sims died alone and indigent, probably a resident of the county poor house—his sad end an indication of just how marginal economic survival could be for free blacks. [102]

By 1850, the cost of a coffin had increased to $5, the sum paid to John Pierce, John Pierce, Jr.'s oldest son, for "a coffin and burying a Negro." As late as 1870, another of Milly's grandsons William H. Pierce, continuing what was by then almost a family tradition, was paid a dollar a day to guard prisoners "because of the insecurity of the jail." In the same year, Milly's granddaughter Martha Jane Cousins, "restaurant keeper at Goochland Courthouse," received $4.80 from the court for providing dinner to jurors hearing a felony case. In the following year, Martha Jane's older brother Philip presented an account to the court for $30 incurred in his capacity as an Overseer of the Poor. That a black man should occupy this particular position is deeply ironic,

---

[102] GOB 1844-1852, p. 416 [John Pierce paid for coffin]; Circuit Court Common Law Order Book 5 1863-1883, pp. 149, 184, 272, 318 [William Pierce paid for guarding jail]; GOB 1862-1871, p. 455 [Martha Jane Cousins paid for feeding jurors in Commonwealth versus Mat Jasper]; *ibid.*, p. 565 [Philip Cousins Overseer of Poor]; Hening, *op. cit.*, XII, pp. 27-28 [Overseer's duties]. Although the circumstantial evidence indicates that Philip Cousins was a son of Milly's daughter Lydia, there is some question about this.

Milly Pierce

considering that the Overseers had hounded and haunted free blacks for eighty years prior to the Civil War. Granted, Reconstruction turned the old order on its head, but a mere six years before Philip became an overseer, the job would have required him to place free black bastards in involuntary apprenticeships, to hire-out free black vagrants and to sell free black tax delinquents into slavery. [103]

A FREE BLACK AND HER SLAVE

Milly's relatives were not the sole beneficiaries of her good standing at the Courthouse. Her slave, Franklin, also found paid employment there. Beginning in 1846, the Goochland court awarded Franklin "an annual allowance" of $5 for "attending the Courthouse square." This unusual arrangement, reminiscent of John Pierce, Sr.'s employment while still a slave, suggests that Milly was to some extent a custodial slave-owner who allowed Franklin a measure of freedom. Significantly, Franklin was paid directly by the county, rather than through Milly. Yet, the fact remains that Milly owned Franklin, a stark fact that begs the question: what was the nature of this unusual relationship? [104]

---

[103] GOB 1844-1852, p. 131 [Franklin paid $5 allowance]

[104] Acts 1847-1848, pp. 119, 120. The law forbade blacks to assemble and forbade a slave to remain on anyone's property for more than four hours without his master's permission. For good discussions of the relationships between free blacks and slaves, see Russell, *Free Negro*, pp. 130-137 and Berlin, *op. cit.*, pp. 269-70.

In the course of their daily lives, the difference in legal status between Milly and Franklin was probably seldom an issue between the two, their relationship more that of employer and hired hand than overseer and slave. Whatever distinctions existed were more likely based on the differences in their economic and social positions. Yet, bound by a common heritage, a shared culture and their mutual experience of slavery, they were in most ways more alike than not. If Milly were typical of the majority of free blacks, she mingled easily with slaves, or at least slaves of the "right sort." She did, after all, have her somewhat elevated status in both the black and white communities to maintain. While Milly may have exercised some discrimination about those slaves with whom she associated, it was the white population that would have viewed her consorting with slaves with suspicion and disapproval. Such relationships had long been discouraged as potentially explosive, and eventually the legislature actually attempted to limit them by law. [105]

Milly may have harbored few if any prejudices against slaves (after all she had "married" one), yet her own freedom must have mattered greatly to her—even if the benefits it conferred were often intangible, even if the distinctions between the free and the enslaved continued to diminish. Possibly as she dictated her will, Milly was stirred by memories of that long ago day in 1795 when she herself had become a free woman, perhaps the image of John, finally freed at 58, loomed before her, for Milly's legacy to her slave Franklin was his freedom. In her will Milly stipulated that "I leave my man Franklin free after he shall have served my two daughters, Mary and Jane

---

[105]GDB 36, p. 222 [Milly's will]; GOB 1852-1862, p. 46 [Franklin allowed to register]; GFN # 957 Franklin registered in 1853.

Milly Pierce

Pierce, for two years after my death." She concluded with the "wish that the County of Goochland suffer him to remain in this state." In 1852, with the consent of Milly's executor, William W. Cosby, the court allowed Franklin, aged 59, to register as a free man of color. [106]

Franklin's freedom was not all that Milly apparently bequeathed her slave. Within a few months of Milly's death, Franklin assumed some of her duties at the Courthouse. In the spring of 1850, Milly was paid $8 for tending the Courthouse while the circuit court was in session; in the fall, Franklin was paid the same. By 1852, Franklin, now called Franklin French, was on the County payroll receiving Milly's former salary of $70 a year for "keeping the Courthouse" and an additional $5 for tending the public square. The seamless transition suggests that Franklin may have actually performed these services for some time before Milly's death. [107]

If Franklin's new status as a free man made little real difference to the quality of his life, he was, ironically, more fortunate than most. Freedom for many newly emancipated blacks was hardly an unalloyed good. Accustomed to being provided with shelter, clothing and food and often emancipated in old age with few skills, most former slaves struggled to survive. Franklin, in contrast, had inherited not only his

---

[106]Circuit Superior Court of Law and Chancery Order Book 1847-1863, p. 110 Milly paid in April and p. 198, Franklin paid in September; GOB 1844-1852, p. 521 [Franklin's pay]

[107]Frazier, *op. cit.*, pp. 192-205, 300-313; Berlin, *op. cit*, pp. 57, 247 [privileged position of mulattos]. The Goochland tax records are inconsistent throughout in the designations of individuals as free Negroes or mulattos, but at various points both John and Milly are described as mulatto; GFN #128 John Pierce, Jr., 1814; *ibid.*, # 662 Judith Pierce, 1842; *ibid.*, # 683 Mary Pierce, 1843; *ibid.*, # 957 Franklin French, 1853.

freedom but a job, both perhaps expressions of Milly's appreciation and affection for "my man Franklin."

ALMOST FREE, ALMOST WHITE: HUE MAKES A DIFFERENCE

It was probably not incidental to the Pierce's privileged position at the Courthouse that they and most of their connections—even Franklin French—were mulatto rather than black. Although white southerners deplored miscegenation, free mulattos were generally more successful than free blacks in securing remunerative employment in the white community. Both John and Milly were mulatto; John Pierce, Jr. was "yellow"; his older sister Judith "yellow, hair nearly straight"; and their youngest sister Mary "very bright yellow." When he registered in 1853, Franklin French, too, was described by the clerk as "yellow." [108]

If white attitudes toward all free blacks were ambiguous and complex, their attitudes towards free mulattos were even more ambivalent. A mulatto represented what many considered the moral depravity of all blacks, and a moral lapse, at least, on the part of some whites. Mulattos also portend one of the most horrifying prospects envisioned by those who opposed universal emancipation: an inevitable mixing of the races. Imagining such an outcome, Thomas Jefferson, and many who favored the

---

[108]Thomas Jefferson, *Writings: Notes on Virginia* (The Library of America, New York, 1984), p. 270 [racial mixture]

banishment of all freed slaves, believed that they must be "removed beyond the reach of mixture." [109]

Yet, it was this very mixture which made mulattos more palatable as intimates than those of pure African ancestry. To what degree the choice was conscious is unclear, but many whites preferred personal servants who were partially white. This preference toward mulattos was a curious corollary of the belief that blacks were innately inferior—"a brutish sort of people"—and suited to only the most menial work. A Negro, lightened with a tincture of white, was a superior, improved Negro. [110]

Mulattos were the most troubling—and privileged and successful—element in a troubling caste. Certainly the most conspicuous example of white ambivalence toward mulattos was Thomas Jefferson. Jefferson consistently expressed his horror of the mixing of the races, yet for most of his adult life, surrounded himself with his mulatto in-laws as house servants. Owner of some 200 slaves, he only manumitted eight—all of whom were mulatto and believed to be direct descendents of his father-in-law, John Wayles. [111]

---

[109] For discussions of white preference for mulattos, see Berlin, *op. cit.*, p. 151 and Frazier, *op. cit.*, pp. 145-146; Morgan, *op. cit.*, p. 314 [brutish sort]

[110] Paul Finkelman, *Slavery and the Founders: Race and Liberty in the Age of Jefferson* (Armonk, N.Y., 1996) pp. 129, 142-143. [Jefferson's slaves]

[111] _____. Legislative Petitions, Goochland, MS. A7095-1831 [petition for removal of free blacks]

While the Pierces' white connections will probably never be known, it seems likely that skin color was a factor in John's positions as Dr. Brydin's personal servant and county jailer and in the close relationships enjoyed by both Milly and Lydia Pierce Cousins with the Woodson family. Unquestionably, character and diligence were major factors in the family's successful interaction with the white community, but, ironically, being almost white may have been almost as helpful as being almost free.

WHITE AMBIVALENCE

The continued favor with which Goochland's white leaders regarded the Pierces was far from typical of their attitude toward free blacks as a class. Several of the prominent men who were in daily contact with Milly and John Pierce and found them worthy employees signed a printed petition, circulated throughout Virginia in 1831, which expressed the desire that all free blacks be removed "to other lands." [112]

Their objections to free blacks were threefold. According to the petitioners, free blacks fostered, even promoted, "impracticable hopes" and "wild and visionary schemes" among those who were "even more ignorant and unreflecting" (read slaves). Marked by Nature as unsuitable for the fullness of freedom and protected by law from enslavement, free blacks were "of necessity, degraded, profligate, vicious, turbulent and discontented." Furthermore, "pursuing no course of regular business, and

---

[112] *Ibid.*

Milly Pierce

negligent of every thing like economy and husbandry," they were a burden on the community. [113]

Although only sixty-three Goochlanders signed the petition, several of the signatures suggest the pervasive and profound character of white ambivalence about free blacks. Former county clerk William Miller had for many years worked alongside and paid John Pierce. His son and successor Narcissus W. Miller worked daily with Milly. Dr. George W. Harris, Dr. John Morris and John Fleming were Milly and John's immediate neighbors. Each of these men had ample opportunity to observe that Milly and John were hard-working, thrifty, seemingly content and hardly wild-eyed visionaries. Even so, they signed a petition which labeled Milly and John the "bane" of their country's "prosperity, morality and peace" and urged that they be shipped off to "other lands." [114]

CHANGING ATTITUDES: SLAVES REBEL, FREE BLACKS SUFFER

However conflicted Virginians may have been about free blacks, the views expressed in the petition were widely held. Virginia's lawmakers had continued slowly

---

[113] *Ibid.* Harris, Morris and Fleming each owned land that according to the land tax records adjoined Milly's at one time or another.

[114] Examples of increased legislative pressure on free blacks: _____, Acts 1819, p. 22-23. Overseers to check every three months for free Negro self-sufficiency, if not, declared vagrants. Not allowed to deal with slaves without consent of master; if do so, declared vagrant; Acts, 1822, p. 35. Instead of punishment in penitentiary for two or more years, stripes and banishment; Acts, 1824, p. 37. Punishment for grand larceny to value of $10 or more punishable with stripes, sale and banishment.

but deliberately to tighten the screws on free blacks during the prior decade, and the legislature of 1831-1832 produced some of the most vicious rhetoric and repressive law yet directed toward the Commonwealth's free black population. The law, always an uneven, shifting ground beneath the feet of Virginia's free blacks, began to look like a slippery slope towards slavery. [115]

Despite the legislature's earlier efforts to reduce the number of free blacks in Virginia, their numbers continued to increase, and they remained an ever-present and uncomfortable reminder that blacks were not, by nature, suited only to slavery. Free black population growth had slowed and the number of manumissions had declined, yet Virginia's free black population numbered 47,348 in 1830, an increase of 10,474 or 8% from 1820. The percentage of increase was only slightly less than that for whites and slaves. Goochland's growth in all categories was marginally higher than that for the state as a whole, reflecting the attraction for many Virginians of the more sparsely settled western counties. By 1830, Goochland's white population had grown by almost 10% to 3,857. Slaves now numbered 5,706, an increase of 10.3%. Free blacks accounted for only 7.7% of the total population, yet their numbers reached an all-time high of 795 in 1830, an increase of 8.5% from 1820. Free blacks were keeping pace with over-all population growth in Virginia, a fact that did not go unnoticed by the legislature. [116]

---

[115] Berlin, *op. cit.*, pp. 136, 397, 399 [Virginia population figures]; USCG 1820 and 1830 [Goochland population figures]

[116] Kenneth S. Greenburg, *The Confessions of Nat Turner and Related Documents* (Bedford Books of St. Martins Press, Boston, 1996), pp. 21, 22 [Nat Turner Rebellion]

Milly Pierce

Demographics alone, however, were not sufficient to account for the frenzy of repression directed towards Virginia's free blacks in the 1831-1832 legislature. Once again, in reaction to a slave revolt, Virginia's lawmakers vented their fury and frustration on the free black population. In 1831 Nat Turner, a Bible-reading and visionary slave who believed he was on a divine mission to lead his people from bondage, led a savage attack on the white population of Southampton County. In the course of two days, Turner and his followers slaughtered 55 people, including Turner's owner Joseph Travis, his wife and three children. Turner was eventually captured and executed on November 11, 1831. Of the 50 slaves who were arraigned in the matter, nineteen were hanged and twelve banished from the state. [117]

Five free blacks were identified and charged as participants in the Turner massacre. One was discharged and four were tried in Superior Court. Of the four who went to trial, three were released, and one was tried and hanged. These five free blacks, guilty or not, were all that was necessary to reinforce the fear and loathing that many whites felt toward all free blacks. So strong was the reaction against free blacks in Southampton County that, in fear of their lives, possibly as many as 300 or one fifth of the county's free black population accepted transport to Liberia. [118]

---

[117] *Ibid.*

[118] _____. Documents of the Virginia General Assembly, House of Delegates 1832, Document 1, p. 1 [Governor Floyd's remarks]; Goochland County Minute Book 1811-1818, pp. 440-441 [George, Grandison and Plato ordered to be hanged between 11 am and 3 pm, June 5, 1818]; *ibid.*, p. 439 [John Binns charged and acquitted]

CeCe Bullard

THE DANGERS OF FRATERNIZING WITH SLAVES

The "banditti of slaves" who had "participated in the bloody tragedy, have expiated their crimes by undergoing public execution," Governor John Floyd assured the citizens of Virginia in his 1831 address to the Virginia legislature. Nat Turner and his confederates were, however, only the most recent and visible of the rebellious slaves and allegedly subversive free blacks who terrified white Virginians. On June 5, 1818, three dark bodies had hung from the gallows at Goochland Courthouse. A stark image against the broad blue sky of central Goochland, the three executed slaves dangled almost at Milly Pierce's doorstep. Although intent upon the care of her children and the cultivation of her land—and relatively secure in her freedom—Milly must have shivered at the sight. Another free black, John Binns, had almost become a fourth victim of the hangman's noose. [119]

The son of Sally and Gabriel Binns (one of the slaves emancipated by Thomas Pleasants in 1782), John was indicted along with the three slaves—George, Plato, and Grandison—for "feloniously plotting and conspiring in the murder" of a white man Henry D. Carver, overseer on Randolph Harrison's "Dover" plantation. The case against Binns was based upon his loan of a gun to the slave Plato, the same gun with which George murdered Henry Carver. Two slaves, Milford and Charles, allowed

---

[119] John Binns [Bins] was the son of Gabriel and Sally Binns. Gabe Binns registered in 1814 as GFN #150 and cited his emancipation by Thomas Pleasants, Jr. His wife was named in the 1813 GPPT; John Binns never registered; Goochland County Minute Book 1811-1818, pp. 440-443 [Testimony in the trial of George, Grandison and Plato]

to testify only because the defendants were slaves, gave evidence that George had sworn to kill Carver after Carver had whipped him. A white witness, Daniel Rowlett, testified that on another occasion when Carver had punished George, the slave had "called for assistance from the Negroes and cursed them and asked if they would suffer him to be treated so." In response, Plato advanced with his plow whip clubbed within 15 or 20 steps" and refused to retreat when ordered to by Carver. Rowlett had intervened, and Plato had "stopped and after a little while retreated." [120]

John Binns and his friend Royal Cowig, grandson of Clarissa Cowig, another of Thomas Pleasants, Jr.'s former slaves, also testified in the case. Cowig had borrowed the gun in question from a Mr. Pleasants. While Cowig was in Richmond, his wife loaned the gun to John Binns who wanted to shoot a flock of partridges. Binns, in turn, had loaned the gun to Plato "to shoot a wild hog that the Overseer Carver had given to the Negroes which they could not catch with the Dogs." When Cowig asked for his gun back, Binns had agreed to go with him to "Dover" to retrieve it. When they arrived at "Dover," Milford had informed them that there was "a great alarm" at the stables and that George had "flashed the gun at Carver." Plato, however, knew where the gun was—behind a fence about 150 yards from the stable—and returned it to Royal Cowig who, the next day, returned it to Mr. Pleasants. [121]

---

[120] GFN # 138 Royal Cowig registered at 21 in 1814. GFN # 758 Clarissa Cowig or Cowigg registered in 1847 and cited her emancipation by Thomas Pleasants, Jr.; Goochland County Minute Book 1811-1818, p. 441 [Testimony Binns and Cowigg]

[121] Goochland County Minute Book 1811-1818, pp. 439-440 [Sentencing of slaves]; _____, Acts of 1817 (Richmond, 1818), p. 5 [Appropriation for executed slaves]

Defended by John S. Fleming, Binns was found "not guilty." Fleming, the court-appointed counsel for the slaves, was rather less successful in pleading the cases of George, Grandison and Plato. The court was unanimous in finding all three guilty and sentenced "to be hanged until he be dead." At the end of each death sentence, the Court recorded its valuation of the condemned man. George was worth $850; Grandison, $750; and Plato, $700. Randolph Harrison's loss of $2,300 in personal property was almost exactly a third of the $7000 the Virginia legislature had routinely appropriated for "slaves executed or transported" in the year 1818. [122]

As John Binns' narrow escape shows, consorting with slaves had real risks for free blacks. It is little wonder that some kept a safe distance from their enslaved brethren. Even so, there were often strong family ties between free blacks and slaves. In fact, John Binns' wife was a slave whom he owned. Binns' association with Randolph Harrison's slaves, however, had almost cost him his life, and his involvement in the affair must have intensified the suspicion and hostility that all free blacks faced, even in a fairly tolerant environment. Following the trial, John Binns left Goochland. [123]

---

[122] GPPT 1817 John Binns owned 1 horse or mule and 1 slave over 16 years; After 1817, John Binns disappears from this and all Goochland records.

[123] _____, Documents of the Virginia General Assembly, House of Delegates, Document 1, p. 2. [Governor Floyd's remarks]

Milly Pierce

LIBERIA: "THE LAST BENEFIT WE CAN CONFER"

Whenever slaves aroused the fear and anger of the white populace, those feelings quickly spilled over onto the free black community. Once Governor Floyd had finished congratulating himself on the quick and thorough suppression of the Turner rebellion, he quickly turned his attention to "free people of colour." It was his belief that outside agitators had fostered discontent among free blacks as well as slaves, having "opened more enlarged views, and urged the achievement of a higher destiny, by means for present less violent, but not different in the end from those presented to the slaves." [124]

Without any apparent irony, the governor observed that the legislature had heretofore treated free blacks "with indulgent kindness" and that there were "many instances of solicitude for their welfare" in the law. Banishment from their homes upon emancipation and imposition of the excessive poll tax apparently slipped his mind. Oblivious to any point of view but his own, Floyd expressed indignation and surprise that "This class...has been the first to place itself in hostile array against every measure designed to remove them from amongst us." Arguing that "it will be indispensably necessary for them to withdraw from this community," he asserted that "the last benefit we can confer upon them" would be an annual appropriation "for their removal from this Commonwealth." [125]

---

[124] *Ibid.*

[125] Jefferson, *op. cit.*, p. 264-270 [deportation]

Colonization, an elegant euphemism for deportation, had been floated as a solution to slavery even before the Revolution. Among its earliest champions was Jefferson who, in his 1771 *Notes on Virginia*, argued the necessity of deporting all emancipated slaves. Once slavery had been accepted as a necessary evil, however, colonization schemes were focused primarily on free blacks and pursued with growing enthusiasm, although, contrary to Governor Floyd's expectations, they found little favor with those targeted as potential colonists. [126]

Among the laws passed in 1832, one required the local sheriffs, who traveled the counties collecting taxes, to ask all free Negroes if they were interested in emigrating to Liberia. The Goochland sheriff was so ordered by the court, but there is no indication that he received any favorable responses. Certainly, there were none from the Pierce family. The belief that fully acculturated free Americans, although black, would eagerly emigrate to a distant and foreign place is matched in its absurdity only by the 1856 law which conferred upon free blacks the unique right to select a master and voluntarily become a slave. Needless to say, none of the Pierces availed themselves of this special opportunity either. [127]

---

[126]GOB, p. 216 [Sheriff to interview free blacks]; _____, Acts 1855-1856, p. 37 [right to be a slave]

[127]Jefferson, *op. cit.*, p. 264 [Deep rooted prejudices]

Milly Pierce

THE AMERICAN SOCIETY FOR COLONIZING THE FREE PEOPLE OF COLOR

Among the early proponents of colonization were many slave-owners of the Revolutionary period who were troubled by the moral contradiction in a nation founded on principles of liberty and justice that, simultaneously, supported institutionalized slavery—and was supported by it. Qualms of conscience aside, most white Virginians could not conceive of living in a society which included a large number of former slaves. As Jefferson agonized over the question of emancipation and colonization, he mirrored the feelings of many Virginians when he wrote: "Deep rooted prejudices entertained by whites; ten thousand recollections by the blacks, of injuries they have sustained; new provocations, the real distinctions that nature has made; and many other circumstances make freedom within Virginia impossible." Although Jefferson's observations were inspired by his apocalyptic vision of wholesale abolition and its consequences, these words from America's greatest proponent of freedom and equality suggest just how difficult it was to be both black and free in Virginia. [128]

Slave-owners who feared free blacks as an incendiary force and those who fostered deep racial prejudices were not alone in favoring colonization as a solution to the free black problem. Among the earliest and most ardent proponents of the movement were committed abolitionists, especially the Quakers. Slave-owners simply wished to be free of their guilt and fear; the Quakers believed that as long as slavery

---

[128] Worrall, *op. cit.*, pp. 290-291 [Quaker interest in colonization]

endured in this country, free blacks would never be allowed to live in peace, secure in their freedom. [129]

Eventually, the concerns of both groups converged in 1817 with the formation of the American Society for Colonizing the Free People of Colour. Among those instrumental in the promotion of the Colonization Society was another member of the Quaker Pleasants family, James Pleasants, who lived at "Green Level," a few miles east of the Pierces. The Pleasants family had arrived in remote Goochland in the seventeenth century, refugees from the Church of England's persecution of Quakers. Their beliefs and their own experience led many members of the Pleasants family to decry the immorality of slavery and the persecution of free blacks. The family produced many distinguished members and several ardent abolitionists; among the more prominent was James Pleasants. [130]

A lawyer by training, James Pleasants was elected to represent Goochland in the Virginia House of Delegates in 1796 and became clerk of that body in 1803. From 1810 to 1818, he served in the United States House of Representatives, and in 1822, he was elected Governor of Virginia, an office he held by annual re-election until 1826. During and after his years as Governor, Pleasants was active in the Colonization Society and its efforts to establish Liberia as a colony where America's free blacks

---

[129] Agee, *op. cit.*, p. 170. James Pleasants was born at "Green Level" (later called "Contention") at Crozier, Va. In 1769 and died there in 1836.

[130] *Ibid.*, pp. 179-180 [Pleasants' career]; *The Annual Reports of the American Society for Colonizing the Free People of Color of the United States*, Volumes 1-10, 1818-1827 (Negro Universities Press, NY, 1969) Seventh Annual Report, p. 169, 1824 and following. [James Pleasants involvement]

could live fully free. The Honorable John Marshall, Chief Justice of the United States, served as the president of the Colonization Society's Richmond auxiliary, and His Excellency James Pleasants as first vice president. [131]

Although some Quakers persisted in the hope that Liberia would prove a humane solution to the free black dilemma, many were eventually disillusioned by the failure of the Society's slave owning majority to embrace what the Quakers believed to be the concomitant cause of abolition. With the loss of widespread Quaker support, the Society focused exclusively on freeing the slave states of a people whose existence both philosophically and symbolically undermined the institution of slavery. Liberia remained the centerpiece of the plan, but its creation did not resolve a critical issue: how to remove free blacks to that far-off place. As Governor Floyd noted, there was hardly mass enthusiasm among free blacks for this new venture, but the slave owning constituency was undeterred. [132]

EVEN LESS FREE THAN BEFORE: THE LAW OF 1832

While the Commonwealth could not force a free, albeit black, people to leave, it could attempt to make their lives sufficiently miserable that abandoning their home of several generations might appear more appealing. That, and general suppression, was the intent of the 1832 act for "reducing into one the several acts,

---

[131] Worrall, *op. cit.*, p. 291 [Quaker disillusion]

[132] _____, Acts of 1831-1832, pp. 20-24 [act for reducing into one...]; _____. Journal of the Senate of Virginia, 1832, Bill no. 6

concerning Slaves, Free Negroes and Mulattoes [sic]." Unquestionably, the multitude of free black laws that had proliferated over the years required legislative consolidation. From a legal perspective, consistent enforcement was difficult. From a free black's point of view, the laws had become a maze of proscriptions in which it was all too easy to make a fateful misstep. The act of 1832 succeeded in simplifying the application of the free black laws; it did nothing to clear the minefield of prohibitions and sanctions that every free black was forced to negotiate. In fact, it rendered every move that much more difficult and treacherous. [133]

Among the most serious blows to the collective strength of free blacks and to their sense of community were the suppression of black preachers and the denial to all blacks of the right to assembly for religious or other reasons. With the specter of Nat Turner still looming large in the white imagination, any gathering of blacks was viewed not only as suspicious but also as a possible prelude to rebellion. Long condemned to live in constant fear and insecurity, individual free blacks were now isolated as never before, deprived of the solace of a shared faith and sustaining fellowship. [134]

In an effort to end what was believed to be widespread trade in stolen goods between slaves and free blacks, the 1832 law stipulated that livestock and agricultural

---

[133] _____, Acts 1831-1832, p. 20 [no preaching or assembly]

[134] *Ibid.*, p. 21 [certification of agricultural products]; United States Agricultural Census, Goochland County, 1850. Only this census which lists her real estate as 23 acres suggests that Milly still held the 2 acres at the Courthouse, although it was listed as the property of John Pierce deceased through 1855.

produce could only be sold by free blacks when "a discreet freeholder" certified in writing that the goods were "honestly acquired." Such a restriction would have been a nuisance, at best, for free black farmers like the Pierces. The first agricultural census in 1850 indicates that Milly's twenty-three acres produced twelve bushels of wheat, seventy-three bushels of Indian corn, thirteen bushels of oats, two bushels of peas or beans, three bushels of Irish potatoes, fifty pounds of butter, twenty tons of hay and homemade items valued at $6, more than enough to sustain a household consisting of an eighty-year-old woman, her two adult daughters and a slave. What was not consumed by the family and one horse and three working oxen would have been sold or bartered. Milly, well connected as she was, would have found having her produce certified a minor inconvenience, but such red tape would have been an impossible tangle for many free blacks. [135]

Farmers were not the only hard-working free blacks to be penalized by the new laws of 1832. A free black who refused the opportunity to emigrate to Liberia at public expense could no longer practice his or her trade or handicraft without special permission from the local court, nor could he or she take apprentices or teach their trades to anyone other than a family member. The sole exception was "Coloured barbers," a southern institution. Barbering, requiring little capital and physically undemanding, was still considered servile "nigger work." As a consequence, there

---

[135] *Ibid.*, p. 22 [trades]; Russell, *Free Negro*, 151 [barbers]; Berlin *op. cit.*, pp. 235-236 [barbers]

were few white competitors, and barbers, indispensable to their white customers, were among the more prosperous free black tradesmen. [136]

The new laws not only complicated and more narrowly circumscribed the lives of free blacks, they also narrowed the gap between freedom and slavery. Freedom as applied to a black was increasingly more nominal than real. Free blacks were now denied the right to a trial by jury, except for crimes punishable by death, and were henceforth to be prosecuted and punished in the same manner as slaves. "Justice" was swift, and often harsh. Free blacks had never been tried by a true jury of their peers, but they had benefited from the deliberate course of due process. Now, they were to be tried by the courts of oyer and terminer, established in 1692 for the "speedy prosecution of slaves…without the sollemntie of jury." In this venue, a panel of five local justices heard cases within ten days of arrest; there was no right to appeal; and punishment was prompt. "Thirty-nine lashes on the bare back, well laid on" was the preferred sentence for misdemeanors. Crime for crime, punishment was much more severe than that meted out to whites. Even slaves, most often disciplined by their masters, were spared the public humiliation of a free black at the whipping post. [137]

The 1832 law continued in a long litany of former rights revoked, among them, the right to own firearms. Today, the right to bear arms may be a largely political issue; then, it was a practical matter of protecting livestock and crops and

---

[136]*Ibid.*, p. 24 [no trial by jury]; Russell, *Free Negro*, 104-106 [trial and punishment of free blacks after 1832]

[137]*Ibid.*, p. 21 [no firearms]; GOB 29, p. 449 [Austin Isaacks to keep a gun]; GOB 32, p. 80 [search for guns]; _____, Acts 1839, p. 24 [firearms search]

Milly Pierce

hunting game to put food on the table. Previously, a free black of good character had been allowed to own a gun and ammunition with permission of the local court. In May of 1816, Milly's son-in-law Austin Isaacks had petitioned the court and been granted this privilege. In 1832, however, the Goochland Court ordered the constables "to visit every free Negro house...and make diligent search for fire arms, ammunition and unlawful weapons of any description and take possession of all...they may find in the houses or possession of any free Negro." Those found in violation of the law were to be brought immediately before a Justice "that they may be dealt with as the law directs." The guilty were "punished with stripes...not exceeding thirty-nine lashes." In 1839, the law was strengthened to allow the constables to batter down the doors of free black homes, if necessary, in their search for firearms. [138]

Even the Virginia legislature acknowledged, although indirectly, the severity of the 1832 law, when in 1833 it passed a law primarily for the protection of Native Americans. This law granted "any person of mixed blood" who was not a free Negro or mulatto a certificate "to protect and secure such a person from and against the pains, penalties, disabilities and disqualifications imposed by law on free Negroes and mulattoes [sic]." [139]

How did Milly respond to the diminution of her rights and to the hostility implicit in the 1832 law? Sixty-two years old and widowed, she lived within a stone's throw of the Courthouse square where her fellows were flogged for petty crimes. In

---

[138] _____, Acts 1833, p. 51 [mixed blood exception]

[139] _____, Acts 1832, p. 21 [slave ownership]

charge of maintaining the Courthouse, she routinely rubbed elbows with the white men who supported and enforced laws intended not only to restrict rights she had previously enjoyed but to drive her from their midst. As the mother of twelve children, she must have feared for their futures. Where would this repression end? For herself, she most probably kept her nose to the grindstone, determined to preserve the relatively safe cocoon of white respect and economic security that she had created for herself and her family.

THE COMPLEXITIES OF FREE BLACK SLAVE OWNERSHIP

Among the restrictions in the new law which would have had minimal impact on most free blacks was that which revoked their long-standing right to purchase and own slaves. Spouses, children, and inherited slaves were the only exceptions. Given the will and the ability to raise the money, free blacks could still attempt to keep their families intact. As rescued family members accounted for the majority of black-owned slaves, this new limitation on slaveholding would have affected only a very few free blacks. Among those who might have felt the impact of this new restriction, however, were several members of the Pierce family. [140]

---

[140] USCG 1810. Milly owned two slaves; GPPT 1810 through 1860. Pierce, Cousins, Isaacks, and Moss slave ownership. Milly owned 3 slaves in 1812 through 1814 and 4 in 1815. Austin Isaacks paid taxes on three slaves in 1818. Daniel Moss paid tax on three slaves in 1819. GOB 30, p. 165 [Austin Isaacks collateral]

Milly Pierce

Milly Pierce had been a slave-owner since at least 1810. Milly's daughter Lydia and her husband, Henry Cousins, paid personal property taxes on two or three slaves at various times, although after 1830, they owned a single female house servant. Lucy Pierce and her husband Daniel Moss owned as many as three slaves at one time, as did Susan Pierce and her husband, Austin Isaacks, a carpenter. In 1821, Austin Isaacks secured his debt on twenty acres purchased in 1814 with "personal property." The only personal property he owned of any value was a male slave under the age of 45. [141]

In 1840, the census taker reported that Judith Pierce's household consisted of two free children and one male slave between the ages of twenty-four and thirty-six. Unlike the slaves owned by her siblings, Judith's slave was most probably not merely a bound laborer. In all likelihood, he was her husband. In the previous census, Judith Pierce had been listed as a single woman, without husband or children, and it seems likely that in the intervening years, she had "married" and purchased her spouse. [142]

"Marriage" between free blacks and slaves, although never legal, was not uncommon. Indeed, Milly had done the same. Prior to passage of the 1806 emancipation law, there were really no negatives to a union between a free black woman and a slave. Her children would be free, despite their father's status, and her husband's owner would still have been responsible for providing him with the necessities of life. Following 1806, however, there was always the danger that a slave

---

[141] USCG 1840, [Judith's household]; USCG 1830 [Judith's household]

[142] Russell, *Free Negro*, p. 77, p. 170 [Free blacks owning their spouses]

spouse might be sold and shipped far away. In order to keep her family intact, Judith had apparently purchased her husband. He remained technically a slave to avoid the risk of banishment from the Commonwealth. Situations such as Judith's accounted for many, but not all, instances of free black slave ownership, and among the Pierces, it appears to have been unique. [143]

Despite the history of slave ownership in the Pierce family, however, the only Pierce to whom the 1832 prohibition on slave ownership would have made a major difference was the most ambitious member of the family, John Pierce, Jr. who, at the time, owned ten slaves and would add to that number periodically over the next several years. Although several continued to own slaves, no other family member purchased a slave after 1832. [144]

DEATH AND TAXES

Slave ownership, however, was not the sole measure of Milly's ambition or success. During her eighty years, she raised a large family, owned significant real estate and personal property, and paid her not inconsiderable taxes. Denied many of the rights accorded any white person, she was never relieved of the responsibility of paying taxes. Fortunes rise and fall, friends and family come and go, but taxes, it

---

[143] GPPT 1832 [John Pierce, Jr.'s slaves]

[144] Hening, *op. cit.*, IV, p. 133 [1723 disenfranchisement]; Hening, *op. cit.*, VI, pp. 39-40 [1782 law]; _____ Acts 1849-1850, p. 7 [penalty on taxes]

Milly Pierce

seems, go on forever, and the size of Milly's tax bill and her ability to pay it reflect the extent of her material excess. After all, the majority of free blacks never owned any property worth taxing. Paying taxes may seem a routine, if onerous, matter, but for free blacks it was much more. By virtue of a 1782 law, free blacks who failed to pay their taxes were reduced to temporary servitude and hired out by the Overseers of the Poor to work off their debts. Later, as tolerance for free blacks ebbed, Goochland routinely offered free Negroes for sale at public auction for non-payment of their taxes. [145]

In addition to the routine levies assessed all taxpayers, free blacks were periodically subjected to special taxes. In 1813 through 1815, they alone were required to pay the special poll tax, allegedly to finance the War of 1812. Perhaps the most extraordinary special tax imposed on free blacks, however, was the one dollar charged all free black males between 21 and 55 to pay for their own deportation to Liberia. Among the eleven Goochland free blacks unable to pay this tax and offered for sale on the Courthouse steps in 1857 was "Moses Mayo (dead)." Neither Moses Mayo nor the ten living miscreants were sold "for want of bidders." [146]

The $1 poll tax may not seem an enormous burden, but the average wages of Goochland workers make its severity readily apparent. In 1850, Goochland's farm

---

[145] *Ibid.* [$1 poll tax]; GDB 38, p. 494 [Moses Mayo dead]

[146] United States Social Census Goochland 1850 [Goochland wages]; Russell, *Free Negro,* p. 147 and Berlin, *op. cit.*, p. 229 [free blacks work for less]; Luther Porter Jackson, "The Virginia Free Negro Farmer and Property Owner 1830-1860," *Journal of Negro History*, 24 (1939), pp. 394-395 [value to small farmer]

laborers were paid 60 cents a day. Free blacks—who often worked cheap in order to compete with white workers—made less. Most often, free blacks worked as occasional and inexpensive labor for small farmers who could not afford slaves. In this capacity, they actually filled a critical niche in Virginia's economy, and non-slave owning farmers were among the few who consistently argued against their mass deportation. [147]

Milly both paid more taxes and enjoyed more success than many of her contemporaries. When she died in 1851, she bequeathed to her three youngest children—Mary, Thomas, and Jane—a productive 21 acre farm valued at $600 and a personal estate including several beds, two looking glasses, two tables, a dozen chairs (a reminder of her once-large family), one Negro man and one mare colt; the whole appraised for $235.25. Compared to most free blacks and many whites, Milly had done well economically, but not without long years of hard work and the careful cultivation of powerful white patrons. [148]

---

[147] GDB 36, p. 222 [Milly's will]; GLT 1851 [Value of Milly's farm]; GDB 36, p. 311 [Inventory of Milly's estate]

[148] GDB 20, p. 530 [Samuel Woodson's will]; GMR, 1812, p. 353 [Pierce m. Cousins]; USCG 1850 Henry Cousins gave his profession as cooper. His father Francis was also a cooper. Henry Cousins first appears in the Goochland records when he is listed in the column for "white male titheables" in the personal property ledger for 1809. The tax collector's assumption that all free taxpayers must be white gives some small indication of how oxymoronic "free black" was to the white mind. To designate those taxpayers who were not white, "free Negroe" or "f.n." was noted next to the appropriate names. GLT 1811 [location of Lydia's ½ acre]; The deed to this ½ acre and to 134 acres purchased 1841 are in Lydia's name only and both were carried in the land tax ledger in her name only.

Milly Pierce

A PIONEER PAVED THE WAY

    Milly Pierce's rise from the severe limitations of slavery and the dependency it fostered was a rare journey without a road map. Empowered by her freedom, she made her way with purpose and self-sufficiency until she and her family were securely established. In a quiet and distinctly feminine way, yet with steely determination, Milly had bent the system to her will and made herself indispensable to the white patriarchy. As a nation, Americans had subverted the oppression of the English monarchy; as an individual, Milly subverted a legal system designed to crush her.

    If Milly, the pioneer, was a subversive, undermining a seemingly intractable social structure, her children were perhaps predictably conventional. Defying the expectations of white society, Milly had traversed unknown territory and created a secure place in a hostile world for her children. Her children, in turn, embraced the culture of the very society that both feared and oppressed them.

    Milly had made her own way; her offspring adopted the white way. All of Milly's children responded to their mother's subversion and courage by adopting the mores and values of the dominant culture. Most of them settled into unremarkable lives of modest prosperity and left as little mark on the landscape of history as the majority of ordinary people living ordinary lives. And, like most Americans, their energies appear to have been concentrated on the acquisition of property.

III

LYDIA PIERCE COUSINS: THE MIDDLE GROUND

Lydia Cousins stood straight and tall at the funeral of her father-in-law Francis Cousins. Secure in her stature and status in the community—or as secure as any woman of color might be—she may have listened with some pride as the white minister praised her father-in-law for his service to his country and concern for his family. When she bowed her head in prayer, she may have given silent thanks for the white men of conscience who had freed them both, for the mother who had made her a strong and independent woman, and for the rare peace and prosperity that surrounded her.

Although born a slave, Lydia Pierce enjoyed the advantages not only of her mother's grit, determination and modest success, but also of the Woodson family's gratitude and generosity. In 1810, when she was only in her late teens, Samuel Woodson's will had provided her with a small plot of land and a home of her own. Two years later, she married Henry Cousins, a well-established cooper and member of another solid, propertied freed black family. The couple set up housekeeping on

Lydia's half acre just southeast of the Courthouse. Like mother, like daughter, Lydia continued to hold this property in her own name after her marriage. [149]

Milly had worked long and hard to claim a place, however marginal, among the free, and her land had both signified and assured that freedom for herself and her family. Building on her mother's legacy, Lydia sank deep roots into the land, roots that held against the whirlwind of an increasingly hostile, predominantly white, world. Her brother John, in contrast, appears to have been caught up in the whirlwind, swept away from his family and his roots as he chased the elusive ideal of white success. John, the son of a man emancipated in his old age, had something to prove. Lydia, daughter of a woman who apparently deployed her family as a small army against poverty and white oppression, had the example of her mother's strength and faith in family solidarity.

Milly had not only raised a large family, she had also forged a place for herself in the world of white male authority. Lydia, in turn, followed a far more conventional path. She devoted herself to her family and pursued the nineteenth century ideal of domesticity in which women were valued, above all, for their skills in housework and child-rearing. Had she not made herself somewhat conspicuous when she became the largest free black female landowner in Goochland, she might well have been "the over-looked woman." Much like his wife, Henry Cousins, too, conformed to conventional expectations and proved an able provider for his wife, four

---

[149]Lebsock, *op. cit.*, pp. 17-18 [19th century marriage]; USCG 1820 Cousins household; two sons, two daughters; USCG 1830 Cousins household: four sons, four daughters

sons and four daughters. Lydia was less bold than Milly, but then there was less need to be. [150]

EMANCIPATION AND REACTION

In 1823 at the age of 31, Henry Cousins presented himself at the Courthouse to be registered as a Free Negro and stated that he had been emancipated by the wills of John and Jonathan Pleasants. Henry had not, in fact, been born when the Pleasants, father and son, had written their remarkable wills. His father Francis, however, had been owned by the Pleasants whose extraordinary act of conscience ultimately bestowed freedom on several hundred slaves. [151]

Few, if any, Virginia families were responsible for more emancipations or more active in the abolition movement than the Quaker Pleasants. And few acts of manumission were more spectacular and more hotly contested than those of John and Jonathan Pleasants. In 1771, defying the legal prohibition against private manumission, John Pleasants attempted to liberate his "poor slaves" in his will,

---

[150] GFN # 000 1823 Henry Cousins registered at age 31 and cited the Pleasants' wills as his source of freedom. The lack of a number suggests there may have been some question about his registration, although it seems to have caused him no problems. He registered again in 1852 as # 868 at age 65. Francis Cousins registered as "Frank" # 290 at age 66 in 1822 and cited the Pleasants' wills.

[151] Stephen B. Weeks, *Southern Quakers and Slavery* (Baltimore, 1896), pp. 213-215 [Pleasants prominence]; Daniel Call, *Reports of Cases Argued and Adjudged in the Court of Appeals of Virginia* [Richmond, Michie Co., 1900], vol. 2, p. 329 John Pleasants' will

stipulating that this should occur when they arrived at the age of thirty and "the laws of the land will admit them to be set free without their being transported out of the country." [152]

Six years later, John's son Jonathan wrote a similar will, in which he expressed the belief that "all mankind have an undoubted right to freedom" and his wish that his slaves might "in good degree partake of and enjoy that inestimable blessing." To this end, he ordered that "as the most likely means to fit them for freedom, that they be instructed to read…and that [when] they arrive to the age of thirty years [they] may enjoy the full benefit of their labour in a manner most likely to answer the intention of relieving their bondage." He concluded with the instruction that "whenever the laws of the country will admit absolute freedom to them…they will become free." Like his father, Jonathan left his slaves to various relatives, their ownership limited by his hope and intention that eventually the law would allow their emancipation. [153]

It was left to Jonathan's brother Robert to make that hope a reality. A committed abolitionist, Robert Pleasants had begun lobbying the Virginia legislature in 1770 "to repeal the law [of 1723] which prevents a man from rewarding faithfulness with freedom for his servants." For more than ten years, Robert Pleasants and other committed Friends labored to this end. Finally, in 1782, their efforts bore fruit, and

---

[152] Call, *op. cit.*, p. 330 [Jonathan Pleasants' will]

[153] Worrall, *op. cit.*, pp. 225-226 [Robert Pleasants and law of 1782]

under the terms of John and Jonathan Pleasants' wills, both those slaves mentioned in their wills and the children of those slaves were entitled to their freedom at age 30. [154]

The confluence of Quaker activism and Revolutionary idealism which had inspired the Pleasants father and son waned along with the eighteenth century, and in 1800, Robert Pleasants found himself before the Virginia Court of Appeals, defending his father's and brother's wills against the opposition of other heirs reluctant to part with their slaves. As an heir of John Pleasants and executor for both John and Jonathan Pleasants, Robert Pleasants had requested the other heirs, now defendants, to emancipate the slaves; they had refused. The Pleasants heirs were not unique in their desire to hang on to their chattels, and when one of their lawyers argued that "although it may be true that liberty is to be favored, the rights of property are as sacred as those of liberty," it was made abundantly clear that attitudes towards freedom for blacks were changing. "The glare of hostile public opinion not only dissuaded many would-be manumitters," Berlin has observed, "but also encouraged avaricious heirs and creditors to challenge the slaves' right to freedom." The year of the Pleasants' lawsuit, 1800, marked the beginning of a significant decline in the number of manumissions. [155]

The lower Court of Chancery had found for the dissident heirs of the Pleasants, and Robert Pleasants was forced to appeal. The case was argued largely on question of "perpetuities and executory limitations." As those who opposed the wills

---

[154]Call, *op. cit.*, p. 31 [property versus liberty]; Berlin, *op. cit.*, p. 101 [changing attitudes to manumissions]

[155]Call, *op. cit.*, pp. 329-341 [arguments in the Pleasants case]

pointed out, the emancipations stipulated by the Pleasants had been predicated upon laws not yet written. A further consideration, introduced by those who opposed the intent of the wills, was "the principle of convenience," applying here primarily to Mary Pleasants Logan whose husband, Charles, had used the slaves in question as collateral for debts. [156]

Perhaps the most serious obstacle to the plaintiff's case was the legal requirement that he indemnify the Commonwealth against the support of those either too old or infirm to support themselves. This obstacle was surmounted by a proposal in which the slaves themselves would by their labors contribute to a trust fund. Fortunately for Francis Cousins and all of the slaves covered by the Pleasants' wills, the justices agreed with lawyer John Marshall's contention on behalf of Robert Pleasants that: "If justice requires it, the Court may compel the Administrators to emancipate; and the legatees, by taking their legacy, bound themselves to perform the trust. Of course, they may be compelled to a specific performance of it." [157]

Following the Appeals Court's decision, a number of the Pleasants' former slaves registered in Goochland as free blacks. As the wills covered not only those slaves serving at the time of the Pleasants' death, but also "their increase," it is impossible to determine exactly how many free blacks owed their liberty to John and Jonathan Pleasants, but in Goochland alone, at least thirty-six slaves who had actually been owned by the Pleasants registered and settled in the county. Curiously,

---

[156] *Ibid.*, p. 333 [Marshall quote]

[157] GFN Only those who were born prior to 1800 and cited the Pleasants' wills when they registered are included in these figures

considering Mary Logan's reluctance to part with her slaves, six of those emancipated by the court case chose the surname Logan; only three adopted the name Pleasants. [158]

FREE BLACK FREEDOM FIGHTER

Among the earliest of the Pleasants' former slaves to settle in Goochland was Henry Cousins' father, Francis. Francis promptly availed himself of one of his new rights as a free man, and on April 16, 1801 married Chloe Cousins—who had apparently assumed his surname long before. Their wedding was witnessed by Edward Fuzmore, a free black who worked alongside Francis as a planter on Robert Pleasants' plantation. The dates of the Pleasants' court case and of his marriage indicate that Francis was newly freed, yet there is a likelihood that he had been quasi-free for many years. Most probably he was one of the slaves left directly to Robert Pleasants who unlike his siblings may well have viewed his role as custodian rather than owner. This seems the only plausible explanation of the fact that Francis Cousins, while still

---

[158] GMR p. 78 [Francis m. Chloe Cousins]; GPPT 1801 Both Francis Cousins and Edward Fuzmore are listed as planters on Robert Pleasants' land. Luther Porter Jackson, *Virginia Negro Soldiers and Seamen in the Revolutionary War*, (Guide Quality Press, Norfolk, Va. 1944), p. 33. He is listed as Francis Cozens in *Virginia Soldiers of the American Revolution*, compiled by Hamilton J. Eckenrode (Virginia State Library, Richmond, 1989), p. 116 and in the NARS Revolutionary War Service Index, Reel 12, General Index Card 2273. For a thorough history of free blacks in the Revolution see Benjamin Quarles, *The Negro in the American Revolution* (University of North Carolina Press, Chapel Hill, 1961).

deprived of his personal freedom, embraced the larger cause of liberty for all Americans and enlisted in the Continental Army. [159]

Both slaves and free blacks served in the Revolution; slaves as substitutes for their owners, some free blacks as draftees, and others as freedom-loving patriots. Slaves were rewarded, although sometimes tardily and only upon the threat of law, with their freedom. The motives of free black enlistees, as opposed to those who were drafted, were rather more complicated. On the one hand, their service in the pre-Revolutionary militia and their right to bear arms had been among the badges of their freedom. On the other, their freedom had been systematically compromised by the very leaders who now sought their service. Some free black enlistees were, no doubt, attracted by the land and monetary bounties offered in return for service—among the rewards offered in Virginia was the choice of a healthy sound Negro 10 to 30 years of age or 60 pounds in gold or silver. Many free blacks, however, were moved by a belief that the American cause was just and by the hope that the Americans' commitment to liberty and justice for all might prove real rather than rhetorical. Although whites were ambivalent about allowing either free Negroes or slaves to serve—the thought of arms-bearing blacks alarmed many—they were, in the end, allowed to do so because, as one Virginia Governor observed, "they could best be spared." [160]

---

[159] Quarles, *Revolution*, p. 183 [legislature forces masters to free slave soldiers]; *ibid.*, p. 8 [free Negroes in militia]; *ibid.*, pp. 80, 108-110 [bounties]; Berlin, *op. cit.*, p. 19 [best be spared]

[160] Jackson, *Virginia Negro Soldiers*, p. 33 [Francis enlists]; Hening, *op. cit.*, IX, p. 280 [Certificate of Freedom required]; Russell, *Free Negro*, p. 110 and Jackson, *Virginia Negro Soldiers*, p. vi [Negro roles in army]; Jackson, *op. cit.*, p. 1 [Banks]; Jackson, *ibid.*, and "Virginia Negro Soldiers and Seamen in the American Revolution," *Journal of Negro History*, vol. XXVII, no. 3

Milly Pierce

Francis Cousins enlisted as a private in the infantry, presumably with Robert Pleasants' permission, and probably prior to 1777. So many runaway slaves had posed as free blacks and enlisted—pursuing military service as a route to freedom—that after 1777 black enlistees were required to present a certificate of freedom. Francis would have been in his late teens at the time, and according to law and practice may have served as a drummer, fifer, pioneer, forager, orderly or laborer. Not that all free blacks served in roles that were either menial or did not require them to carry arms. John Banks, a Goochland native, was the rare free black who joined cavalry. Several other Goochland free blacks served in the Revolution, among them Elizabeth Grantham's son, James Mealy. Mealy, drafted in 1781 at the age of eighteen, served under Lafayette and fought in the final engagement at Yorktown. Following the war, he and his brother Archer were both arms-bearing members of the Goochland militia. [161]

(July, 1842), pp. 247-287 [other Goochland free blacks in Revolution]; Margaret Walker, "Goochland's Post-Revolutionary Militia," *Goochland County Historical Society Magazine*, vol. 4, no. 2, p. 14 [Mealys served]. John Banks, born free in Goochland in 1749, served for two years 1779-1781 in TheoderickBland's regiment and was awarded an annual pension of $90 per year in 1818. His brother Jacob served as a wagoneer in the service of supply. Others from Goochland who served were George Tyler, Isaac Howell, James Johns, James Cooper, John Cowigg, and James Mealy.

[161] PPT 1815 [Francis last on R. Pleasants dec'd. land]; USCG 1810 Cousins household; GPPT 1805 Francis a cooper; GPPT 1811 Francis a planter or farmer; GPPT 1804 Francis owns first horse; GDB 21, p. 137 [Page to Cousins]; GDB 22, p. 191 [Francis emancipates Ridley]; GFN # 238 Ridley registered in 1822 at 30 citing the court decree and her ownership by Charles Logan. GMR, p. 366 [Ridley Cousins m. John Copland]; GFN # 231 registered in 1819 at 30 as former property of Charles Logan's estate. Copland is also spelled Coupland and Copeland. Why Ridley, alone, of Francis Cousins' children remained in bondage in 1816 is unclear. Henry is listed in the 1809 GPPT as a free male and was only in his early twenties in 1812 when he married Lydia Pierce, yet, although he was not yet 30, both are evidence that he enjoyed the privileges of a free black. Conceivably, Robert

CeCe Bullard

Following his Revolutionary service and his emancipation, Francis Cousins remained on Robert Pleasants' land where he worked as a planter and a cooper. Although he supported a household of eight, Francis still managed to save enough money to purchase his own 60 2/3 acre farm in 1816. More importantly, he was in a financial position to secure the freedom of his still-enslaved daughter Ridley and her children, Frank William and Lucy Ann. Ridley, aged 24, had not yet obtained the magic age of 30 when she would have been automatically freed by the Pleasants' wills. Consequently, Francis purchased his daughter and grand-children from Robert Pleasants in January of 1816, and on March 18th, "for the good will and affection I have for them," he emancipated them. Given permission to remain in Virginia, Ridley settled in Goochland, and in 1824 married John Copland who owed his freedom to the Pleasants' wills. [162]

Pleasants had given all of Francis's family in his possession their freedom once the court case was settled, but Ridley, owned by Charles and Mary Logan, had remained under their control awaiting the outcome of a few relatively minor legal questions referred back to the lower court by the Court of Appeals. Mary Logan had opposed the emancipations, pleading that "her husband had died indebted to several persons," those debts secured by the slaves in dispute (Call, *op. cit.*, p. 330).

[162] USCG 1830 Cousins household; GPPT 1818 Cousins' slaves; there were two sons between the ages of 10 and 24 in the Cousins' household; USCG 1840 Henry Cousins household included one female slave 10-24 years of age.

Milly Pierce

MIDDLE-CLASS SECURITY

Francis Cousins and Milly Pierce had much in common, as did, evidently, two of their children. Emancipated as adults, they nevertheless were able to shed the yoke of slavery and with single-minded determination pursued the American dream— and both emerge stronger figures through the mists of time than any of their children. Milly and Francis belonged to the first generation of blacks emancipated following the Revolution, and that first surge of freedom in a generally sympathetic climate seems to have generated a particular energy and focus that produced some remarkable individuals. The convergence of increasing repression and increased economic security in subsequent years resulted in lower profile and less notable accomplishment in the next generation. John Pierce, Jr., the exception to this generalization, was remarkable in ways his parents' generation would no doubt have disapproved.

Lydia and Henry Cousins, in contrast to John Pierce, Jr., were model middle class citizens, although deprived of some of the rights the word "citizen" implies. The 1830s and early 1840s appear to have passed peacefully and prosperously for them, or as peacefully as possible for the parents of four sons and four daughters. Henry's cooperage was sufficiently busy to have required the assistance of two slaves at one time; now he had sons old enough to help him with the work. Nor did Lydia have to work her fingers to the bone looking after her large family. Three of her daughters were old enough to be of some help, and by 1840, she had acquired a female slave to help with the housework. In the midst of this middle-class idyll, Lydia was moved on a spring day in 1841 to walk the short distance to the Courthouse and register as a free Negro. [163]

Why had she waited so long—and why did she bother now? Perhaps, early on, it had seemed unnecessary. After all, she was a Pierce and a woman of property. No piece of paper, no scrawl in a register was needed to affirm her stature and status. To register may even have seemed demeaning, an admission that she was just one more free Negro. Her daughter Elizabeth—more attuned to the less tolerant temper of the times, less reliant on family history—may have been responsible for Lydia's change of heart. Elizabeth, in celebration of her twenty-first birthday, accompanied (or dragged) her 54-year-old mother to the Courthouse where the two women registered and acquired their freedom papers. The clerk described Lydia as "bright yellow" and about five feet five inches tall with a scar on her left wrist. [164]

If her freedom papers asserted her legal status as a free black, Lydia made a strong statement about her stature in the black community when in the same year she purchased 134 acres adjacent to the county Poor House for $469. Of Goochland's 670 landowners in 1842, only twenty-two were black, and just six of these were women. Lydia now owned real estate assessed at $579. Both her acreage and its value far exceeded the holdings of any other black woman. Only Milly's 21 acres appraised at $315 came close. Even though her marriage was both legal and more traditional than

---

[163] GFN # 637 Lydia Cousins and # 636 Elizabeth, "about 21 and yellow."

[164] GDB 36, p. 305 David Royster to Lydia Cousins, GLT 1841 23 free black landowners. The women were: Lydia Cousins, 134 ½ acres; Polly Cousins (no relation), 2 ½ acres; Milly James, 9 ¼ acres (jointly with Timothy Pleasants); Charlotte Lynch, 1 acre: Milly Pierce, 21 acres; and Rissa, 1 acre.

her mother's, Lydia still retained some degree of independence. She continued to hold her new acreage, as well as her inherited half-acre, solely in her own name until her death. [165]

Why, exactly, Lydia purchased the 134 acre tract in unclear. Possibly she leased it, although there is no lease on record; perhaps she maintained a garden there, but there is no evidence of any significant agricultural activity. In fact, when her son John Cousins sued to settle his father's estate, he described the property as "poor land." For Lydia, owning the land may have been an end itself. Property was, after all, the distinctive emblem of a successful free black. [166]

PROPERTY, STATUS AND LITIGATION

Henry and Lydia Cousins' peaceful existence came to an end when Henry's father Francis died in 1844. In his will, Francis left his sizeable estate to his wife Chloe for her lifetime and then to his four sons: Samuel, Frederick, Henry and Walter. The estate consisted of more than 240 acres of land seven miles west of the Courthouse, a mill and personal property valued at $246.17. In addition to a quantity

---

[165] There is no record of agricultural production in either Lydia or Henry's name in either 1850 or 1860 (US Agricultural Census Goochland), and in his 1869 suit to settle Henry Cousins estate, Lydia's son John described this 134 acres as "poor land" (Chancery Cases, File 6).

[166] GOB 1844-52, p. 35 [Francis Cousins will proved November, 1844]; GDB 34, p. 41 [Francis Cousins' will]; GLT 1844, Francis Cousins taxed on 4 tracts west of the Courthouse totaling 236 1/6 acres; GDB 34, p. 89 [Francis Cousins' inventory]

of farm equipment, tools and livestock, Francis' estate included several amenities indicative of a comfortable life—a desk, a clock, a spinning wheel, a carriage and china. [167]

Francis's will reflects not only his material provision for his family but a deep concern for his daughter Milley. The legacies to his older sons, Samuel and Frederick, were contingent upon their "supporting in a proper manner…my daughter Milley who is unable to take care of herself." He further stipulated that should they fail to do so, he wished the Goochland court to appoint a committee with the power to take as much land from Samuel and Frederick as was necessary "to support the said Milley in a comfortable way." Despite the court's role in the persecution of free blacks, Francis, product of an earlier and more benign era, still had confidence in the legal system and the court's respect for his wishes. [168]

While Francis's will left Chloe and Milley well provided for, it also spawned a number of minor legal squabbles among his ultimate heirs, a scenario repeated more than once following a death in the Cousins family. There must have been a well-beaten path from the Cousins' households to the Courthouse. Some of the difficulties were simply the result of unresolved questions regarding the disposition of an estate. Other disputes point out just how important property was to free blacks. Property ownership—and the privilege of paying taxes on it—was one of the last remaining

---

[167] GDB 34, p. 41 [Francis Cousins' will]
[168] Russell, *Free Negro*, p. 88 [property rights]; GLT 1792-1860 [free black landowners]; twenty of these relatively rare propertied free blacks were members of the Pierce-Cousins clan, both blood relatives and relatives by marriage.

rights left to this class by the Virginia legislature on the eve of the Civil War. The distinctive emblem of a successful free black, land not only separated the free from the enslaved, it also signaled an elevated status within the free black community. From Goochland's creation in 1727 through 1860, only 81 free blacks acquired real property. Free blacks in a position to own some land clung fiercely to their property rights. [169]

Walter (Watt) Cousins, Francis Cousins' third son and a wheelwright, was designated administrator of his estate, and Henry Cousins stood as security for a bond of $400. Neither of Francis's older sons were available to carry out their father's wishes. Samuel had moved to Ohio, a popular destination for many of Goochland's free blacks, and Frederick to a neighboring Fluvanna County. Walter, selected by default, not only proved somewhat inept in handling his responsibilities as executor but eventually left his own affairs in something of a muddle. Less than a year after Walter qualified as Francis's executor, the Court ordered three prominent white men, two of them lawyers, to audit his accounts. [170]

In 1846, Walter, as Francis's administrator, initiated a lawsuit against his sister Charlotte's husband, Henry Lynch, to collect rents due the estate. After several

---

[169] GOB 1844-1852, p. 42 [Walter Cousins appointed executor]; GDB 37, p. 380. This deed of May, 1848 refers to Samuel and his wife Frances as living in Ohio and Frederick and his wife Phebe in Fluvanna; GOB 1844-1852, p. 115. Walter's accounts were audited by Walter Coles, Thomas B. Gay, Esq., and James B. Ferguson, Esq.

[170] GOB 1844-1852, p. 114 [Walter sues Henry Lynch]; *ibid.*, p. 163 [Walter fails to appear; judgment against him]; *ibid.*, p. 211 [Thomas James qualifies as Chloe's administrator]; *ibid.*, p. 214 [Walter protests]

continuations, Walter still failed to appear in Court, and a judgment was entered for the defendant, the court costs to be paid from Francis's estate. No doubt in response to Walter's incompetence, when Francis's widow Chloe died in 1847, her white neighbor Thomas James, rather than one of her sons, was appointed administrator. Walter promptly moved that "the letters of administration granted by the court to Thomas James" be revoked, but his motion failed. [171]

In the meantime, Francis's grandchildren, James, John Henry, Louisa and Evelina Copland, children of Ridley and John Copland, filed suit against their uncles Walter and Henry Cousins to obtain title to ten acres John Copland had been in the process of purchasing from Francis. In 1835, John had paid $30 on a contract for a piece of Francis's property on the Stage Road from Richmond to Charlottesville. Before the purchase had been finalized, John Copland died, leaving his children to settle to matter with their uncles. Following the instigation of the lawsuit, Henry and Lydia Cousins and Walter and Maria Mayo Cousins transferred the property to John's heirs upon receipt of an additional $30. [172]

In 1850, Walter almost lost all of Francis's land when he failed to pay the land taxes, and Francis's property was "sold for non-payment of taxes and purchased by the Commonwealth." Luckily, the Commonwealth was forgiving of such

---

[171] GOB 1844-1852, p. 230 [Coplands sue]; GDB 35, p. 172 [Francis Cousins to John Copland]; GOB Book 1844-1852, p. 269 [Cousins to Copland]; *ibid.*, p. 273 [Copland suit dismissed]

[172] GLT 1850 Francis's land listed as sold for taxes; GLT 1852 taxes paid, and Francis's land stricken from sold for taxes list. Chancery Suits File 6, Goochland Courthouse [Philip Cousins v. Cousins heirs]

oversights, and when the back taxes were paid in 1852, the land was stricken from the inventory of confiscated properties and restored to the estate. Walter's poor management and legal difficulties survived him. He died intestate and childless, and in 1878, his nephew Philip Cousins was forced to sue the rest of Francis Cousins' heirs or their descendants to achieve a fair disposition of the 50 acres Walter had inherited from his father and to recover the taxes Philip had paid on the land since Walter's death. [173]

FAMILY PROBLEMS, APPRENTICE PROBLEMS

Henry Cousins' difficulties related to his father's death did not end with the Copland suit. Henry's oldest son Philip had married his cousin Lucy Ann Lynch in 1846, and not long after, had purchased 39 ¾ acres of his grandfather's land from the estate. In 1854, Philip, now the father of two young daughters, Elizabeth and Martha Anne, made an agreement with Henry to buy an adjoining 30 acres of what was known as Francis's "Hodges" tract. In order to fulfill his agreement with his son, Henry was forced to sue Walter's heirs to obtain his half of a hundred acres Francis had left to the

---

[173] GMR p. 332 [Philip Cousins m. Lucy Ann Lynch June 22, 1846]; GDB 37, p. 380 [39 ¾ acres to Philip Cousins, May 1848]; GDB 37, p. 436 [Agreement between Henry and Philip for 30 acres also adjoining the property of his aunt Charlotte and her husband Henry Lynch]; Goochland Record Order Books 1852-1862 p. 270 [Henry sues for his ½ of 100 acres]; *ibid.*, p. 330 [Henry awarded his 50 acres]; *ibid.*, p. 349 [Henry and Lydia Cousins acknowledge deed of Jan. 19, 1858 to Philip for 50 acres]

two brothers. Finally, in 1858, Henry was able to deed the promised property to Philip. [174]

Francis's special provision for his daughter Milley meant that Chloe Cousins' estate required an administrator long after her death. In 1858, Henry, the only son still living in Goochland, qualified as Chloe's administrator; his uncle, John Pierce, Jr., served as his security. The next year, the Court appointed Henry's son Philip as "the Committee" to look after the interests of Milley Cousins, "a person of unsound mind." Presumably appointing Henry, Chloe's administrator, as Milley's "committee" would have created a conflict of interest. Nevertheless, a conflict emerged, and, in 1861, Henry made a motion to the court that Philip, having failed to render an accounting, be removed as Milley's committee. A year later, Henry's sister Evalina Lynch file a similar motion. The motions, never acted upon, may have been the result of genuine dissatisfaction with Philip's management. They may also have been legal maneuvers to hasten the settlement of Chloe Cousins' estate, for Milley, "insane" and in her mid-seventies, had finally died. It was indeed fortunate that Francis Cousins had provided so carefully for his daughter. [175]

Henry's legal headaches during these years were not entirely confined to family matters. In 1847, Nancy Kinney brought suit against him in the Goochland

---

[174] GOB 1852-1862, p. 373 [Henry qualifies as executor]; *ibid.*, p. 437 [Philip appointed committee for Milley; James Copland his security]; *ibid.*, p. 610 [Henry moves to Philip's removal]; *ibid.*, p. 671 [Evelina moves to remove Philip]; USCG 1850 and 1860. In 1850, Milley is listed as age 66 and "insane." She does not appear in the 1860 census.

[175] GOB Book 1844-1854, p. 208 [Kinney versus Cousins]; GOB 32, p. 125 [1832 order to bind out]

court to have the apprenticeships of her children James and William Kinney revoked. The long-standing law requiring the compulsory apprenticeship of free black bastards remained on the books, although a Goochland court order of 1832 indicates that its intent had changed with the times. No longer was there even an ostensible concern with imparting a trade or a rudimentary education. Instead, the Overseers of the Poor were instructed to "bind out all free Negro children whose parents are not able to support them and who do not bring them up in honest and industrious habits." [176]

Interestingly enough, Goochland's Overseers of the Poor often placed free black apprenticeships with free black masters. There is, in fact, some evidence that the Overseers attempted to make compassionate placements, assigning their young charges to their parents' neighbors or benefactors. John Pierce, Jr., for instance, had been placed with Samuel Johnson, the white farmer who leased his mother's land. Even so, there may have been some special tension when free black children were "bound out" to other free blacks. Social and economic stratification being what it was in the South, some may well have preferred placement with a more affluent and powerful white family. Francis Cousins had been similarly challenged by a mother in 1830 when Hannah Powder moved to have the apprenticeships of her children Ben, Robert, Frank and Davy revoked. In Henry's case, Nancy Kinney apparently failed to

---

[176]GOB 24, p. 205 [John Pierce, Jr. bound to Samuel Johnson]; GOB 31, p. 449 [Powder versus Cousins]; USCG 1850 [Henry Cousins household includes Kinneys]

have the apprenticeships annulled, for in 1850, James Kinney, 13, was still in Henry Cousins' household and had been joined by Horace Kinney, 8. [177]

Property, however, remained central to most of the Cousins family's litigation, and a death in the family almost inevitably embroiled them in another round of lawsuits. When Milly Pierce's daughter Mary died in the early 1870s, Margaret Cousins, Mary's niece and Lydia's daughter, sued all of the other potential heirs both in her own right and as a creditor. [178]

BLACK AND WHITE COMMON-LAW MARRIAGE

Margaret Cousins, Lydia and Henry Cousins' oldest daughter, was yet another independent and unmarried Pierce woman, although hers was independence with a slightly different twist. Whereas her grandmother, Milly Pierce, had, in the end, remained unmarried by choice, marriage for Margaret was never an option.

Around 1855, Margaret, a relatively mature woman in her early thirties, joined the household of John J. Cragwall, a carpenter and farmer. Cragwall, several years her senior, was white and unmarried. By 1860, the Cragwall household also

---

[177] Goochland Chancery Order Book 1871-1873, p. 10 [Cousins versus Pierce]

[178] USCG 1860 Margaret Cousins, 40, living with Cragwall and an infant Henry Cousins; USCG 1870 Henry Cousins, now John J. Cousins, 10; Goochland Circuit Court Common Law Order Book 6 1883-1916, p. 88 John J. Cragwall, administrator, sues for Margaret Cousins' estate. In USCG 1850, the only member of Cragwall's household was Edward Cooper, an 84 year old farmhand.

included Henry Cousins, a one month old mulatto infant. The nature of Margaret's relationship with Cragwall may be guessed from the curious evolution of Henry's name. By 1870, he was known as John. J. Cousins, and in 1886, as Margaret's executor, he had become John J. Cragwall. [179]

Almost from the moment blacks arrived in Virginia, intimate relationships between black and white were subject to severe social and legal sanctions. In 1691, the General Assembly acted decisively "for prevention of that abominable mixture and spurious issue" by outlawing both mixed race marriages and illicit interracial relationships. Although couples who defied the law risked both severe legal sanctions and the possibility of violence from their white neighbors, common-law liaisons between free blacks and whites continued. In Goochland, at least six interracial families can be identified between 1840 and 1860. Most of them, for good reason, led inconspicuous lives. [180]

In one instance, however, a mixed race relationship in Goochland went beyond local gossip and was brought to the attention of the General Assembly, although not for the obvious reason. In 1850, Mary J. Terry petitioned the legislature

---

[179] Hening, *op. cit.*, III, pp. 86-87 [1691 law regarding white/black relationships]; USCG 1840, 1850, 1860: Five white men can be identified as co-habiting with a free black woman when there is no other adult female in the household: Jack Ragland, M.F. Anderson and E. Johns in 1840. George W. Cox with Evy Gray and Elijah Cragwall with Betsy Randolph in 1850; and John J. Cragwall with Margaret Cousins in 1860. One white woman Anna Thurston, age 65, lived with John Jenkins, 65, a free black male in 1860.

[180] Legislative Petitions, Goochland, 1850 ms. (no number) divorce petition of Mary J. Terry.

for a divorce from her husband of fifteen years, Wiliam B. Terry. Two years prior, Terry, a farmer, had "taken up with a free Negro woman living in the neighborhood and with her left the county and State" for Ohio. Abandonment must have been a severe blow to Mrs. Terry, left with five children to raise, a blow made all the heavier by the color of her husband's paramour. [181]

The most conspicuous of the interracial couples who remained in Goochland were John J. Cragwall's younger brother Elijah and Elizabeth Randolph, a free mulatto. The Cragwall-Randolph family stands out both because of its size and its relative material success. In 1850, Elijah R. Cragwall, a forty-four year old white carpenter, owned $1500 in real estate, and his household consisted of Betsy Randolph, aged thirty-five, and eight mulatto children ranging in age from 14 years to three months. By 1860, Cragwall's land had appreciated in value to $1670, and he reported $600 in personal property. Elizabeth Randolph, her occupation given as "marketwoman," owned $300 worth of personal property in her own right. The couple now had twelve children ranging in age from twenty-seven to one. Their daughter, Mary, 27, was employed as a house servant, and their son John, 24, was, like his father and uncle John, a carpenter. [182]

Although John Cragwall was not the only member of his family to have an on-going relationship with a free black woman, he was a somewhat unlikely candidate

---

[181] USCG 1850 and 1860 Elijah R. Cragwall household

[182] Legislative Petitions, Goochland, 1831, ms. 7095 [John J. Cragwall, a signer]; Agee, *op. cit.*, p. 135. John and Elijah Cragwall's father, Samuel N. Cragwall, and his wife Nancy donated the land on which Bethel Methodist Church was built in 1834.

Milly Pierce

to have numbered among those few white men who defied law and convention to live as man and wife with a free woman of color. Some twenty years before Margaret Cousins became a permanent member of his household and apparently bore his son, he had added his signature to the 1831 petition requesting that all free blacks be shipped to "other lands." Had he experienced a change of heart before he met Margaret Cousins? Or, had his heart found an exception to his dislike of free blacks in general? As in many instances of prejudice, John Cragwall may still have found free blacks as a group offensive, yet face to face with Margaret Cousins could not justify or sustain his position. Perhaps his parents, both devout Methodists, had long ago sown the seed of tolerance in their son, although living "in sin" and outside the law with a free black woman was a peculiar expression of the Methodist's early opposition to slavery. [183]

Ignoring the law and defying social opprobrium—and apparently overcoming any reservations John Cragwall had about free blacks—Margaret Cousins became and remained the only adult female in the Cragwall household. By 1870, however, John Cragwall was sixty-eight years old, and Margaret's future might well have been precarious. But, Margaret was not without resources. She was a seamstress, a profession popular among enterprising free black women. Not only did she have a trade to rely on, she had further secured her economic future when in 1866 she purchased 107 ½ acres at Sabot in Goochland. Perhaps to avoid any confusion or opposition at Cragwall's death, she had paid $1000 for the land which was owned by

---

[183] USCG 1870 [John Cragwall age]; USCG 1860 [Margaret identified as a seamstress]; Lebsock, *op. cit.*, pp. 97-99 [seamstresses]; GDB 40, p. 466 [Cragwall to Cousins]; USCG 1870 [all property in Margaret's name and values]

John Cragwall. Thus, although Cragwall was still living in 1870, all property, both real and personal, was listed in Margaret's name. Her real estate in one of the county's most beautiful and affluent neighborhoods adjoined James M. Morson's "Dover" plantation and was assessed for $1164 including a house valued at $400. [184]

At what personal price had Margaret achieved her economic security? She was, presumably, the housekeeper cum concubine of an aging white farmer, an illegal and dependent position. Like her mother and grandmother who had secured the good will of the Woodsons by their faithful service, Margaret made her way in the world by catering to the needs of white men. From today's perspective Margaret' situation especially might appear a questionable compromise, yet white patronage in one form or another was virtually indispensable to the security of all free blacks, male or female. Whatever judgment her path to economic security may invite, whatever her motives and the exact nature of her relationship with Cragwall, Margaret enjoyed a life of privilege relative to the majority of her peers. An incident on John Cragwall's farm in 1854 makes this abundantly clear.

A SLAVE IS WORTH A LOT MORE THAN A FREE BLACK WOMAN

In March 20, 1854, Peyton, "a Negro man slave the property of John J. Cragwall," was charged with "feloniously, premeditatedly, and of his malice a fore

---

[184]GOB 1852-1862, p. 97, [Peyton charged]; Hening, *op. cit.*, III, p. 102 and IV, p. 127 [Courts of Oyer and Terminer-slave trials]; _____, Acts 1832, p. 24 [free blacks denied trial by jury]; GOB 1852-1862, p. 99 [Peyton's trial]

Milly Pierce

thought" killing Rebecca Peyton, a free woman of color. At the court hearing, Peyton was accused not only of killing Rebecca Peyton, but of having abused her previously "by wounding with his fists and by smoking with sulphir [sic] and other ill treatment. While justice in Goochland often proceeded at a leisurely pace, slaves and, after 1832, free blacks were tried as quickly as possible after their arrest. Consequently, Peyton was brought to trial the following day, represented by John S. Fleming, his court appointed attorney. The Gentlemen Justices found Peyton not guilty of first-degree murder but rather of "voluntary manslaughter only." His punishment? Thirty-nine stripes on his bare back. Thirty-nine stripes was the value of a free black woman's life in the opinion of a white court. A slave, even if temporarily damaged, was worth far more, and the court was apparently loath to deprive Cragwall of his valuable property.[185]

Margaret Cousins, however awkward her situation in life, was determined to be nobody's victim, and in 1872, she was intent upon collecting both as a creditor and as an heir from the estate of her aunt Mary Pierce. Mary's estate was inextricably bound with that of Jane Pierce, the sister with whom she had lived virtually all of her life, and the lawsuit revolved around 86 acres at Cedar Point which the sisters had owned jointly. Ultimately, the commissioners who had been appointed to gather the facts in the case determined that 39 acres belonged to Lee Pierce, Jane Pierce's minor

---

[185] GOB 1872-1873, p. 10 [Cousins versus Pierce]; GDB 38, p. 715 [Mary and Jane Pierce deed for Cedar Point]; Goochland Chancery Order Book 1874-1785, p. 45 [Mary Pierce's land divided]; *ibid.*, p. 207 [Margaret's case as creditor dismissed]; Goochland Circuit Court Common Law Order Book 6 1883-1916, p. 88 [Cousins versus Cocke]

child, and that the remaining 47 ½ acres could not be fairly divided among the almost two dozen potential heirs. Consequently, the commissioners sold the property and distributed the proceeds. Margaret, like the rest, must have received a pittance. As for her position as a creditor, the case was dismissed, and Margaret was liable for the cost of the proceedings. She was equally unlucky in a later lawsuit against Magnolia and E.B. Cocke whom she sued over money owed for their purchase of her property. Although she won, she was long dead by the time the case was settled. [186]

FREE BLACK WOMEN AND THE IMPORTANCE OF INDEPENDENCE

Margaret Cousins was party to yet another lawsuit involving members of the Pierce-Cousins clan, this time as an heir of her mother Lydia. Lydia's life, although not without striving, was ultimately most notable for its quiet self-sufficiency. If Lydia's struggle for a secure place in this world was much less arduous than her mother's, her life still echoed Milly's in many ways. Both women honored first of all their commitment to family, yet neither relinquished a distinct sense of personal independence. This rather modern model was not atypical of free black women. Dependence on anyone, even a spouse, seems to have been anathema, especially to those who had formerly been slaves, and economic self-sufficiency was the hallmark

---

[186]GOB 1862-1871, p. 3 [Cousins versus Cousins]. Details of the case are in File 6, Goochland Chancery cases. Lebsock, *op. cit.*, pp. 100-111 [Independence of free black women]

of those who, whether by choice or necessity, assumed responsibility for their own destinies. [187]

Possibly as an outgrowth of this self-reliance and in recognition of the fundamental importance of financial independence, free black women were inclined to be quite specific in their wills, addressing, as Lebsock has suggested, "inequalities of love and loyalty, inequalities of need." This attention to love, loyalty and need often took the form of particular concern for their female heirs. In this regard, Lydia's will, written a year before her death of "paralisis" in 1860 at age 68, was typical. Lydia bequeathed to her four daughters, "Elizabeth, Margaret, Mary Francis, formerly Mary Cousins, and Martha Cousins all of my estate both real and personal to be equally divided." Included in her estate was the bulk of the Cousins family land holdings: her half-acre and house at the Courthouse and the 134 acres adjacent to the Poor House. No mention is made in the will of Lydia's four sons. Granted, Philip, aged 40, was well established in his career as a boatman on the James River and had acquired approximately 70 acres from his grandfather Francis's estate. Her oldest son John had registered in 1842 at 24 and left Goochland. So, too, may have Fields, who registered in 1852 at 21 and Henry, who had registered in 1856 at 24. Lydia's husband Henry,

---

[187]Lebsock, *op. cit.*, p. 136 [quote] and p. 142 [concern for female heirs]; United States Social Census, Goochland 1860 [Lydia's death]; GDB 39, p. 295 [Lydia's will]; USCG 1860 Philip identified as propertied boatman; GMR, p. 332 Philip Cousins m. Lucy Ann Lynch, June 22, 1846, James Copland and Walter Cousins, witnesses. Lucy Ann was the daughter of Henry Cousins' sister Charlotte Lynch; GFN # 866 Fields Cousins registered; GFN # 654 John Cousins registered and disappears from Goochland records; GFN # 995 Henry Cousins registered; USCG 1860 Henry Cousins household.

74, was presumably well taken care of, and at the time of Lydia's death, Elizabeth, 40, and Martha, 20, were still living with their father. [188]

Lydia left no doubt when she wrote her will that she was primarily interested in the welfare of her daughters. Free black women in general, and the notable number who were unmarried mothers in particular, seem to have been especially concerned that their daughters have some degree of economic autonomy and self-determination. A nineteenth century woman, black or white, faced limited options, her fate circumscribed by both custom and law. Marriage, the common route to economic security, marked the end of a woman's personal and financial independence. A married woman was not only expected to take a subservient role to her husband, she also ceded to him all of her property rights. Personal freedom, however, was often the road to penury. [189]

The free black woman's situation was even more narrowly circumscribed. If she chose to marry, the pool of potential husbands, especially in rural areas, was small. Some, like Milly Pierce "married" slaves—in fact, if not in law. Others, like Lydia,

---

[188] Lebsock, *op. cit.*, p. 103-111 [Non-marriage among free black women]

[189] GFN # 707 Philip Cousins registered at 21; in his 1878 lawsuit (Chancery Case File 6), Philip Cousins lists his wife as Lucy Ann, the daughter of his paternal aunt Charlotte Lynch. Mary Cousins does not appear in the marriage register, but Lydia refers to her in the will as Mary Francis; Margaret Cousins in her 1872 suit names her as the wife of Robert Francis; and she registered in 1863 as Mary Ann Francis, formerly Cousins, GFN # 2033, age 37, and "bright yellow." According to the marriage register, an Elizabeth Cousins married James S. Woodson in 1853 (p. 390), but Lydia's daughter Elizabeth was still at home in 1860, and it appears that she died prior to 1871 when her executor sued her aunt Evelina Lynch over rents which may have been owed to her father's estate (OB 1862-71, p. 526). Margaret Cousins was living with John Cragwall when Lydia died.

Milly Pierce

found suitable free black husbands, although relatively few were available. The choice of mates was even more limited for free black men. When Lydia's oldest son Philip came of age in 1845, there were 166 free black males between the ages of 10 and 35 in Goochland; there were only 132 females in the same age group. Philip settled upon his first cousin and neighbor, Lucy Ann Lynch. Despite the numeric odds in their favor, many of Goochland's free black women remained single. Only an unmarried woman of independent means remained mistress of her own fate, both legally and economically—this was the full meaning of Lydia's bequests to her daughters. Although Mary was already married to Robert Francis, Elizabeth, Margaret and Martha were still single and would remain so. [190]

Ironically, Lydia's wishes as expressed in her will were undermined by her marital status, and the will became the subject of yet another lawsuit between members of the Cousins clan. Despite Lydia's explicit request that her property go to her four daughters, she had forfeited all control over that property when she married. Under common-law, her marriage invalidated her will, and her estate passed intact to her husband. Her will was proven on June 18, 1860, yet when Henry Cousins died in 1868, Lydia's property was part of his estate. Unlike his wife, Henry died intestate, allowing the law to determine the distribution of his estate among his heirs. [191]

---

[190] Goochland Chancery Cases, File 6. In his statement to the court, John Cousins states that Henry died in 1868, intestate.

[191] GOB 1862-1871, p. 359 [John Cousins sues other heirs]; details of the case are in File 6, Goochland Chancery cases. The case was not settled until 1876.

CeCe Bullard

In 1869, Lydia and Henry's son John, now a resident of Roanoke County, filed suit in Goochland to settle his father's estate. Elizabeth was, by this time, dead, but Lydia's three remaining daughters and other potential heirs were named as defendants in the suit. The estate in dispute consisted primarily of Lydia's 134 ½ acres. There was, however, too little land to be fairly divided among too many heirs. Consequently, the land was sold. 66 2/3 acres were purchased by the adjoining landowner George H. King for $263.66, and the same acreage for the same amount was acquired by Martha J. Cousins. Martha, as an heir of Henry and Lydia Cousins, was not required to pay as "her share [of the estate] would at least equal the amount she gave for the lot." The suit was not settled until 1876 when a final distribution was made. Margaret may have been dead by this time and is not mentioned in the settlement; Mary's share was paid to her widower, Robert Francis. [192]

Martha Jane alone benefited as her mother would have wished—not that she actually needed her inheritance. The 1870 census describes her as a literate 35-year-old mulatto with $355 in real estate and $125 in personal property. In 1861, with the assistance of three white "special partners"—R.G. Banks, William Miller and A.M. Hamilton—she had purchased property at the Courthouse where she ran a restaurant. Among her clients was the powerful Courthouse crowd whom her grandmother Milly Pierce had served so faithfully. When meals were needed for jurors, Martha Jane was asked to provide them. As a single, working mother, Martha Jane employed a black

---

[192] USCG 1870 [Martha Jane Cousins household and assets]; Common Law Order Book 1870, p. 294, Martha Jane and partners sued over the purchase of the Courthouse property and prevail. No deed could be found. GOB 1862-1872, p. 455 [Martha Jane paid for jurors' meals]

Milly Pierce

housekeeper to care for her two children, Margaret, 6 and Lydia, 10. Lydia Cousins, unlike Milly, was honored with a grandchild named after her. A mother may well have been more endearing to her children than a hard-driving matriarch, although Martha Jane appears to have followed closely in her grandmother's footsteps. [193]

---

[193] Berlin, *op. cit.*, p. 279 [quote]

IV

JOHN PIERCE, JR.: WHITE AMBITION

Richmond in 1862 was a bustling capital destined for destruction, and as John Pierce, Jr. looked out of his window on the city, he may have seen a reflection of his own life—a meteoric rise to prosperity, prelude as it turned out, to a disastrous fall—and raged against the harshness of his fate and color.

FREE, BLACK AND A COMMERCIAL SLAVEOWNER

Milly Pierce had committed herself to the formidable task of securing a foothold for her family in the world of the free. Lydia Cousins and most of her extended family were content enough to settle for a yeoman farmer's self-sufficiency and respectability. They led what would now be called solid, middle class lives, very much like the lives of most of their white neighbors. Lydia's brother John wanted more—much more. John's model was the white aristocracy, and all of its accoutrements, including slaves. As Berlin has remarked, "...wealth and a light skin remained the most common prerequisites for membership in the upper crust of free Negro society...[and] elite freemen came to venerate economic success and to idealize the style of life of the white upper class." John Pierce, Jr., aspiring to the "upper crust," pursued the worst of the white world's ambitions and conventions with a vengeance. Yet, the more successful an ambitious mulatto such as John Pierce, Jr.

became, the more ambiguous and difficult his place in antebellum society. Whether black or white, slave or free, many resented his success and regarded him with suspicion. He was destined to wend his way through a social and political no-man's land. [194]

Unlike his parents and siblings, John Pierce, Jr. did not deal in sweat equity, at least, not his own. A man with something to prove, John was intent on establishing himself as an equal to successful whites, at least in the one arena where he had a fighting chance—the accumulation of wealth. His style was more that of the late twentieth century stock speculator or corporate raider, more intent on making money at any cost than on making a concrete contribution to society or to the economy. Even when John Pierce, Jr. invested in farming or brick making, he was not actively engaged in the enterprise. Instead, his energies were focused on exploiting slaves for profit and land speculation.

Despite the evidence that slave owning was an acceptable practice in the Pierce family, it is still somewhat surprising that John Pierce, Jr., born the son of slaves, established himself as a commercial slave-owner. In 1817, at the age of twenty-four, John Pierce, Jr. made his first appearance in the Goochland personal property tax ledger as the owner of two slaves. By 1820, he owned five slaves, a number which rises to six in 1822, then drops to 3 in 1826, and rises again to 9 in 1829—fluctuations which seem to indicate active buying and selling. In 1832, he paid personal property

---

[194]GPPT 1817, 1820, 1822, 1826, 1829, and 1832. [John Pierce's slaves]

Milly Pierce

taxes on eight slaves over sixteen, two slaves over ten, five horses or mules and a barouche valued at $100. [195]

Somehow, John managed to circumvent the restrictions on black slave ownership imposed by the 1832 law, for there is every indication that he continued to buy and sell slaves throughout the next two decades. In general, Goochland officials appear to have been relatively tolerant of the county's free blacks and somewhat lackadaisical in the strict enforcement of laws pertaining to them. Yet, their apparent indifference to John Pierce's three decades of slave trading is still surprising. The court's benign neglect of John's slave business (benign to John if not his human property) may have been, in part, a reflection of their respect for Milly and John Pierce, Sr. and the family's close connection to several powerful whites. John himself proved adept at finding white allies, especially when there was the potential for mutual profit. [196]

---

[195] GPPT 1832-1858 [evidence of John Pierce's slave trading]. The tolerance of Goochland's officials towards free blacks is evident not only in the lax enforcement of some free black laws but also by the fact that the county had the second largest population of free blacks of any of the Piedmont counties in 1860. One of every nine blacks in Goochland was free; one of six in Loudon County (Russell, *Free Negro*, p. 15).

[196] William Bolling, "The Diary of Col. William Bolling of Bolling Hall (1836-1839)," Part II, *Goochland County Historical Society Magazine*, vol. 9, no. 2 (Autumn, 1977), p. 23 [flood and John Pierce's boat]; *ibid.*, Part V, vol. 11, no. 1 (Spring, 1979), pp. 36-37 [ships tobacco with John Pierce]; *ibid.*, Part VII, vol. 13, 1981, p. 64 [pays for shipping wheat].

CeCe Bullard

UPWARDLY MOBILE

How the younger John Pierce first accumulated the cash to launch his slave trading enterprise is a mystery. Certainly, he may have worked on his mother's farm, although payment in cash seems unlikely. Possibly, he worked for a wage on the boat for carrying cargo on the James River that his father purchased in 1811. Working the river seems the most plausible source of John's initial capital, for it appears that John Pierce, Jr. carried on his father's business in river commerce after the latter's death.

In August of 1836, Colonel William Bolling, one of Goochland's most distinguished citizens and an inveterate diarist, described his difficult return home from a trip to Richmond. The rains were so hard and the road so bad that "the fat passengers had to walk up the hill" (Colonel Billing was slim), but when they reached Beaverdam Creek, experiencing the "highest freshet...that has ever been known," they could go no further. Determined to get home, the next morning, Colonel Bolling "rode up to John Peirces [sic] where he took us in his boat thro' Stannards, Seldens and my own low grounds," and thence home to Bolling Hall. John Pierce may have ferried the Colonel home as a favor, but two subsequent entries in Bolling's diary make it clear that John was actively engaged in river commerce. In June of 1837, he records "Tobacco shipped...3 Hhds. To make up Billy Martin's [a free black] load with six he took at "Pocahontas" [another Bolling plantation] and 9 Hdds. On board John Pierce's boat." In an entry of October 1838, Bolling noted that he had "settled with John Pierce for freight of wheat." [197]

---

[197] GPPT 1822 [John Pierce's holdings]; GDB 25, p. 144 [loan to father]

Milly Pierce

Although the Bolling diary sheds light on John Pierce's commercial activity in the late 1830s, it still does not explain how, prior to his father's death, he initially accumulated enough capital to begin his business as a commercial slave-owner. That he was shrewd and avid in the acquisition of money is certain. By 1822, when he was about twenty-eight years of age, he not only owned six slaves and three horses or mules, he was able to loan his father $200 on which he expected to earn interest. That he may also have been conscienceless in his pursuit of wealth is suggested by the possible outcome of that loan. [198]

MAKING MONEY ON OTHER MEN'S BACKS

As a commercial slaveholder, John Pierce's inventory in 1830 consisted of two males under 10, two males 10 to 24, 10 males in the prime years of 24 to 36, one male over fifty-five, two females under 10 and one female between 24 and 36. Typically, these slaves would have been hired out for a fee to work for others, used as cheap labor by their owner or sold at a profit. [199]

While fluctuations in the number of his slaves indicate that John Pierce indulged in some buying and selling for profit, he may also have made money on his

---

[198] USCG 1830 [John Pierce's slaves]; Luther Porter Jackson, *Free Negro Labor and Property Holding in Virginia* (New York, 1942), pp. 210-211 [practices of slave owners].

[199] Schwarz, *op. cit.*, p. 393 [boatmen and others owned slaves]; GOB 32, p. 95 [Court ordered Pierce's hands to work road]. Eight of Stanard's hands to work on one road, and John Pierce's hands to work on another.

investment in human property by using some of his slaves to man his riverboat or boats. Boatmen, along with blacksmiths, coopers, barbers and carpenters, were the free blacks who most commonly owned slaves. Pierce apparently generated additional income by hiring out his slaves. In 1837, the Goochland Court directed that "John Pierce's hands do work on the road of which Rice Carter is surveyor," and an entry in the Bolling diary of the same year seems to confirm Pierce's practice of hiring out his slaves as construction workers. [200]

In June of 1837, the tireless Bolling rode the long way home from a visit to James B. Ferguson who lived at "La Vallee" in the same Rock Castle neighborhood. From Mr. Ferguson's, Bolling wended his way "via Selden's to the line of canal which John Pierce, Morris and Shelton are working." Apparently, John Pierce was working under contract to the James River and Kanawha Canal Company, using his slaves to work on the canal's expansion which was proceeding west from Maiden's Adventure through Goochland. A commercial slaveowner hiring out his slaves for profit is hardly surprising; what is surprising, however, is Bolling's next remark: "Dined at John Pierce's." Still a distance from home, Bolling, apparently, had fetched up at John Pierce's in time for his mid-day meal. Unlike many of his contemporaries, Bolling evidently did not find color an insurmountable deterrent to sociability—or a good meal. Well-fortified, the Colonel rode home after lunch and spent the afternoon supervising the tobacco planting. [201]

---

[200]William Bolling, *op. cit.*, vol. 11, no 1, p. 36 [John Pierce's hands working the canal]; Bolling, *ibid.* [dines at John Pierce's]

[201]Bolling, *op. cit.*, vol. 11, no. 2, p. 83 [Tom Pierce fiddler]; *ibid.*, vol. 15, p. 66 [Madison Pierce builds pillars]

Milly Pierce

As one of Goochland's Gentleman Justices, Colonel Bolling spent a great deal of time at the Courthouse, and was, unquestionably, acquainted with both Milly and John Pierce, Sr. and their children. In describing a Christmas party in 1837, he noted that "The young people managed to get George Walker (Thomas Vaughan's fiddler) and Tom Pierce [John Pierce's younger brother], first rate ballroom musicians" to play. In December of 1839, he employed John's son Madison Pierce, a bricklayer, to put up four pillars to support the columns for an extension of the south porch at Bolling Hall. It is more than likely then that Colonel Bolling had known John Pierce, Jr. for most, if not all, of the younger man's life, and another diary entry six weeks after his lunch at John Pierce's, reinforces the impression that the aging white aristocrat was happy enough in the younger black man's company—and that John Pierce interacted easily with whites. [202]

In the course of "an agricultural ride" with his son Thomas, Bolling "sat an hour on the River bank with Nelson Shelton, Mr. Steel and John Pierce..." Nelson Shelton who owned land at Cedar Point was Bolling's neighbor; Steel, a contractor building an aqueduct for the James River and Kanawha Canal Company. What the voluble Bolling, who considered the canal a plague upon the land, especially his land which had been condemned for the project, had to say to Steel, one can easily imagine. The two gentlemen farmers probably discussed their crops and the weather. And John

---

[202]Bolling, *op. cit.*, vol. 11, no. 1, p. 41 [sits on riverbank with John Pierce]; in 1847, Pierce bought 451 acres owned by Shelton (GDB 35, p. 67).

Pierce? Perhaps he was imagining what it would be like one day to own some of the fertile river bottom that lay behind them. [203]

FREE BLACK SLAVEOWNER, A RARE AND DUBIOUS DISTINCTION

While the Bolling diary gives some notion of John Pierce, Jr.'s activities during the 1830s, and indicates how he may have employed his slaves, the suspicion that John Pierce, Jr. was a commercial slaveowner who did some trading on the side was first aroused by the Goochland and Richmond personal property tax records. The very number of slaves he owned was conspicuous. When coupled with fluctuations in the numbers and the fact that the slaves were definitely not family members, the evidence seemed strong. What was, however, just a suspicion initially was later confirmed by Luther P. Jackson whose own observations were verified by "George W. Lewis of Richmond, born in 1857, [who] testified to the writer that the Pearces of Goochland and Richmond were commercial slaveholders." Jackson also indicates that John Pierce hired out his slaves in Richmond as well as Goochland. [204]

Owning slaves was a rare and dubious distinction among free blacks. As Philip K Schwarz has observed: "In the 1830s, probably the peak of such ownership,

---

[203] Jackson, *Free Negro Labor*, p. 211 and 211n [John Pierce commercial slaveowner].

[204] Schwarz, *op. cit.*, p. 319 [Number of free black slaveowners];
_____, Acts 1832, p. 21 [slave owning restricted]. Both John Pierce's family and his wife's family were free; there appear to have been no enslaved family members.

Milly Pierce

no more than 1000 of the 55,000 free Negroes in the Old Dominion help human property for any reason." Most commonly, free blacks owned slaves who were family members. The purchase of an enslaved spouse was not uncommon, and following passage of the law of 1806, those purchased remained technically slaves rather than face the possibility of banishment from the commonwealth. After 1832, free blacks were barred by law from buying slaves other than members of their immediate families. Familial slave ownership was an indication of the ever more desperate situation of free blacks and the length to which some would go to preserve their families. Those free blacks who owned family members often made enormous sacrifices to keep their loved ones near. John Pierce, Jr., however, did not own members of his family, nor is there any evidence that indicates he was a humanitarian or custodial slave-owner. [205]

John Pierce, Jr., instead, belonged to that small group of free blacks who owned slaves primarily for profit. He may have employed some of his slaves on his boat or boats working the James, yet, curiously enough, this was one profession that was common among free blacks in Goochland and elsewhere. John's nephew Philip Cousins was a boatman, as were Philip's cousins, Sam and James Cousins. The driving force behind John Pierce's slave owning, and his life for that matter, appears to have been financial gain, and those slaves whom he did not keep for his own use or as hands for hire were a ready source of extra cash. [206]

---

[205] USCG 1850 [Philip and Sam Cousins, boatmen]; USCG 1860 [James Cousins, boatman]

[206] Russel, *Free Negro*, pp. 130-137 and Berlin, *op. cit.*, pp. 57, 269-273 offer good discussions of the relationships between free blacks and slaves.

CeCe Bullard

A BLACK MASTER

Financial considerations aside, what was John Pierce's attitude toward slaves? And how did his slaves regard him? The majority of free blacks maintained close and easy relationships with slaves, some of whom were their blood relatives. The frequency of intermarriage between free blacks and slaves further indicates the ease with which the two groups commingled. Indeed, the close connections between free blacks and slaves were profoundly troubling to many slave-owners. The conventional wisdom among whites was that free blacks were slave sympathizers, willing conduits for property stolen by slaves from their masters, and fomenters of rebellion. [207]

The sympathy between free black and slave, however, was not universal. Sometimes, as James Madison observed, "...a freeman immediately loses all attachment and sympathy with his former fellow slaves." Although Madison's generalization was far too sweeping, there were a number of free blacks, like John Pierce, who simply turned their backs on their "former fellow slaves." Strongly identified with white culture, those free blacks who abandoned their own typically had close associations with whites, were light-skinned and determinedly upwardly mobile. And, as in the case of John Pierce, their identification with white values sometimes

---

[207] Gaillard Hunt, ed., *The Writings of James Madison*, (New York, 1900-1910). 9 vol., vol. 1, p. 107 [James Madison on free blacks. Letter to Joseph Jones, Nov. 28, 1780]. Berlin, *op. cit.*, pp. 271-277 [attitudes of upwardly mobile free blacks]

extended to owning slaves. Like white slave-owners, John Pierce, Jr. appears to have regarded his slaves as little more than chattels. [208]

How did John Pierce's slaves regard their black master? They almost certainly envied his material success and aspired to his status as a free man. Did the desire for freedom burn more intensely in their breasts upon seeing one of their own free and successful? This was certainly the fear of most whites. Although John's slaves probably admired his position in the world, they may well have distrusted him as a man. White was the color of oppression; a black master may well have inspired a cruel combination of hope and betrayal in the men he owned. As a black slave-owner, John Pierce was truly caught in the middle; neither slave nor white master, he lived in an awkward and ambiguous relationship to both.

THE LURE OF THE CITY

The income from his slaves and boat business was not apparently sufficient to satisfy John Pierce's ambitions, and the commercial opportunities in a rural backwater like Goochland were limited. Around 1840, John moved to the city of Richmond where he began to invest in real estate.

---

[208] John Pierce, Jr. appears in neither the Goochland nor the Richmond census for 1840. In 1841, he appears in the Richmond Personal Property taxes, paying tax on 2 slaves, 1 horse or mule and a carry-all (vehicle). He reappears in the Goochland personal property taxes in 1846 with a note that he was a resident of Richmond and paid taxes on 3 slaves and 3 horses/mules. Berlin, *op. cit.*, p. 175 [statistics re: urbanization]

Pierce was not alone among free blacks or within his own family in his belief that cities were more congenial than the country to enterprising free blacks. Free blacks in large numbers were attracted to the south's urban centers. Although free black in the south, like whites and slaves, were a predominantly rural population, the number of free blacks in urban areas increased much more rapidly during the nineteenth century than did the free black population as a whole. By 1860, over a third of the free black population lived in cities as opposed to 15% of whites and 5% of slaves. [209]

About the same time that John moved to Richmond, his sister Judith, accompanied by her 10 year old daughter Harriet, registered in Goochland as a free mulatto woman. Her registration was apparently in preparation for her move to Richmond, and in 1846, she purchased a house on Third Street in Jackson Ward, a district that would become the center of the city's black cultural and commercial life. Their sister Phebe had long been a resident of Richmond where she had relocated in 1820 immediately after her marriage to Page Carter, a native of the city. John's younger brother Thomas settled in Danville, a small city in the western part of the

---

[209] GFN # 662 Judith registered in 1842 at age 50; RDB 69A, p. 94 [Judith purchased Lot 12 on west side of Third St. from David Judah]; USCR 1820 [Page Carter is listed as a resident]; USCR 1830 [Phoebe Carter is listed as a resident]. An 1852 deed of gift (GDB 37, p. 101) refers to Thomas as "now residing in Danville." He appears in the Personal Property taxes in Goochland through 1849. RDB 56, p. 635 [William Henry Pierce buys Duval Street Lot from David Judah]; RDB 56, p. 636 [William Henry Pierce "of Goochland" sells Duval Street lot]; RDB 72B, p. 24 [James Madison Pierce's property]; Goochland Chancery Order Book 1871-1873, p. 4 [Cherry St. property sold to settle Henry Cousins' estate. Chancery Cases, File 6 describes property. Could not find deed.]

state, not long after his mother's death in 1850. William Henry Pierce who was probably John's son moved to Richmond in 1846 and like his aunt Judith purchased a lot in Jackson Ward. William lived on Duval Street until 1849 when he sold his house and returned to Goochland. City life was not for everyone. Another son, James Madison Pierce, owned property in Richmond near the corner of Broad and Twenty-second Streets from 1852 to 1857, although he appears to have followed John's lead and made the purchase solely as an investment. Similarly, Lydia and Henry Cousins had purchased "a house and small lot" on the north side of Cherry Street in Richmond.[210]

For free blacks especially, cities afforded greater economic and social possibilities than the country. By tradition, free blacks dominated certain trades in southern cities, working as barbers, milliners, seamstresses, and blacksmiths among other occupations, and for those without a trade, occasional employment was readily available. Cities not only offered a better chance at economic self-sufficiency, the anonymity of a large urban population afforded greater freedom. At the same time, their concentration in greater numbers enabled free blacks to develop a sense of community and social institutions, both of which were generally lacking in rural areas. In contrast to their urban peers, rural free blacks had less opportunity and generally

---

[210] Russell, *Free Negro*, p. 150 and Berlin, *op. cit.*, 273-274 [lure of the city]; Russell, *Free Negro*, pp. 150-151, Lebsock, *op. cit.*, 97-99, and Berlin, *op. cit.*, p. 218, 234-238 [Free black occupations]

less success. A tiny minority, they were both conspicuous and isolated in ways that urban free blacks were not. [211]

John Pierce, as a free black exploiting other blacks, may have had special reason for preferring the anonymity of urban life. By 1830, John must have been fairly conspicuous within the narrow confines of Goochland. He was one of only seven Goochland free blacks who owned slaves. Most owned only one slave, although John Lynch owned eight. John Pierce owned eighteen.[212]

A FREE BLACK OWNS HIS WIFE AND CHILDREN

John Pierce never emancipated a slave. John Lynch did. Prior to his death in 1839, John Lynch, although illiterate, carefully crafted a will in which he freed his slaves: his wife, "Alla," whom he had "heretofore purchased" and their four children, Mary, Mahala, James and Sally. Worried that his family was "subject to disposition as property," he desired that "when my personal protection of them shall cease by my death to invest them with all liberty I can confer." John Lynch requested that his executors, "my friends James Poor and William Lynch," ask the Court to permit Alla and their children to remain in Goochland and hoped that "the humanity of the Court

---

[211] USCG 1830 Number of black slaveowners and John Pierce's and John Lynch's households

[212] GDB 32, p. 33 [John Lynch's will]; GDB 31, p. 368 [Poor to Lynch-John's farm]

will allow them to continue where they have heretofore resided"—the 102 ¾ acre farm he bequeathed to them. [213]

John Lynch, a blacksmith by trade, left his family well provided for. In addition to his farm, his estate also included his blacksmith tools, two yoke of oxen, fifteen sheep, five cows, a good horse, a shot gun which had apparently escaped confiscation by the Sheriff, two spinning wheels (his mother Polly had been a "spinner"), a loom and substantial household furnishings. All of this, valued at almost $2000, was left to Abba for her lifetime and then to the children. John Lynch concluded his will with a request that his executors "render every act of kindness and attention to my helpless family." There is ample evidence that James Poor, his white neighbor, and William Lynch, his brother, heeded his words. [214]

Although left comfortably fixed, Abba, age 46 at John's death, was apparently unprepared to assume management of John's finances and farm. For the next fourteen years, the executors, primarily James Poor, administered John Lynch's estate for the benefit of the family. They paid Lewis Chaudoin for "preaching" John's funeral, they bought clothing for the family, purchased seed corn and wheat for the

---

[213] GDB 32, p. 320 [John Lynch's estate]; Polly Lynch is identified as a spinner living on Sarah Bowles land in the GPPT in 1804 and after. John and Billy (William) are listed with her.

[214] GDB 32, p. 474 [Wm. Lynch pays for clothes, gives cash]; GDB 32, p. 475 [James Poor pays Chaudoin, buys corn]; GDB 33, p. 211 [Poor collects debts]; GDB 35, p. 408 [Poor collects rents]

farm, and allocated cash for miscellaneous necessities. They also collected debts owed John Lynch and rents on his land. [215]

Freedom for a woman liberated in middle age was an unsettling and uncertain bequest, and there were no guarantees that she would be allowed to remain in quiet possession of her home. As stipulated in John Lynch's will, Poor and William Lynch made a request in 1839 for a hearing regarding Alla and the children's permission to remain in Goochland. After a second request to the Court in 1840, however, they let the matter drop. There was, ironically, greater safety and more security in remaining a nominal slave than in claiming one's freedom with its attendant risks. For the next twelve years, John Lynch's wife and four children were recorded in the tax records as slaves, the property of John Lynch deceased's estate. Their peculiar situation confused even the census taker. In 1840, the surviving Lynches were counted as free blacks; in 1850, Alla, her four children and nine grandchildren appear in the Slave Schedule as the property of John Lynch rather than in the census of free inhabitants. [216]

Alla, wary of the consequences, made no further attempt to claim her freedom and retain her home until 1850. Finally, in 1851, she and the children received a hearing on their petition to remain in Goochland as free blacks. Although James Poor retained attorney John Coles Rutherfoord to represent the Lynches, the Gentlemen Justices of Goochland determined that "the applicants have produced no

---

[215]GOB 1836-1844, p. 209 [executors request hearing 1839]; GOB 1836-1844, p. 232 [second request]; GPPT 1840 to 1850 [John Lynch's estate taxed]; USCG 1840 [Lynches listed as free blacks].

[216]GOB 1844-1852, p. 487 [hearing]; GDB 37, p. 206 [Poor paid Rutherford and court costs]. For more about Rutherfoord's beliefs, see p. xx this ms.

proof of their being of good character, sober, peaceable, orderly, and industrious…and permission [is] unanimously refused by the Court." No proof was presented to show that the Lynches did not possess these traits either. How effectively their case was argued is certainly open to question, considering that their counsel, also a state legislator, would soon emerge as one of the most vocal proponents of the involuntary deportation of all free blacks to Liberia. [217]

With the Court's decision, Alla and her children were effectively given notice to leave the only home they had ever known. Shortly after the hearing, John Lynch's executors began to sell his land. The final sale was consummated in 1853—the same year that Alla, aged 60, Mahala Ann, 29, Sally Ann, 27, James, 23, and Mary 22, registered as free Negroes, presumably in preparation for their departure from Virginia. Their names never again appear in the Goochland or Virginia records. A year after Alla was denied permission to remain in Goochland, Milly Pierce's former slave and current Courthouse caretaker Franklin French was allowed to stay. For free blacks, character and connections were critical.[218]

---

[217] GDB 36, p. 196 [Poor and Lynch to Bibb-1853]; GFN 1853 # 894 James Lynch, # 896 Sally Ann Lynch, # 897 Mahala Ann Lynch and # 898 Alley [sic] Lynch. All cited John Lynch's will as the source of their freedom; GFN 1853 # 957 Franklin French registered.

[218] GPPT 1846 [John Pierce, Jr. resident of Richmond]; RDB 41, p. 182 [Abbott to Pierce]; Richmond Land Tax (RLT) 1841 [Description as Southgate Garden]; RLT 1850 [value of property]; RDB 59, p. 153 [Pierce to Sterns]. Although Navy Hill was just east of Jackson Ward, a hub of the free black community, there does not appear to have been a concentration of blacks on the Pierce property. Housing in Richmond was not segregated at this time, although there were pockets of primarily black households (Elsa Barkley Brown and Gregg D. Kimbell, "Mapping the Terrain of Black Richmond," *The Journal of Urban History*, vol. 21, no. 3 [March, 1995], pp. 296-346).

CeCe Bullard

JOINING THE WHITE GENTRY

Alla Lynch and her children presumably disappeared from Goochland with funds sufficient to begin a decent life elsewhere. Several years earlier John Lynch had departed the county with enough cash in hand to launch a new career as a real estate investor. Exactly when John Pierce made his move to Richmond is uncertain. The Goochland records do not specifically indicate the move until 1846, yet he does not appear in the 1840 Goochland census, nor in the Richmond census, for that matter. In 1840, however, John Pierce of the County of Goochland paid Josiah B. and Catherine Abbott $2000 for approximately fourteen acres with buildings on Navy Hill in Richmond. The property, described in the real estate assessments as lots 55 through 76 of Southgate Garden, was bounded by Eighth Street and Shockoe Creek. This purchase marked the beginning of John Pierce's career as a landlord and land speculator in Richmond. By 1850, this same property was valued at $2500 and generated an income from rents of $100. Pierce made a handsome profit when he sold it that year to Franklin Sterns for $5000. [219]

In 1846, however, John Pierce made a real estate purchase which, like his slave trading, said as much about his character as it did about his financial acumen. Returning to the county of his birth, John Pierce, now a resident of Richmond, purchased 246 acres on the James River for $2212.87. The land was sold by George

---

[219] GDB 34, p. 481 [Pope trustees to Pierce]; GLT 1846 [Holdings of Pierce and Sampson]

Milly Pierce

W. Harris and James W. Logan, guarantors of a deed of trust from lawyer Charles H. Pope who, along with Dr. John Morris, became John Pierce's neighbor. John Pierce, Jr. had now established himself in the midst of Goochland's landed gentry. He had also become Goochland's second largest free black landowner, his acreage surpassed only by that of Jacob Sampson who held a total of 288 ¼ acres in five parcels. In 1847, however, John Pierce added 451 acres to his Goochland holdings, far outstripping Sampson. [220]

John Pierce, Jr. must have made something of a splash in Goochland's small pond when, on a cool November day, he stepped forward at a public auction held on the Courthouse steps and placed the winning bid of $4000 for 451 acres on the James River. He now owned more land than the majority of Goochland's white landowners, and his holdings dwarfed those of all of the county's free blacks. Of Goochland's 29 free blacks who owned any real estate, 22 owned fewer than 50 acres and of these, eight owned fewer than five. John had big dreams, however. Ten years earlier, John had sat on the riverbank with the property's owner, Nelson Shelton. Perhaps he had coveted the Cedar Point tract ever since, and now Shelton's financial distress had made his dream a reality.[221]

Once again, John laid claim to a prime parcel, this tract adjacent to "Blithewood," a plantation owned by Judge Robert Stanard of Richmond. Stanard was

---

[220]GDB 35, p. 67 [Miller (Shelton's trustee) to Pierce]; GLT 1847 Free black landowners

[221]William S. Wight, *The Story of Goochland* (Richmond, 1935), pp. 20-23; Agee, *op. cit.*, pp. 94-99, 167-168 [Morsons and Seddons]

only one of several prominent and wealthy Richmonders who settled on Goochland's fertile and beautiful riverfront land around mid-century. Others who found the Goochland countryside an appealing alternative to city life were the Bruce sisters, Ellen and Sallie, who with their husbands, James M. Morson and James Alexander Seddon, both attorneys, settled on the rolling hills above the river at Sabot, a few miles east of John Pierce. The sisters and their families envisioned a long and happy future on their adjoining estates, the Morsons at "Dover" and the Seddons at "Sabot Hill"—a future cut short by the Civil War during which Seddon served as the Confederacy's most able secretary of war. John Pierce could be said to have been part of a fashionable trend when he purchased river front land in Goochland, but he alone among the wealthy Richmonders was black. [222]

STABBED IN THE BACK

Wealthy Richmonders laying claim to some of the county's most beautiful and productive land served to intensify a divide within Goochland that was both geographical and social. From the first, those who lived along the river and enjoyed the bounty of the fertile lowlands were generally more prosperous than the yeoman farmers who tilled the red clay fields of the backcountry. Blessed with a certain amount of leisure and relatively easy access to Richmond, the river families were often well connected socially and politically, and active in both spheres. Some resentment

---

[222] CeCe Bullard, *Goochland: Yesterday and Today, A Pictorial History*, (Donning, 1994), p. 12. Wight, *op. cit.*

Milly Pierce

among less affluent and less influential locals was inevitable. Throw into the mix a free black with pretensions to joining the gentry and resentment easily escalates into something more lethal. In the case of John Pierce, Jr., the conspicuous return of a native son was not, apparently, an entirely welcome turn of events. [223]

John Pierce, Jr. placed the high bid on what was known as the Cedar Point property on November 6, 1847. On November 16, David Mims, a well-to-do white Goochland farmer and member of an old Goochland family, was brought before the county court and "charged with unlawfully, maliciously and feloniously stabbing with intent to kill John Pierce, a free man of colour." [224]

According to witnesses the stabbing occurred on the towpath of the James River Canal as it passed through the Morson's "Dover" plantation. Witness James S. Agee "saw both riding very rapidly, the prisoner on a white horse and in pursuit of Pierce, each had a switch in his hand." While Agee "did not see any wound inflicted or see any weapon," William Pollard, another witness, not only "saw the race between the prisoner and John Pierce," he also "saw a motion from the prisoner's hand and heard Pierce say he had been stabbed—immediately afterwards he [Mims] left Pierce, both were riding very fast and prisoner in pursuit of Pierce." Pierce was wounded in the center of the back and bleeding profusely when William Pollard had him "conveyed in a cart to one of Mr. Morson's servants houses." There, he was examined by Dr. William S. Wight, a neighbor of Morson's who found that Pierce "had received

---

[223] GOB 34, pp. 237-238 [Indictment of Mims]

[224] GOB 34, p. 237 [testimony in Mims hearing]

a wound inflicted with some sharp instrument in the back near the spine." Although there was "considerable flow of blood," Dr. Wight determined that "Pierce's pulse was not excited and his breathing not difficult [and] there was no evidence of injury to the lungs." [225]

Upon hearing the evidence against Mims, the Gentlemen Justices expressed the opinion that the prisoner was guilty of the offense and should be tried in the Circuit and Superior Court of Law and Chauncery. James M. Morson, William Pollard, William S. Wight, John Morris, Thomas Curd, James S. Agee and Francis Blankenship (near whose shop the alleged stabbing had occurred) were ordered to appear as witnesses and "give evidence on behalf of the Commonwealth against David Mims." Although the justices had originally determined that the "prisoner is not bailable," upon further pleadings by Mims' counsel, they agreed to set bail at $5000. Peter Guerrant, Thomas Massie, William Pollard, Thomas W. Vaughan, Charles Massie, John S. Fleming and Edward Pettit stepped forward as securities for Mims. This group of Mims' supporters included not only members of some of Goochland's more prominent white families, but also, and most curiously, one of the witnesses called against him. [226]

On April 20, 1848, the case of "David Mims, late of the Parish of St. James Northam and County of Goochland, farmer" was heard in Superior Court, Judge John B. Clopton, Esquire presiding. Twenty-four potential jurors were assembled, and of

---

[225] *Ibid.*

[226] Goochland Superior Court Order Book 4, p. 56 [Trial of David Mims]

these, eight were struck from the panel by the prisoner. Impaneled to hear the case as jurors were: Daniel S. Carter, Henry Anderson, Casper W. Armistead, James H. Turner, James F. Jennings, John Michie, William O. Ragland, James H. Merewether, James T. Isbell, Thomas W. Herndon, Richard Powell, and James Nash. No details of the proceedings are recorded, but "the jury sworn as aforesaid having heard the evidence upon their oath do say that the said David Mims is not guilty." [227]

How the jury arrived at this verdict can only be a matter of speculation. Certainly, William Pollard's eye-witness account of the stabbing would have been pivotal. On the one hand, Pollard went so far as to note in his deposition that "the blow was given by the right hand." On the other hand, he also stated that when he witnessed the incident "he did not know it was the prisoner [Mims] but believes it was," although like the other witness, James Agee, Pollard observed that Mims, positively identified by Agee, "was riding a white horse." Perhaps Pollard's failure to identify Mims absolutely at the time of the stabbing was the loophole David Mims walked through. Considering that Pollard volunteered as a security for Mims' bail, he may well have spun his testimony in a manner favorable to the defendant. [228]

---

[227] GOB 34, p. 237 [Pollard and Agee testimony]

[228] GLT 1848 and GPPT 1848 [Property of Pierce, Mims and jury]. Richmond Personal Property Tax (RPPT) 1848 [Pierce property]. The only wealthy juror was John Michie who owned 804 acres and 22 slaves.

CeCe Bullard

FREE BLACK SUCCESS AND WHITE REACTION

John Pierce, Jr. was probably a less than sympathetic character to many of Goochland's white citizens, and this, too, may have had some impact on the Mims verdict. Pierce, a free black, now owned more property and appeared to possess more wealth than most of the white, yeoman farmers who constituted the jury of his so-called peers. In 1848, he owned 697 acres of valuable lowlands in Goochland, 14 acres in Richmond, ten slaves in Goochland, three in Richmond, several horses and mules and a carriage. Witness William Pollard, whose testimony may have been critical to the verdict, owned no land and a single slave. With one exception, none of the jurors in the Mims case came even close to owning either as much real or personal property as John Pierce. [229]

Pierce had not only conspicuously challenged conventional presumptions of white superiority and inserted himself in the midst of Goochland's elite, he had acquired his land at the expense of white owners who were unable to satisfy debts secured by their property. Taking advantage of respected white gentlemen in financial difficulty was not apt to win a free black much favor in the white community. Nor had John Pierce hesitated to take on his white "superiors" in court. During the 1840s, he filed several lawsuits against members of prominent Goochland families—John B.

---

[229] Both the Pope and Shelton properties had been sold because the owners were unable to meet the terms of their deeds of trust (mortgages); GOB 20, p. 468 [Pierce versus Gay]; Circuit Superior Court of Law and Chancery Order Book, Goochland, 1837-1842, p. 358 [Pierce versus Robert R. Watkins] and p. 384 [Pierce versus Robert and John Watkins]; Superior Court Orders 1831-1855, p. 356, and Chancery Cases File 20 [Pierce versus Pope].

Milly Pierce

Gay, Robert R. Watkins, John R. Watkins and his neighbor Charles F. Pope—for monies owed, and he prevailed. [230]

There was nothing subtle about John Pierce's style. Aggressive about asserting his rights under the law, he also enjoyed the conspicuous display of his success. Flush with the profits of his slave business, he had driven around Goochland in the late 1830s in a $100 barouche, one of only three free blacks to own a conveyance of any kind. Even among whites, such a vehicle was not common; just 135 of the county's 968 taxpayers paid personal property taxes on carriages, carry-alls and gigs in 1839. Not only was owning a vehicle conspicuous, but a barouche was hardly a purely utilitarian mode of transport. Four wheeled, it required two horses; configured with two, facing double seats, it had a box for a driver; it also featured a collapsible top. It was made for display. [231]

Pierce—ambitious, aggressive and high profile—was a likely lightening rod for the racial, economic and ideological fears of his white neighbors. As Berlin has observed: "Ironically, the more the free Negro became like them, the more enraged whites became. It was easy for a people who professed to love freedom to despise a slave; whites needed reasons to hate blacks who were free," especially demonstrably successful ones. All things considered, resentment may well have figured both in John Pierce, Jr.'s trial and his interaction with whites in general. [232]

---

[230]GPPT 1838 [Pierce paid tax on barouche; other vehicle owners]

[231]Berlin, *op. cit.*, p. 89 [quote]

[232]United States Agricultural Census, Goochland 1850 [Mims' real estate]

CeCe Bullard

A WHITE FATHER AFFIRMS: THESE FREE BLACKS ARE MY CHILDREN

John Pierce, slave trader and uppity, nouveau riche free black, was almost inevitably a controversial figure, but what kind of man was David Mims? Even if he did not stab John Pierce, it seems clear that there was an altercation of some sort. What provoked it? Envy and racism would be the obvious answers, yet neither really seems to apply. David Mims appears to have had little cause for feelings of envy or resentment toward John Pierce. He was a member of an old and respected family, and men of like background rallied to his side as his securities for bail. He was a successful farmer who in 1850 owned real estate valued at $7000 and would eventually leave a sizeable estate. [233]

Was Mims, whose slave holdings reached a high of thirty-nine in 1840, a racist, convinced that free blacks were a threat to the status quo? How then to explain the free blacks who also lived on his farm? Over the years, the number of David Mims' slaves declined, and in 1860, when he was 70 years old, his household consisted of 10 slaves, several of them aged, a white housekeeper, her grandson, and 11 free blacks: Agness Pleasants, her three children, Harriet Gray and her five children. The census enumerations alone indicate that David Mims was not bedeviled by an irrational prejudice against free blacks, but the evidence about Mims' attitude

---

[233] USCG 1840 slaves owned by David Mims. There were also 7 free blacks on his property. USCG 1860 Mims household

toward free blacks is both more complex and compelling than that. David Mims was the father of several mulatto children. [234]

On March 1, 1850, Goochland's county clerk Narcissus W. Miller recorded David Mims' deed of manumission to "a woman slave named Matilda, sometimes called Matilda Mims…a bright mulatto woman about five feet six inches high and will be twenty-five years old on the 10th day of March instant." Matilda's freedom may have been a wedding present, for on March 5, she married Tarlton Tyler, a young man "of yellow complexion" and member of a long-established free black family. Tyler's grandfather George Tyler had been born free in Goochland around 1754 and had served both in the Revolution and afterwards in the Goochland militia. In October of the following year, a second deed of manumission from Mims was entered in the deed book, this one liberating "Judy, a mulatto woman, sometimes called Judy Mims, and her seven children, Tom about twenty-three years of age, James about twenty, David nineteen, Shadrack seventeen, Salmon fifteen, Jane thirteen, and Phoeby, a girl about ten years of age." On the fact of it, there is nothing unusual about a benevolent white owner emancipating what appear to have been favored mulatto female servants. [235]

The full significant of these deeds of manumission only becomes apparent in light of David Mims' will, written in 1853 and proven in 1865. Mims bequeathed

---

[234]GDB 35, p. 600 [Mims emancipates Matilda]; GMR, p. 334 Matilda Mims m. Tarlton Tyler. GFN # 1083 Tarlton Tyler registered in 1860 at age 33; GFN # 159 George Tyler registered at age 60 in 1814; Jackson, *Free Negro Soldiers*, p. 45 [George Tyler in Revolution]; Margaret Walker, *op. cit.* p. 14 [George Tyler in militia]; GDB 36, p. 323 [Mims emancipates Judy and children]

[235]GDB 1862-1871, p. 111 [Mims' will]

$1200 to Jane Mims, $1200 to F---yby [Phoeby?] Mims and "$1200 to my son James Mims who shall hold the same in trust for the benefit of my daughter and his sister Matilida...the remainder of money to the following male members of my family—Thomas, James, David, Shadrack and Salmon Mims." [236]

To this point, Mims' will is reasonably straightforward, if revealing, in terms of the earlier deeds of manumission. What follows is equally revealing, but rather odder: "Giddeon Mims who is now about nine years old is now entitled to his freedom as a white boy, but to avoid all dispute, I now set him free, and I also give to him for his natural life the following named slaves and the increase of their families, to wit: Harry, John, William, Martin, Needham, Winny, Dick, John Henry, Pleasant and Nelly [?]." Mims goes on to qualify this bequest, stating that Giddeon cannot sell these slaves, must give them "a portion of their labor" and should he "part with either of the said slaves or slave, those Negroes thus parted with shall be free, my object being that he should hold the said slaves and treat them humanely." [237]

When these slaves were freed is uncertain, but Martin, known as Martin Robinson after he was freed, cannot have enjoyed his liberty for long. In 1864, as Union Colonel Ulric Dahlgren marched through Goochland, laying waste to anything that stood in his path, he enlisted Martin's help in finding a safe place to ford the James River. Thwarted in his plan, not by treachery but by a river at flood stage,

---

[236]*Ibid.*

[237]Agee, *op. cit.*, pp. 99-101 [Martin Robinson]

Milly Pierce

Dahlgren angrily ripped a rein from his bridle and hung Martin from an oak tree. The locals left him hanging there, a warning to all would-be collaborators. [238]

David Mims' will, far from portraying him as a man irrationally prejudiced against free blacks, shows him to have been a concerned slave-owner, and beyond that, a concerned father. The will concludes with an acknowledgement of his mulatto off-spring: "…being perfectly satisfied that the legatees above named are my children, I have given them my name and consider it my sacred duty to provide for them…" David Mims' mulatto children were his only descendants and heirs. He never married, and his slave Sally may well have been his wife in fact, if not in law. His genuine affection for their children is reflected not only in the terms of his will but also in the choice of family names, including his own. Shadrack, Salmon, Gideon and David were all names which graced one or more of their distinguished white forebears and relatives. [239]

Nor was David Mims' sympathy for free blacks confined to his immediate family. In 1831, he guaranteed a loan to Lydia Pierce Cousins' brother-in-law John Copland, and in 1848, the year of the stabbing, he assisted Lydia's son Philip Cousins, john Pierce's nephew, in the purchase of some land. While the origin of David Mims' disagreement with John Pierce will never be known, it seems likely that their dispute was personal rather than racial. David Mims may have disliked John Pierce, but

---

[238] GDB 1862-1871, p. 111 [Mims' will]; Samuel Mims, *Leaves from the Mims Family Tree: A Genealogic History* (Minden, La., 1961) [Family names]

[239] GOB 32, p. 57 [Mims and Copland sued by Cousins]; GOB 36, p. 221 [Mims security for Philip Cousins]

nothing suggests that he disliked free blacks either individually or as a group. Ironically, John Pierce was, in many ways, what he might have hoped his children would become: successful, self-assured and literate free mulattos.[240]

THE THREAT OF FORCED DEPORTATION

If David Mims harbored no hostility toward free blacks, he was unusual, rather than typical, in this regard. The majority of Virginia slave-owners wished nothing more than to see the last of this unsettling presence in their midst. Various schemes for the voluntary emigration of free blacks to Liberia had been tried over the years, but with little success. By 1850, many of Virginia's legislators were ready to force the issue. All vestiges of earlier tolerance for free blacks had vanished.

While the patrician and absolutely secure Colonel William Bolling, who mingled easily not only with his own kind but with poor whites, slaves and free blacks, represented an older, more accepting generation, John Coles Rutherfoord who settled just down the river from "Bolling Hall" at "Rock Castle" epitomized the more anxious and angry white attitudes toward free blacks at mid-century. The only son of former Virginia Governor John Rutherfoord who had purchased "Rock Castle" in 1843, John Coles Rutherfoord was a lawyer and powerful Democratic member of the

---

[240] Agee, *op. cit.*, p. 174 [Rutherfoords and Rock Castle]

Virginia House of Delegates representing Goochland. He was also a vigorous advocate of compulsory free black deportation. [241]

During the 1853 session of the General Assembly, several proposals for "the removal from the Commonwealth of the free colored population" reached the floor of the House of Delegates. Rutherfoord rose to speak in response, delivering a lengthy speech which was so highly regarded (perhaps by its author) that it was privately printed for general distribution. In a voice recaptured by the Dixiecrats of this century, Rutherfoord spoke in support of the forced deportation of all able-bodied free blacks under 50. His oration moved uneasily from protestations of his own sense of fairness and sense of the greater good to vicious denunciations of free Negroes as depraved and disruptive.[242]

Arguing that the "evil" represented by free blacks far outweighed any evil attending their removal, Rutherfoord supported this view by stating that "as a class, they can be idle, ignorant, degraded and immoral, filling our courts with culprits and our penitentiary with convicts, consuming more than they produce…" He supported this assertion by citing the increase in crimes committed by free blacks: "During the first thirty years of this century, their crimes are estimated to have been as three to one to crimes among the whites; now they are as nine to one." Rutherfoord's remarks

---

[241] _____, Journal of the House of Delegates, 1853 (Richmond, 1853); John C. Rutherfoord, *Speech of John C. Rutherfoord of Goochland in the House of Delegates of Virginia, on the Removal from the Commonwealth of the Free Colored Population, Delivered February 18, 1853* (Ritchie and Dunnavant, Richmond, 1853).

[242] *Ibid.*, p. 4 [idle, ignorant]; pp. 6-7 [crime figures]; Russell, *Free Negro*, p. 165 [remarks of Gov. William B. Giles]

about crime among free blacks were essentially accurate, although their defenders argued that this was a result of their grinding poverty and lack of opportunity. A free black's chances of ending up in the penitentiary were also enhanced by the ever-changing and quite specific free black laws—a virtual trap for a generally uneducated and peripheral population. Once incarcerated, a free black faced a longer sentence than a white charged with a comparable crime. As one fair-minded Virginia Governor observed, "the laws, in some instances, have been administered against this class more in rigour than in justice." It was little wonder that free blacks over-flowed the penitentiary. [243]

One of Rutherfoord's more creative arguments for relieving the Commonwealth of this "idle and vicious class" was his contention that free blacks were "a class of unproductive consumers—consuming more than they produce…constituting, in fact, a charge and burden upon the labor of the slave." Twice, Rutherfoord hammered home the point that free blacks consumed more than they produced, but without explanation. Presumably, he was referring to the cost of housing the criminal element in the penitentiary and the aged or incompetent in the county poor houses. While crowding in the penitentiary was a legitimate concern—one compounded by the fact that white criminals did not wish to mix with black criminals—the issue of the poor houses was more political than real. Virginia law ensured that any able-bodied free black debtor or indigent was either bound out as a laborer by the overseer of the poor or sold into slavery. In 1850, Goochland's poor

---

[243]Rutherfoord, *op. cit.*, p. 8 [burden to slaves]; USCG 1850 Residents of Poor House

house had three black residents: George Scruggs, aged 100, a "pauper and idiotic," and two young children, Mary Scott, 8 and Tom Scott, 3. [244]

Rutherfoord's most serious charge against free blacks, however, was their threat "to the peace and happiness alike of the master and the slave," a peace and happiness dependent on the slave's docile acceptance of his lot in life. In daily contact with free Negroes and "connected with him by ties of blood and affinity," the slave would feel "dissatisfied that his equal socially should be his superior politically." Not only did free blacks, according to Rutherfoord, encourage the slave's discontent, they filled him with the "poison" of abolitionism. If white southerners were to continue to enjoy "the security of our firesides, as well as the value of our property," free blacks must be banished from the state. [245]

FROM DEGRADATION IN AMERICA TO A DEMOCRATIC PARADISE IN AFRICA

Perhaps the most remarkable rhetoric and logical contortion performed by Rutherfoord was his attempt to suggest that free Negroes, living lives of incredible indolence and squalor in Virginia, would be miraculously transformed into energetic and resourceful citizens of the republic Liberia and, indeed, the hope of all Africans. In justification of "compulsory hiring" of free Negroes so that their wages, and not the

---

[244] *Ibid.*, p. 5 [threat to peace and happiness etc]

[245] *Ibid.*, pp. 13-14 [horrors of free Negro life]

taxpayers' money, would finance their deportation, he explained that such forced labor would pose no hardship, indeed, it would be a positive good:

> In the country, where the bulk of these people live, their expenses are small. They have generally no rent to pay for their cabins. They own truck-patches and hen-houses, and the fields, hog-pens and the barns of neighboring proprietors will continue to support them with the means of subsistence and the means of trading for the supply of their wants. Indeed, such is their general idleness, that it by no means follows that when you withdraw the able-bodied laborers…you thereby lessen very greatly the actual amount of productive labor amongst them. In many cases, it is as among savages: the women are made to do all the work for their lazy, whiskey-drinking lord. [246]

Against this picture of the deplorable state of the free Negro in Virginia, Rutherfoord painted an idyllic vision of their future life in Liberia. He imagined that:

> …we will confer a great blessing upon this unhappy class of persons by sending them to Liberia. They will be transferred to a country, where, no longer a degraded class, they will enjoy both social and political equality; where, on a soil teeming with fertility, in a climate more favorable than our own to their health and vigor, citizens of a

---

[246] *Ibid.*, p. 9 [life in Liberia]; *ibid.*, p. 20 [agents of providence]

republican government, the strongest stimulants will exist to elevate their character and arouse their energies.

At the conclusion of his oration, Rutherfoord outdid himself, as he envisioned the destiny of America's free blacks in Africa where "they may be made the agents, under Providence, of a vast and noble work of human good—the suppression of the slave trade, which has so long desolated Africa, and the final civilization and enlightenment of her unhappy and benighted millions." [247]

LIBERIA, "A PATHETIC HOPE"

Rutherfoord may not have fully realized and certainly could not have acknowledged the full import of this miraculous transformation, but within his remarks rested the tacit admission that treated as equals and given unlimited opportunities, free blacks could become productive citizens of the republic, whether it be in America or Liberia. Yet, as long as Rutherfoord and his fellow white southerners tried, ever more desperately, to rationalize the involuntary servitude of millions of African Americans, such an admission was impossible. As Berlin has noted: "The tenacious support practical men gave an impossible plan [colonization] suggests the pathetic hope of whites to be rid of blacks, especially free ones." [248]

---

[247] Berlin, *op. cit.*, p. 104 [pathetic hope]

[248] _____, Documents of the Virginia General Assembly 1854 (William F. Ritichie, 1853-40), Document 1, p. 15 [Governor's remarks]

Liberia as a solution to the free black problem was, indeed, a vain hope. In his 1854 address to the General Assembly, Virginia's Governor Joseph Johnson reviewed the results of the 1853 law for the removal of free blacks to Liberia. He noted that although 240 Negroes had been deported in the first six months under the new law at a cost of more than $10,000, the reality remained that Virginia's free black population was estimated to be $55,000 and growing. Furthermore, since 1820, the total number of emigrants from Virginia to Liberia totaled only 2800. Considering the magnitude of the problem, he concluded that "This act [of 1853], designed to rid us of this evil, will fail of its purpose, unless more urgent inducements be used to cause this class of persons to consent to their removal." This sentiment became an increasingly angry and despairing refrain in the various Governors' messages in the years leading up to the Civil War.[249]

FEAR OF THE VERY FEW

Despite his oratory in support of views such as the Governor's, Rutherfoord ended his lengthy speech with a personal disclaimer of sorts, stating that his "secret sympathies and inclinations have strongly opposed the conclusions to which my reason and observations have unwillingly led me." He admitted that "there are a few [free blacks], but they are very few, who have the qualities to make good citizens, if our laws or prejudices would allow it." Ultimately, however, he had submitted to the

---

[249]Rutherfoord, *op. cit.*, p. 20 [secret sympathies]

Milly Pierce

dictates of reason and to the will of his "constituents [who] feel so deep an interest in this subject, that, though a quiet and home-staying people, they have assembled in public meeting at their court-house, to express their sentiments." [250]

Could Rutherfoord actually have had Milly and her family in mind when he alluded to the "very few?" He may well have made the acquaintance of the Pierce clan in the course of his legal work at the Courthouse. Certainly the Pierces and Cousins were among those free blacks with whom it would have been hard to find fault, yet ironically, it was just such self-sufficient and upwardly mobile blacks, manifestly suited to freedom, that whites found most frightening. The criminals and the poor were easily dismissed as evidence of the oxymoron "free Negro"; their failures merely buttressed the arguments of pro-slavery and anti-free black apologists. Those who flourished in freedom, however, appeared a threat not only to the rationale of slavery, but also to the three-tier legal structure that insured white superiority. Although "the very few" were far too few to pose any real threat of rebellion, they did threaten the peace of mind of many whites.

As one of the very few, Milly had built her life on the goodwill and good faith of men such as Rutherfoord. Mercifully, she was not around to hear Rutherfoord's cruel verdict on the history and future of her class. Her youngest daughters, Mary and Jane, however, still lived in the house on the Courthouse square. What did they make of their fellow Goochlanders' public demonstration of support for

---

[250] Mary and Jane Pierce apparently lived in the Courthouse house until 1855, the last year it is listed as the property of John Pierce deceased, when they moved to Cedar Point [GDB 38, p. 715 Cedar Point purchase]

ridding their county of free blacks? Did they cower behind closed shutters, terrified? Or did outrage overtake their fear? Conceivably, they experienced neither emotion. Numbering themselves among the free black elite and closely connected to the white establishment, they may actually have been sympathetic to what they might have perceived as condemnation of only the basest of their class. [251]

BETRAYAL: THE WHITE SIDE IS THE RIGHT SIDE

John Coles Rutherfoord's depiction of Virginia's free blacks as active abolitionists and insurrectionists was actually far from accurate. Most free blacks were realists, not revolutionaries. In general a cautious and conservative class, free blacks were more concerned with preserving those few prerogatives they possessed than with demanding greater freedoms for themselves or liberation for those still enslaved. Rather than agitating for universal emancipation or conspiring in slave revolts, free blacks were much more inclined to maintain the status quo—even if that involved betraying their own. A few years after Rutherfoord's speech to the General Assembly, a Goochland free black woman, Caroline Henley, eschewed the loyalties of race for the loyalties of preference. Just as Delegate George Mason had predicted in the 1806 legislative debate on ending emancipation, Caroline Henley, a free black, found it in her best interest to give information of a slave insurrection. Caroline secured not only

---

[251]Berlin, *op. cit.*, pp. 270-271 and Genovese, *op. cit.*, 273-275 [Discussion of free blacks and slaves]

the favor of the white community but also a tract of land when she exposed a plot by several slaves to poison their owner. [252]

Caroline Henley, her husband, James, a boatman, and their son Albert, lived east of Goochland just up the River Road from Powell's Tavern, home of Samuel S. DuVal, a wealthy farmer and slave-owner. In early 1859, some of DuVal's slaves decided to poison their master. Unable to purchase the poison themselves, they threatened to kill Caroline Henley if she did not procure it for them. This she did, but immediately informed DuVal of the plot against his life. Upon learning of the conspiracy, DuVal severely whipped and then sold the rebellious slaves, ridding himself of the trouble-makers without losing his investment in them. [253]

Both Caroline Henley and Samuel DuVal attended nearby Dover Baptist Church—as did several of DuVal's slaves. In the same year in which she saved DuVal's life, Caroline Henley was received as a candidate for baptism by the Dover congregation. The slave conspirators—Mahala, Cornelius, Francis, Pone and Albert—were excommunicated. Even when the church dropped "the colored portion" of its membership following the Civil War, Caroline Henley, arriving in her ox cart, continued to attend until her death in the early 1900s. By betraying the slave conspiracy against DuVal, Caroline Henley had obtained the white community's seal

---

[252] USCG 1860 [Henley household]; Helene B. Agee, "Dover Baptist Church, Manakin, Virginia," *Goochland County Historical Society Magazine*, vol. 21, 1989, pp. 37-38, 39 [the plot].

[253] Agee, *Dover*, pp. 37-38, 39 [Consequences of DuVal plot]; Mrs. Bernard Henley who died at 100 in 1996 told the author she remembered seeing Caroline arrive at Dover.

of approval; she also acquired a free black's badge of success when DuVal rewarded her with a parcel of land. Like Milly Pierce, Caroline Henley, in her own way, blurred the harsh outlines Rutherfoord had drawn in depicting the character of free blacks. [254]

FREEDOM PAPERS OR JAIL

Undeterred by either legislative or personal assaults, Milly's son John continued to build his financial empire. The only impact the attitudes expressed by Rutherfoord may have had on John Pierce was, that after living in Richmond for several years, he finally registered with the court in 1853. Although any black "going at large" without his or her freedom papers was, by law, presumed to be a slave, registration compliance and enforcement were both historically lax. In the past, free Negroes had most commonly registered only when they needed to travel to another country or city, a risky business without one's "freedom papers," when they sought employment or when they wished to establish the status of their children. Wary of white officialdom, many free blacks never registered.

The mood reflected in Rutherfoord's remarks, however, suggests just how intense the scrutiny of free blacks had become. Indeed, the Richmond court records show an increasingly large number of free blacks jailed for failing to carry copies of their registers. One William Cousins was picked up for this offense and remained in jail for three months until the next quarterly session of the Hustings Court. When his

---

[254]Hustings Court Minutes Richmond (RCM), 23, p. 12 [William Cousins to work off jail debt]; *ibid.*, p. 129 [William again in jail]

Milly Pierce

case was finally heard, the court, believing that he was free, ordered him hired out "for so long a time as may be necessary to pay his jail fee" which was $1.30. He was not to be hired out, however, for less than ten cents an hour. A little over two months later, William was caught again; this time he was ordered to work off $3.10 in jail fees. William was caught in a bizarre legal trap—without papers, how could he travel to obtain papers? [255]

With good reason, John Pierce, who periodically eluded both the tax collector and the census taker, now found it in his best interest to declare his presence in Richmond. On Friday, July 15, 1853, John Pierce and family presented themselves in Richmond's Hustings Court and registered. A John Karr, presumably white, identified Eliza Pierce as the free born daughter of WinnyLigon of Chesterfield County. John Pierce presented his freedom papers from Goochland which showed that he had been emancipated by the will of Tucker Woodson. [256]

John Pierce, Jr. and Eliza Ligon, "a free girl," had married in Chesterfield County in 1820, and were now the parents of six children. Also registered as free on

---

[255] John managed to elude the census taker entirely in 1840. He appears in the Richmond Personal Property records only sporadically. RCM 26, p. 102 [John and Eliza register]

[256] Chesterfield County Marriage Register, p. 163 [John Pierce m. Eliza Liggon (sic)]; RCM 26, p. 102 [Pierce children]; GPPT from 1853 on, John Pierce (3) and Madison Pierce are listed together right after John Pierce, Jr. USCG 1860 John Pierce, a 28 year old mulatto was living with James Madison Pierce, a 44 year old mulatto, and William Henry Pierce, a 42 year old mulatto is listed in the household of John Thompson, Jr., hotel keeper. The most logical explanation of Madison and William's parentage is that they were John Pierce, Jr.'s children. They were not Milly's, and based on the ages and marriages of Milly's other children, they could not have belonged to any of them.

175

that July day in 1853 were Mary Jane Pierce, 28, Sarah Pierce, 26, Eliza Pierce, 24, Isaac Pierce, 18 and William B. Pierce, 12, who were identified as the free born children of John and Eliza. In addition to the five children who registered with them, John and Eliza were the parents of another John Pierce who was about twenty-five years old in 1853 and lived with James Madison Pierce on one of John Pierce, Jr.'s Goochland farms. It is probable, even likely, that James Madison Pierce, called Madison, born around 1812, and William Henry Pierce, born around 1818 and a painter in John Thompson, Jr.'s household, were John's sons from earlier liaisons. It would have been in character for him to have given his sons presidential names.[257]

Whatever their attraction to each other, John and Eliza Pierce had, at least, one significant thing in common—independent, land-owning mothers. Milly Pierce had staked out her 23 acres in 1803, and in 1810, Eliza's mother, WinnyLigon, had purchased a lot in Manakinton, a Chesterfield County village. The benchmark of success, especially free black success, had been set. Property ownership mattered, a great deal, not that this exactly set the Pierces apart from most Americans. In fact, it is telling about American values that virtually the only right of free blacks that was never seriously threatened was the right to own property.[258]

---

[257] Chesterfield County Deed Book 21, p. 273 [WinnyLigon buys lot in Manakintown]

[258] United States Agricultural Census Goochland 1850 [Pierce versus Sampson]; GPPT 1850-60 [John Pierce's slaves] and RPPT 1850-60. John never kept more than three slaves in Richmond. Presumably, they were personal and house servants.

Milly Pierce

A FREE BLACK REAL ESTATE SPECULATOR

Regardless of the deteriorating status of his class, John Pierce continued to prosper. His Goochland farms, managed by his sons Madison and John, were productive, although not to the degree they might have been. Owning the land appears to have mattered greatly to John Pierce in light of the debt he assumed to acquire it. Investing in its improvement and productivity—which might have insured his long-term economic survival—seems to have mattered less. In 1850, John Pierce and Jacob Sampson, his only peer as a property-owning free black in Goochland, both had approximately 150 acres under cultivation. The difference in what they produced on this acreage is revealing. Of those crops which were potential cash producers, Pierce raised 140 bushels of wheat compared to Sampson's 200; 250 bushels of Indian corn compared to Sampson's 750 bushels; 30 bushels of oats compared to Sampson's 500 bushels; no hay in contrast to Sampson's 5 tons, and 2 bushels of Irish potatoes in contrast to Sampson's 90 bushels. Presumably, Pierce relied largely on his Richmond real estate deals and continued slave trading to produce cash, as his human holdings ranged from one to fourteen, with fluctuations in between, during the 1850s. [259]

Personally, John Pierce focused on Richmond real estate as his primary business interest during the decade of the fifties. In addition to the Southgate Garden

---

[259] RDB 56, p. 343 [Mayo executors to Pierce]; RDB 59, p. 233 [Two lots on Concord Street]; RDB 60, p. 521 [Sells one of Concord St. lots to John Dwyer]; RDB 59, p. 266 [Goddin to Pierce 100 sq. feet at Marshall and 15th for $900]; RDB 59, p. 267 [Green to Pierce 65 x 100 ft. at Marshall and 15th for $1200. Land was east of 15th and north of Marshall]; Brown and Kimbell, *op. cit.*, p. 301 [Shockoe Valley]

property purchased in 1840 and sold for a nice profit in 1850, Pierce had purchased a lot fronting on Ninth Street in "French Garden" for $35.50 from the estate of Abigail Mayo in 1849. A year later the tax collector valued the lot at $132. In 1850, he added two lots on Concord Street valued at $88.75 from the estate of Jacob Johnson; one of which he promptly sold for $50. His major investment of that year, however, were several lots with houses at the intersection of Marshall and 15th Streets in Shockoe Valley, purchased in two transactions totaling $2100. Just north of the busy docks and commercial warehouses on the James River, Pierce's new property was in an area popular among black residents of the city. Collecting rents was considerably less trouble and more in accord with his image than wresting maximum productivity from the land.[260]

In 1851, John Pierce added another significant Richmond tract to his portfolio, one that resonates with a certain irony. In partnership with William Wilson Morris, a free black cooper, John acquired lot 106 and part of an adjoining lot on the south side of Broad Street at 21st Street for $1278. The seller? Thomas Rutherfoord, uncle of John Coles Rutherfoord, no less. Pierce and Morris held the land for a little over two years and then sold it to Alexander H. Rutherfoord, Thomas's son, for $2000. A member of what John C. Rutherfoord had called "a degraded, idle and vicious class" had turned a tidy profit off of another Rutherfoord. [261]

---

[260]RDB 66, 305 [Rutherfoord to Pierce, Pierce to Rutherfoord recorded at same time]

[261]GDB 34, p. 481 [Harris security for Pope purchase]; GDB 35, p. 67 [Harris and Morris securities for Shelton purchase]

Milly Pierce

THE IMPORTANCE OF WHITE CONNECTIONS

Many whites shared John Coles Rutherfoord's deep suspicion of free blacks, and, based on the Mims case, John Pierce's character may have been as great an irritation to some as his color. Yet, not all whites were averse to dealing with him, especially if those dealings were profitable. When John made his large real estate investments in Goochland in the late 1840s, he had no difficulty in finding prominent white men to serve as guarantors for the significant debts he assumed. Among Pierce's securities for payment on the Pope property was Dr. George W. Harris who was Milly Pierce's neighbor at "Brightly," formerly the Woodson estate. Dr. Harris also served as a security for the $4000 John owed on the 1847 purchase of the Cedar Point tract from Shelton's trustee. The second security for the Shelton property was another of Milly's neighbors, Dr. John Morris, whose estate "Aspenwall" not only adjoined Milly's land but John's newly purchased property as well. John Pierce, Jr., may well have traded on his mother's good name, and, like his mother and sister Lydia, he made the most of his white connections. [262]

Alliances with whites were essential. Within the free black community a John Pierce had few, if any, peers who could provide the financial backing or network of connections he required for his various enterprises. Even for those less ambitious than John, white patrons or protectors were a free black's surest guarantee of peace as well as prosperity. Free blacks who sought to rise in life, however, had little choice except

---

[262]Berlin, *op. cit.*, pp. 339-340 [Alliances with whites]

to cultivate whites who alone could confer access to advancement and a degree of respectability to their endeavors. As a corollary of this white empowerment, many free blacks, and apparently John Pierce was one, found it expedient to distance themselves from their enslaved brethren and even their own less successful peers. [263]

Well-established and highly regarded Dr. Morris and Dr. Harris were the most useful connections for John Pierce, but in John Thompson, Jr., a young white entrepreneur, John seems to have found not only a business partner but a kindred spirit. Like John Pierce, John Thompson was a dealmaker intent on making money; like John Pierce, John Thompson relished a conspicuous position in the community; like John Pierce, John Thompson bought and sold slaves, and like John Pierce, he was willing enough to profit from others' misfortunes. More alike than not, the two men still had one major difference between them, one which in their world was insurmountable: one was black, the other white.

John Thompson, Jr., who first appears in the Goochland records in 1835 when he obtained a merchant's license, would become a prominent landowner in Goochland and an active investor in a variety of enterprises. Initially, however, Thompson focused primarily on making money by serving as the security, essentially the mortgage holder, on any number of deeds of trust. Most often Thompson earned a tidy six percent interest on the bonds he held, but, when pressed, he proved a creative investor. When Lucien Watkins was unable to come up with cash, Thompson settled

---

[263]GPPT 1838 [Thompson merchants license]; GDBs 32-37 are littered with deeds of trust to John Thompson, Jr. GDB 34, p. 461 [Thompson acquires lease of ½ of Ben Dover]; GDB 37, p. 415 [Slaves as collateral]

Milly Pierce

for a one year lease on half of Watkins' "Ben Lomond" estate to satisfy the debt. On another occasion, he accepted slaves as collateral. [264]

Among those indebted to John Thompson, both directly and by various security bonds, was John S. Fleming who owned the valuable and prestigious 379 acre Courthouse tract. As a result of Fleming's financial difficulties, John Thompson acquired the land around the Courthouse for $9878 in 1842. Not only did Thompson obtain valuable property and an expensive house, he acquired both the status and access that would secure his position in the county, a position signified by various official appointments. He also became Milly Pierce's neighbor. [265]

By the time he purchased the Courthouse property, Thompson had accumulated enough wealth to begin trading in horses and slaves, first in partnership with John T. A. Martin, and then on his own. A lawsuit of 1843 indicates that at some point during this period, Thompson also formed a business association with John Pierce, the nature of which is unknown, although their mutual interest in slave trading comes to mind. Thompson and Pierce were named as co-defendants in a suit by David

---

[264] GDB 32, p. 1 [John Thompson security for Fleming]; GDB Book 33, p. 276 [John Thompson, Jr. deed of trust on Courthouse tract. Cannot find actual deed. This deed of trust June 19, 1843. The land is first listed in Thompson's name in the land tax in 1842.]

[265] GPPT, 1841 John Thompson, Jr. and John T.A. Martin paid tax on 4 slaves over 16. In 1842, Thompson only paid tax on 5 mature slaves and 6 horses and mules. Over the next 8 years the number of slaves varies from 0 to 19, the number of horses or mules from 2 to 18, both with fluctuations in between. Circuit Superior Court of Law and Chancery Order Book 1837-1847, p. 378 [David R. Shelton sues Pierce and Thompson for debt]

R. Shelton, executor of Matthew Shelton, for a debt of $100. The court found for the plaintiff, and Thompson paid Shelton the $100 with 6% interest. [266]

A REVERSAL OF FORTUNES

John Thompson and John Pierce were next involved in a business deal in 1849 when John Pierce sold 155 acres of the 451 acre Cedar Point tract to Thompson. Perhaps John Pierce had too eagerly succumbed to the appeal of owning a highly desirable riverfront land normally held by the county gentry, perhaps he had enjoyed the very public assertion of his success, perhaps he had been carried away by the excitement of the auction, but John Pierce both overpaid and assumed a crushing debt when he purchased the Sheltons' land. The property was immediately put under a deed of trust for the full $4000 plus interest. The purchase price amounted to $8.32 per acre; yet, a year later, when Pierce sold the parcel to Thompson, he received only $4.84 per acre. He did a little better when he sold 158 acres to Narcissus Miller for $6.02 per acre. Not all acreage is comparable, and it appears Pierce made his friend Thompson an exceptionally good deal, but possibly, at this point, Pierce was willing to take a loss for cash in hand. The tax assessor's 1851 valuation of Pierce's remaining 167 ½ acres at $6.59 per acre seems to confirm Pierce's ill-advised over payment. [267]

---

[266] GDB 35, pp. 426-427 [Pierce to Thompson]; GFB 35, p. 67 [Pierce buys Shelton land]; GDB, pp. 422-423 [Pierce to Miller]; 1851GLT 1851 [value of Pierce property]

[267] GDB 38, p. 503 [new deed of trust on Shelton property]; GDB 38, p. 327 [new deed of trust on Pope property]

Milly Pierce

Indeed, as the 1850s progressed, John Pierce, now in his sixties, teetered on the financial pinnacle he had attained, ever more desperately juggling debts and assets. While his mother and sister Lydia had paid cash for their land, most of John's property purchases were leveraged. Desperately, John renegotiated deeds of trust on his Goochland holdings. In 1858, he still owed more than $1200 plus 6% on the Cedar Point tract and more than $800 plus 6% on the Pope property. [268]

John was forced to sell several lots in Richmond, and in 1856, placed a new deed of trust on his own Richmond residence to cover a $560 debt to J. W. Shields. Among the lots in Richmond which John let go in the fifties was one near 17th or Valley Street on the east side of the Central Virginia Railroad which he sold to the railroad for $114. This sale not only marked the decline of John's fortunes, it also signaled the beginning of the end for the James River and Kanawha Canal on which John Pierce had made his grubstake, for the railroad spelled the end of the canal's commercial viability. Did John hear the death knell of the canal and his youth in the tolling of the train bell or just the end of the line for his own ambitions? [269]

By 1856, the man who had stretched himself for so many years always grasping for more, was collapsing under the weight of his financial obligations. In

---

[268] RDB 70A, p. 77 [Deed of trust on his residence]; RDB 60, p. 521; RDB 63, p. 610; RDB 64, p. 331; RDB 66, p. 320; RDB 69A, p. 264; and RDB 71A, p. 238; [Pierce sales of Richmond property]; RDB 64, p. 331 [Sale to Central Virginia Railroad]

[269] Details of these suits are covered in John Pierce versus James Madison Pierce, this ms.: GDB 38, p. 715 [Pierce to Jane and Mary Pierce]; GDB 38, p. 620 [Pierce to Haden]; GDB Book, 39, pp. 316-317 [Pierces and Haden satisfy lien]; GDB 38, p. 691 [Deed of release on Pope property]; GDB 38, p. 707 [Pierce to Barret]; GLT 1860 [value of Barret land]

addition to the money still owed on his real estate investments, he was further burdened by liabilities of more than $1000 as the result of numerous lawsuits for debts and damages. Pressured by his growing indebtedness, John Pierce sold 83 acres of the Cedar Point tract for $747 to his sisters Mary and Jane Pierce in 1856. Two years later he sold the remaining 89 acres to James M. Haden for $890. The property was still encumbered by a lien, and Pierce received nothing from either sale. Within a year, he disposed of the last of his Goochland property. On March 21, 1859, he obtained a deed of release on the Pope property, having finally managed to pay off the debt originated 1846. On March 24, he sold the property for $3100 to William N. Barret whose estate "Mount Bernard" adjoined the property. A year later, it was assessed for $3890. [270]

MAKING IT THE HARD WAY: A FREE BLACK OF SUBSTANCE

While John Pierce watched the land he had so avidly acquired slip from his grasp, Jacob Sampson, the only Goochland free black whose wealth eventually eclipsed John Pierce's, remained securely in possession of real estate worth $4000 and personal property valued at more than $2000. A contemporary of John Pierce's and, like him, a conspicuously successful free black, Jacob Sampson was in every other respect a very different kind of man. A hard-working "light yellow" farmer who relied on his sons as well as slaves for help, Sampson managed a very productive, diversified

---

[270] USCG 1860 [Jacob Sampson worth]; GFN 1820 Jacob Sampson registered as #242 at age 25 and a second time as #2002 at age 69 in 1862; United States Agricultural Census, Goochland, 1860 [Sampson farm production].

farming operation. In 1860, his 520 acre farm produced 400 bushels of wheat, 1500 bushels of corn, 1000 bushels of oats, 2000 pounds of tobacco, 80 pounds of wool, 2 bushels of peas and beans, 15 bushels of sweet potatoes, 200 pounds of butter, 5 tons of hay, 2 pounds of beeswax and 16 pounds of honey. His livestock consisted of seven horses, three mules, four milk cows, two working oxen, four cattle, forty sheep and twenty-five hogs valued at $960. [271]

Born a slave in a very modest white household, Sampson had come a long way from his humble origins. Sampson had been owned by Thomas Taurman, a hard-working yeoman farmer whose assets at his death consisted of some cash from the sale of his 83 acres, a bit of livestock, household furnishings, and two slaves, Aggy and her son Jacob. Indeed, Aggy, valued at $55, and Jacob, valued at $110, accounted for more than half of Taurman's personal property. Taurman's will, proven in 1810, is a thoughtful, even touching, document in which he made very specific bequests to each of his six children, insuring that most received a horse, which he seemed to think indispensable, a cow, and assorted household goods. Especially concerned for the well-being of his two daughters, Salley and Frankey, he instructed his executors to purchase a home for them with the cash in his estate. Finally, he "enjoyed the particular attention of my executrix [Salley] and executor [Thomas, Jr.] to my last request: "that his two slaves, Aggy and her son Jacob, should remain with Salley and

---

[271]GDB 20, p. 621 [Thomas Taurman's will]; GDB 21, p. 17 [Taurman's inventory]; GLT 1810 [Taurman owned 83 acres]

Frankey until Jacob reached the age of 21 at which time they should both be emancipated. [272]

In 1820 at the age of twenty-five, Jacob Sampson registered as a free man. With the support of William Pope, Commonwealth's attorney, and John S. Fleming, he was "given leave to remain in the County as a free man." By 1835, he and his wife Frankey were settled on some 38 acres of land on Hockett's Road, 16 miles northeast of Goochland Courthouse, making him one of only 638 free black farm owners in Virginia. He also owned 2 slaves over the age of 16, four horses or mules and a gig valued at $20. One of his slaves was a male over 55 years of age who may well have been his father. [273]

By 1845, Sampson had increased his land holdings to 285 acres, having purchased 100 acres from his emancipator's son Thomas Taurman, Jr., 60 acres from William Anderson, 70 acres from William P. Nuckols and 17 ¼ acres from R. H. Ware. Although he continued to own two or three slaves, Sampson now had home-grown help on his farm, his sons. Robert and Moses were over 21, a third son, Jacob, was over 16, and there were three more sons and three daughters. As his property increased, however, Sampson found himself increasingly dependent on slave labor.

---

[272] GFN 1820 #242 Sampson; GOB 30, p. 81 [permission to stay in Goochland]; GLT 1835 Sampson actually acquired these two tracts in 1830; Jackson, *The Free Negro Farmer*, p. 241 [Number of free black farm owners]; GPPT 1835 [Sampson's slaves, horses and gig]

[273] GLT 1841 Sampson adds land from Taurman and Anderson; GLT 1843 adds land from Nuckols and Ware; USCG 1850 ages of Sampson children; Slave Schedule Goochland 1860 Sampson slaves; USCG 1860 Sampson household

With each new land acquisition, he acquired a few more slaves. By 1860, he owned over 500 acres of land and eleven slaves. He also employed two free blacks, William Cosby and George Harris, who lived on his farm, and he may well have relied on additional help from the sons who remained at home: Moses, 40, Henry, 24, Andrew, 23, a blacksmith, 23, and James, 19, a smiter,~~19.~~[274]

CHARACTER COUNTS: A FREE BLACK "HOUSE OF ENTERTAINMENT"

The growth of Jacob Sampson's farm operations attests to his hard work and thrift. His acquisition of a license to operate a "house of private entertainment" is a testament to his character. Whites were generally opposed to selling spirits to any black person, free or slave, believing it would only hasten the degeneracy of free blacks and inflame slaves to acts of rebellion. Furthermore, the requirements for an ordinary license stipulated that one must be "a person of good character, not addicted to drunkenness or gaming" and capable of keeping "an orderly and useful house of entertainment." That the Goochland Court granted Sampson this license in 1830 suggests that he was truly a man of exceptional character. [275]

Sampson operated his tavern for almost fifteen years, entertaining many white guests and serving as a popular lay-over on the Three Chopt Road for those

---

[274]GPPT 1830 [Sampson first pays license fee]; GOB 1836-1844, p. 44 [qualifications for ordinary owner]

[275]GOB, 1836-1844, p. 5 [Sampson paid fee and granted license]; GOB 1836-1844, p. 8 [Fleming motion to revoke; court splits]; GOB 1836-1844, p. 13 [license revoked]

taking livestock and produce to market in Richmond. In May of 1844, Sampson, as he did annually, appeared in court with a receipt indicating he had paid the clerk $5 for his ordinary license, and the justices ordered it renewed. Later in the same session, however, John S. Fleming made a motion that Jacob Sampson's license be revoked. Why Fleming, who had supported Sampson in his petition to remain in Goochland as a free man, opposed the renewal of Sampson's license is not spelled out. The sitting justices—James B. Ferguson, Benjamin Anderson, Joseph Watkins and Charles Guerrant—were divided on the question, and the motion failed. Two months later, however, at a second hearing on "the propriety of allowing Jacob Sampson, a free man of colour to keep a house of private entertainment," Sampson's license was "revoked and annulled." [276]

Sampson was nothing if not determined, and he pursued the matter to the Virginia Legislature. In December of 1844, Delegate Walter D. Leake of Goochland presented a petition from Sampson to the legislature "praying passage of an act to allow him to keep a house of private entertainment in Goochland." Sampson pointed out that his license had been arbitrarily revoked without "any proof that [he] operated a disorderly house or that he was dishonest or in any way unworthy…" The petition was supported by numerous white citizens from the western counties of Augusta and Rockbridge, all of whom valued the respite of Sampson's hospitality when they made

---

[276] _____, Journal of the General Assembly 1844/1845, p. 36 [petition rejected]; GPPT 1848-1853 [Sampson renews license]; in 1851, 1853 and later years, the General Assembly stiffened the laws regarding slaves, free blacks and alcohol. _____, Acts of the General Assembly, 1851, pp. 51-52 [restrictions on buying a drink]

the long trek east to Richmond. Thirty-one of Sampson's white neighbors described his as "fair, punctual and orderly," and Thomas Taurman, his emancipator's son and now his neighbor, submitted a letter in which he stated that he had known Sampson from birth and that "during his whole life he has supported a fair and unexceptionable character." The committee for Courts of Justice, however, rejected Sampson's petition. Even so, in 1848, the Goochland Court unanimously granted Sampson a new license which was renewed annually until 1853 by which time the legislature had made it virtually impossible for a free black to keep a tavern and "retail ardent spirits." By law, a free black could no longer simply buy a drink without written certification of his good character from three or more justices of the peace. Should he be so bold as to defy the law, the fine was $200. [277]

Loss of his tavern license may have injured Sampson's pride and offended his sense of fairness, but it seems to have had little impact on his long-term well-being. Sampson died a wealthy man in 1870 at about age 84. His wife, Frankey, now 70, was at his side, as were their son Moses, his wife Coraline, their black house servant Rose Hill, and an eight-year-old mulatto child, Isadoria Freeman. Prior to his death, Sampson had transferred his considerable land holdings to his sons Moses and Lewis who now jointly owned 698 acres on which stood three houses, the total valued at $5428. In addition, Moses was sole owner of another nearby tract of 215 acres that, with a house valued at $400, was assessed for $1695.35. Over the course of sixty

---

[277] USCG 1870 [Sampson household]; Jacob's age is given as 84 although, based on his registrations, he may have been about 75. GLT 1870 [transfer of land from Jacob to Moses and Lewis; also, Moses' land holdings]

years, Jacob Sampson had gradually built a solid financial foundation, investing himself in his land and family and enjoying the fruits of his labors to the very end. John Pierce, in contrast, was a flash in the pan, who, within the span of slightly more than ten years had made conspicuously large land acquisitions and lost them all. [278]

UNFINISHED BUSINESS: A FAMILY DISPUTE

John Pierce, although no longer a Goochland landowner, had one last piece of business in the county to settle. In 1860 he filed a suit against James Madison Pierce who was most probably his son. In a written petition, Pierce requested the court to demand an accounting from Madison for all transactions relating to a partnership between the two and to issue an injunction against Madison's "collecting or receiving any partnership debts or other monies." [279]

John Pierce asserted that in January of 1853 he had agreed with Madison Pierce, a bricklayer and plasterer by trade, "to become a partner with him in said trade and business, and, in making bricks for sale and for carrying on the bricklaying business." The brick making business was located on the Cedar Point property, "a tract of land in Goochland County on the James River with suitable clay for making bricks of superior quality," and the partnership also included cultivation of the remaining

---

[278] Goochland Chancery Cases, File 20. All of the information on Pierce versus Pierce is based on the original documents in this file.

[279] *Ibid.*

Milly Pierce

land. The partners were "to share equally in the profits and crops." John was to receive one fourth of all crops as rent for his farm.[280]

John Pierce contended that, although there had been no formal dissolution of the partnership, Madison had "to some extent withdrawn from the business by setting up a brickyard for himself in another place, but had continued to collect the partnership debts and to take and use the bricks belonging to the partnership, and at the same time studiously avoids giving out any money that he receives." John accused Madison of failing to account for more than $500 in monies received, and listed the names of a number of Goochland's prominent white citizens who, he alleged, had paid "large sums of money" to Madison.[281]

Problems with the partnership and the handling of money litter the court records. Beginning in 1857, numerous suits for debts and delivery bonds appear in the chancery order books citing John Pierce, James Madison Pierce and John Thompson, Jr. as defendants. Thompson's participation is never mentioned in either John or Madison's Pierce's statements to the court, although it would have been very much in character for him to have invested in the enterprise. By 1860, John Thompson, Jr. was

---

[280] *Ibid.*

[281] GOB 35, p. 287 [First suit against Pierce, Pierce and Thompson]. Other suits: GOB 35 p. 315, p. 351, p. 381, p. 434, p. 480 and GOB 1852-1862, p. 287, p. 434 and p. 480. United States Agricultural Census Goochland 1860 Thompson's land was valued at $12000 and his livestock at $2500. In 1852, Thompson made an agreement with the James River and Kanawha Canal Company to build a commercial warehouse for wheat and tobacco next to the canal on his land at Cedar Point 9GDB 37, p. 862). He also was a partner with Mark Aldridge and D.W.K. Bowles in the Gilmer Mining Company, a gold mining enterprise in Goochland (GDB 37, p. 900)

a very wealthy man, and his business interests in Goochland ranged from a commercial warehouse on the James River and Kanawha Canal to partnership in a local gold-mining venture, the Gilmer Mining Company. It would appear, however, that those with complaints against the Pierces were mistakenly under the impression that Thompson was a partner, for the complaints were typically re-filed with only the Pierces as defendants. Whether Thompson's involvement was simply assumed on the basis of other ventures with John Pierce or was somehow implied by the Pierces to give greater stature to their endeavor must remain a matter of speculation. In every instance, the plaintiffs prevailed in these suits against the Pierces for damages, debts and delivery bonds. Judgments in excess of $1000 with 6% interest were entered against either John or Madison or both. [282]

FREE BLACK EDUCATION, OR LACK THEREOF

Madison Pierce failed to reply to John's accusations until, apparently under some duress, he finally presented a statement in April 1861. Madison's reluctance to answer the charges leveled against him may be at least partially attributed to his inability to read or write and a self-professed lack of business skills. While John Pierce had written his own petition to the court, Madison's had been dictated and therefore required certification by John Thompson, Jr., as justice of the peace. [283]

---

[282] Chancery Court Cases, File 20. John's statement is written and signed in his own hand. Madison's is written as if narrated by a second party and is certified as his statement.

[283] Russell, *Free Negro*, pp. 137-141 [Education of free blacks]

Milly Pierce

Madison's illiteracy was more typical of his class than John's abilities as a writer. Although uncommon, it was not entirely unusual for free blacks of John's generation to have been taught to read and write. Originally, the terms of free black apprenticeship had required that masters teach their charges these basic skills, and before it became obvious to al that the slave question was insoluble, many whites had viewed the education of blacks as essential preparation for useful lives as free citizens. In turn, blacks, especially free blacks, shared their white neighbors' belief that education was the key to upward mobility and success in American society. [284]

Madison, who registered at 21 in 1833 as a freeborn mulatto, was a generation younger than John, and in that interval, white attitudes had altered radically. Whites had come to view literacy as a potentially dangerous weapon in the black arsenal, both a catalyst and a tool for insurrection. The education of blacks, both slave and free, had been discouraged for many years, and in 1830, opposition to the education of free blacks was formalized when the Virginia legislature made it illegal to teach a free black to read and write. Free blacks caught in the act of learning to read and write were punished with twenty lashes; any white person assisting them could be fined up to $100. As a consequence of the perceived danger posed by literate free blacks, Madison was, at best, semi-literate, and much of his difficulty in responding to John's suit was the result, he claimed, of "his entire want of skill in keeping accounts."

---

[284] GFN # 514 Madison, "light yellow"; _____ Acts of the General Assembly, 1830, p. 107 [education denied free blacks]

Even so, Madison did his best to provide the court with an accounting for the brick making business and farming operation. [285]

TRADESMAN VERSUS ENTREPRENEUR

Madison's defense focused primarily on the true nature of his partnership with John. In his account, the two had formed the partnership solely for the purpose of brickmaking and farming. When he found that the partnership "did not require his whole attention" he began "to work for himself in bricklaying and plastering, which was his trade, to which he had been regularly educated." He went on the point out that John Pierce had no such qualifications. In fact, training in these particular skilled trades was relatively rare among free blacks. According to Madison, there was no reason for forming a partnership "in which he was to do all the work and his partner share in the profits. It would have been absurd." [286]

At this point in his deposition, Madison clearly became upset. In a slightly indignant tone, he elaborated on the absurdity of the complaint:

> ...independent of all work done by him [Madison] for himself, the work he did at the brick yard in making and burning bricks and the general attention bestowed by him on the partnership business far exceeded that of the complainant, who never did any work in the

---

[285] Berlin, *op. cit.*, p. 237 [few free black bricklayers]; Chancery Cases, File 20 [Madison's statement]

[286] Chancery Cases, File 20

brick yard and whose chief services…were in selling the bricks made and crops raised, receiving the money for them and a few other occasional services…

A simpler, less sophisticated man than his accuser, he failed to appreciate that John's contributions of equipment and supplies were in any way comparable to his own hard work as an investment in the partnership. [287]

Madison, adamant that no partnership in the bricklaying business existed, admitted that there was some cause for confusion. He believed that some people had inferred a general partnership based on the existence of the limited one or that John had actually made such a claim without his knowledge and then made agreements for bricklaying in the partnership's name. He admitted that there were "papers which should not have been written, but which respondent either did not have his attention called to or did not deem a matter of any consequence…" Perhaps, Madison simply could not read these papers. Nevertheless, he conceded that papers often included both partnership charges for bricks and his own charges for bricklaying and that he had "never thought of being particular" in separating the two. [288]

"Surprised and offended and distrustful" when he realized that John claimed a share in his bricklaying business, Madison had consulted counsel and "declared the partnership at once dissolved." Furthermore, Madison claimed that John had failed to note the considerable amount of money that he, John, had personally collected for the

---

[287] *Ibid.*

[288] *Ibid.*

partnership. In fact, he believed "that on a fair settlement complainant will be found largely indebted to him." [289]

MONEY MATTERS MOST

Ever the businessman, John, unlike Madison, had kept extensive records of the partnership's expenses and income. Among the many receipts was one for John's purchase of start-up stock which included 70 barrels of corn at $200, a pair of mules for $230, a boat for $100, a brick press for $80 and a two horse wagon for $25.00. Although John bought many supplies in Richmond and shipped them via the canal to Goochland, the partnership also maintained an account at J.M. Haden's store in the county. A copy of the partner's account at Haden's store shows that in addition to purchasing a great deal of lime, the partners consumed large quantities of coffee and sugar. [290]

That the Pierces liked their coffee and liked it sweet is clear. What is less clear is why, included in the partnership accounts, are several agreements for hiring one or two slaves to work in the brickyard. The standard terms were $100 for a year, the slave to be returned "well clothed in the usual manner and to have a hat and

---

[289]*Ibid.*

[290]Chancery Cases, File 20; 1853, 1 slave leased for $97 from N.B. Vaughan; 3 slaves at $100 each from Mrs. Ann L. Miller at different periods in 1854 and 1855; 1 slave from A.J. Mills. In 1853, John paid personal property taxes on 12 slaves in Goochland. In 1854, 12 slaves in Goochland; in 1855, 12 slaves in Goochland and 2 in Richmond.

blanket." This expense is puzzling, for during this period, John owned and paid personal property taxes on anywhere from 12 to 15 slaves, only two of whom were kept in Richmond. Conceivably John felt it best to keep his various business enterprises entirely separate, and the inventory of slaves he maintained for sale or hiring out were not available to the partnership. It seems less likely that the debt-encumbered brickyard was so busy that it was necessary to lease additional hands. [291]

The most serious of the partnership's obligations was a debt to William B. Standard of "Ben Dover," a Richmond lawyer and son of John's former neighbor Judge Robert Stanard. William Stanard had accepted notes from the Pierces for $1270 owed on the 1853 purchase of 31 ½ acres of Robert Stanard's land, land over which Pierce and Pierce "had extended their operations for about three years." By 1857, this debt had accumulated interest of $228.60. Stanard had sued and collected on one of five notes from the Pierces, but even after crediting 5000 bricks at ten cents each to the account, Stanard was still owed $1153.88. Both John and Madison were liable for this amount, but if John expected Madison to satisfy even half of the debt, he was being unrealistic, if not punitive. Madison owned no property, either real or personal, at this time. [292]

Madison's concluding remarks are both plaintive and resentful, the latter an emotion which John Pierce may have inspired in many. If Madison was actually John's son, there is also an element of sadness. Of course, Madison was not the first

---

[291] Chancery Cases, File 20, GPPT and GLT 1860 Madison owned nothing

[292] Chancery Cases, File 20

member of his own family on whom John had tried to make a profit and dealt with harshly. In his final remarks about the partnership, Madison said:

That he has been ever since the partnership was formed a single man, living economically and working industriously, yet he finds himself now as poor as when he went into the partnership. But the complainant has all the while had a large family, a wife and most of the time as many as six children, whom he has supported and who have lived well and dressed well and complainant had little other means than what he drew from the partnership.

When it came to money, John played hardball, whether the victim was his father or his son. [293]

Although it was not unusual for cases to move slowly through the Goochland court, Pierce versus Pierce simply disappeared from the docket for several years. In the meantime, Madison, less ambitious than John, but possessed of a trade, carried on with his life and his work as bricklayer. This, despite the fact than in the course of the Pierce lawsuit, one of their customers George W. Turner had reported to the court that he had paid $35.35 for fourteen hundred bricks and "some brick work badly done."[294]

---

[293] *Ibid.* [Turner quote]

[294] GDB 40, p. 65 [Haden to J.M. Pierce]. At this date, $5 was the customary good faith money to make a deal legal; Chancery Cases, File 20 [obligation to A.J. Mills]

Milly Pierce

MODEST AMBITIONS, MODEST PROSPERITY

As far as his strained relationship with John was concerned, Madison may be said to have had the last word. In 1863, Madison purchased 80 acres of the Cedar Point tract, the same land that John had been forced to sell to James M. Haden in 1858. Madison now owned at least a part of the property John had touted as suitable for making superior brick. The terms of the purchase suggest that, like Milly and other members of the family, Madison maintained a good reputation as a solid citizen with Goochland's white community. Haden sold the land to Madison for $5 "with special warranty." The arrangement was essentially a trust agreement between Haden and Pierce, in that Haden maintained a lien on the land as indemnity against two bonds for $100 each owed to A.J. Mills. Presumably, Madison was to pay off the bonds for which Haden had served as security, as they covered a debt for the annual hire of two of Mills' slaves, a debt incurred by the Pierce and Pierce partnership.[295]

By 1870, Madison, now 56, was well established on his own property, valued at $455, and although still unmarried, maintained a comfortable establishment, his household including Frederick Woodruff, 29, a black farm laborer, Ellen Woodruff, 24, a housekeeper, their small child Francis, and a free mulatto boy, Thompson Leigh, 13. His situation was, no doubt, rendered more agreeable by having his brother William nearby and, until recently, his aunts Mary and Jane Pierce as his immediate

---

[295]USCG 1870 [Madison's household and William's location in Lickinghole district]; Goochland Chancery Order Book 1871-1873, p. 10 [Margaret Cousins versus Madison Pierce et al.]

neighbors. Upon Mary's death around 1870, however, Madison found himself embroiled in yet another family lawsuit. As one of Mary's heirs and her executor, he was the principle defendant in Margaret Cousins' suit over settlement of the estate.[296]

Mary and Jane Pierce, along with their brother Thomas, had inherited all of Milly Pierce's estate, including her 21-acre farm. Shortly after his mother's death, Thomas moved to Danville, and demonstrating a rather different character from his brother John, he had written a deed of gift in 1853 which conveyed "all of my interest in the personal estate of my mother Mildred Pierce" to his sisters Mary and Jane "being desirous of aiding and assisting my said sisters." In 1855, Mary and Jane had sold their two-thirds of Milly's land to their neighbor Dr. George W. Harris, who had eventually succeeded the Woodsons at "Brightly." A year later, when Thomas sold his portion of Milly's land to Dr. Harris, the property that had been the first tangible evidence of the Pierces ascent in the world left the family. Not long after they sold their two-thirds of Milly's land for $350, Mary and Jane Pierce paid their brother John $747 for 86 acres at Cedar Point, and, having satisfied the lien left on the property by John, acquired clear title to it. Although the Courthouse property was desirable, Mary and Jane were, in terms of acreage at least, moving up in the world. Ironically, when Madison arrived as their neighbor in 1863, much of John's Cedar Point property was once again owned by Pierces.[297]

---

[296]GDB 37, p. 101 [Deed of gift from Thomas to Mary and Jane Pierce]; GDB 38, p. 48 [Mary and Jane Pierce to Harris]; GOB 35, p. 22 [Thomas Pierce to Harris. Deed ordered recorded, but cannot find actual deed]; GDB 38, p. 715 [John Pierce, Jr. to Mary and Jane Pierce]

[297]Chancery Cases, File 20 [plaintiff deceased]; Circuit Court Common Law Order Book 5, p. 73 [Thomas W. Pierce versus John Pierce abated]. No will

Milly Pierce

Despite Madison's progress in life, the case of Pierce versus Pierce, still unresolved, may have caused him some lingering uneasiness. Finally, however, in 1866, the court clerk noted on the case file, "plaintiff dec'd." In 1868, the case was dismissed. The termination of John Pierce's lawsuit against Madison and the dismissal of a suit filed against John by his brother Thomas, "abated by the deaths of the parties" in 1867, are the only evidence of John's demise. Curiously, for a man so obsessed with worldly possessions, John left no will. Not that he had much to leave. [298]

FROM FREE BLACK TO FREEDMAN

John Pierce, Jr.'s last years must have been a rather sad denouement to his high-flying life as a would-be gentleman farmer and real estate speculator. Far from dealing in large sums of money, John may well have been hard-pressed to make ends meet. Without a trade, without resources and getting along in years, he apparently found a relatively easy, if illegal, way to generate a little cash. Included in a list of persons indicted by a Richmond Grand Jury in 1859 for "retailing ardent spirits and keeping ordinaries without licenses" was one John Pierce. Apparently John, fallen on

---

for John Pierce, Jr. could be found in either the Richmond or Goochland records.

[298] RCM 26, p. 102 [John Pierce indicted]. There were two John Pierces in Richmond at this time. The second was a white constable which suggests that this refers to the free black John Pierce.

hard times, had resorted to making money in the same way his mother may have when she first faced life as a free woman. [299]

By 1860, John had lost not only his farmlands in Goochland, but also his home in Richmond, probably to foreclosure. His personal property was valued at only $100. His family, too was considerably diminished. Eliza Pierce had died within the year, and only his daughter, Eliza Finney, 32, and her four children ages 8 months to seven years remained with him. His son John was living in Goochland with Madison Pierce, and his daughters, Mary Jane and Sarah, were, presumably, married in homes of their own. John's two youngest sons, Isaac and William, had established themselves in Richmond as barbers, and although barbers typically numbered among the most successful free black tradesmen, neither Isaac nor William lived long enough to enjoy fully the fruits of their labors. Both died in 1860; Isaac, 22, of "consumption," and William, 18, from "dropsy of the chest." [300]

Richmond was a chaotic place in the early 1860s. With the onset of the Civil War, "The city," as described by Virginius Dabney, "was overrun by soldiers,

---

[299] USCR 1860 John Pierce household; his household also included a Margaret Pierce, 53, and Judy Payne, aged 60. Eliza was still alive in 1859 when she acknowledged her agreement to the sale of the Pope property to a Richmond notary (GDB 38, p. 707), but is missing from the 1860 census. USCG 1860 [John Pierce (3) living with Madison]; United States Social Census, Henrico County, Richmond Ward 1, 1870 [Deaths of Isaac Pierce and William Pierce, identified as mulatto barbers]; Russell, *Free Negro*, p. 151 and Berlin, *op. cit.*, p. 235 [Free Black barbers]

[300] Virginius Dabney, *Richmond: the Story of a City* (New York, 1976), p. 163 [quote] and pp. 163-186 [Richmond in early 1860s]. General George McClellen was positioned just southeast of the city, and Richmond was in a frenzy of preparation for an invasion that never came. John Pierce last appears in the RPPT in 1862, suggesting that he died that year.

adventurers, speculators, gamblers, prostitutes and every other type of person who gravitates to the place 'where the action is.'" A much younger John Pierce would, no doubt, have flourished in such an atmosphere. As it was, at 67, he must have been a broken man, an inconsequential failure in a city which had almost overnight doubled in size from its pre-war population of 38,000. By 1862, Richmond was overwhelmed not only by opportunities but also by the wound from earlier battles to the north. It was also a city awaiting imminent invasion. [301]

At some point in this turmoil, in some place not his own, in a city under siege, John Pierce died within the year that Lincoln proclaimed all blacks free. He had lost not only the status of his material success, but also that of his relatively rare, if peculiar, position as a "free Negroe." His only legacy was his lawsuit against Madison which his grandson, Isaac Finney, tried, unsuccessfully, to revive in 1883. [302]

---

[301] Circuit Court Common Law Order Book 5, p. 747 [Isaac Finney versus J.M. Pierce's executor]

[302] Randall Robinson, *Defending the Spirit: A Black Life in America* (New York, 1998), p. 265 [Vernon Jordan disease] and p. 270 [goes along]

V

AN ENDURING LEGACY

In the rubble of Richmond and the rural isolation of Goochland, several thousand black Virginians suddenly found themselves free—at last. Beyond their freedom, they had little else. There were no road maps to the future, and few precedents to follow. Only a Milly Pierce, former slave and successful free black, stood as a signpost to their survival.

Milly Pierce departed this world, a propertied matriarch, surrounded by her children, grandchildren and great grandchildren. Lydia Cousins, like her mother, died a woman of property, a mother with an empowering legacy for her daughters. John Pierce, Jr. died propertyless, with few heirs and little or nothing to leave them. The moral of the story is all too obvious—and much too pat. Similarly, Milly's story begs to be presented as a straight and triumphant upward trajectory; her son John's, its reverse. Yet lives are seldom that simple. Individual stories are less clear in outline and less perfect in the details than the ideal.

Legally, socially and even physically, Milly Pierce bridged the great divide between black and white, but the link she represented was both fragile and frightening in a society based on an absolute separation of the races. Far from pointing the way to reconciliation, a life such as Milly's begged for extermination in the minds of many whites. Yet, caught in the slowly closing vise of ever more limited freedom, Milly secured her own economic independence and paved the way for her children. Member of a class despised and feared by most whites, she survived through white patronage and became a fixture in the white power structure at the Courthouse. Manifestly of mixed race, she embodied the deepest fears of many white southerners, yet her color invested her with a certain status in both the white and black communities. A former slave, she owned slaves.

How to reconcile these contradictions? The paradoxes in Milly's life were, to a large extent, inherent in her ambiguous status as a free black and the particular character of the time and place in which she lived. Born with absolutely nothing—not even control of her own fate—she still made something of herself and her life. Caught in a most irregular crack in a monolithic society, she carved out a small, but safe niche for her family. Viewed in the most favorable light, she was a woman of rare courage and determination. But above all, she was a pragmatist. Some might even say a sell-out and sycophant, a woman willing to sacrifice principle and the interests of her own race for sheer self-interest and success in a hostile world. Today, she might be accused of suffering from what Randall Robinson has called "Vernon Jordan disease," tacitly bowing to the white establishment's belief that "the only good black is a black who 'goes along to get along'" in exchange for a degree of privilege and apparent power.[303]

That would be unfairly revisionist. What conceivable forum could a Milly Pierce have found in which to voice her objections to white exploitation and slavery?

---

[303] The Associated Press, "Black's Rising Suicide Rate, Middle-Class Ties Linked," *Richmond Times-Dispatch,* March 20, 1998, p. A6 [Quote from Carl Bell]

Milly Pierce

There simply was none. Any act of protest would have been an act of suicide. How could she have succeeded in a world controlled completely by whites without ingratiating herself with them? There was no alternative route to economic or personal empowerment. How could she, a former slave, rationalize owning slaves? This last is, from the perspective of the present, the most troubling question about Milly Pierce. After all, a few free blacks did, in fact, hire other free blacks to farm their land or keep their houses. Yet, such instances were rare, and based on her treatment of Franklin French, it appears that Milly was both generous and liberal in the treatment of her slaves. While it is easy to explain, even forgive, Milly her "sins," it is much less palatable to do so in the case of John Pierce. Yet, in most ways, John was merely Milly writ large—with an attitude.

Slaves and their dehumanized condition were the clarion call of those Americans who truly believed in the dream of liberty and justice for all; free blacks were the reality that made that call ring true. Ironically, considering the source, Milly in many ways exemplified the "aristocracy of virtue and talent" on whose shoulders Thomas Jefferson believed the future of this country rested. Whatever her shortcomings from the perspective of that future, she did point the way for generations of blacks to come.

Within her own family, Milly set an example of hard work and self-sufficiency that served them well. Her direct descendants were not, however, the sole beneficiaries of her example. When her entire race suddenly found themselves transformed from slaves to freedmen by a stroke of Lincoln's pen—and a bitter war—free blacks who had survived prolonged persecution and built lives with solid foundations were the only role models available. Post-Civil War African American society was rooted in lives like Milly's. Her example must have given both hope and direction to newly freed slaves. She had shown what was possible, even for a former slave. And, she had demonstrated how to live successfully in a legally hostile environment, an example that would serve blacks well once the repressive Jim Crow laws, based on the earlier free black laws, were imposed.

There are those who might accuse Milly of having been an Aunt Thomasina and reject her example in favor of a more heroic and confrontational model. Milly Pierce's legacy may be imperfect, yet, within the context of her times, she navigated a difficult course with courage, resourcefulness and dignity. She may not have been transcendent, but she did make the best of a bad situation, and even today, her legacy echoes through the generations.

Milly's life has particular resonance for middle class African Americans. Often espousing mainstream American values, middle class blacks still frequently find themselves isolated in a predominantly white society. If white Americans cannot see beyond the color of their skin, the majority of less successful blacks view them as self-aggrandizing traitors to their race. As one mental health expert has observed when confronted with a recent rise in suicides among middle-class black teenagers: "You don't belong in any world. You don't belong in the white middle-class and you don't belong among poor blacks." Like ante-bellum free blacks, modern middle-class African Americans find themselves stranded on an ill-defined middle ground, a middle ground that is, at once, the thorniest immediate problem for those who seek the safety

Milly Pierce

of extremes and quite possibly the ultimate solution to the larger problem of creating a viable multi-racial society. [304]

Milly's legacy, however, transcends race and touches all who are oppressed, whether it be by power or prejudice or stereotype. As an independent, self-sufficient woman, Milly and her story speak directly to every woman who, by necessity or choice, must make it on her own, undeterred by the conventions of the dominant white patriarchy or her more conventional sisters. And although some will take exception to the linkage, Milly's confident assertion of her rights and the place she made for herself in the white, male power structure contain the seeds of feminism—especially when her life is compared to those of most of her contemporaries. As the ultimate outsider, Milly also speaks to those who, failing to conform to prevailing social and cultural norms, find themselves caught in the cracks of a putatively free and open society, living in a social and legal limbo. Her survival in this murky place, defined only by a maze of limiting laws, is a message to all who forsake the simplicity of extremes and attempt to negotiate the subtleties in between.

In her own low-key, but determined way, Milly Pierce, while not directly questioning the mores of her oppressors, did, by her perseverance and success, shake the foundations of the peculiar institution. Like Faulkner's Dilsey, she endured, and that endurance of a free and determined spirit signaled the vulnerability of her oppressors. Few white men could have looked Milly Pierce in the eye and argued that she was nothing more than chattel, a vile and debased creature suited only to the brutal subjugation of slavery. Her life suggests that no oppressor can survive the subversion

---

[304]

of quiet persistence and unflinching purpose, not even those most modern of tyrants—immediate gratification and instant annihilation.

END

NOTES

1. William W. Hening, comp., *The Statues at Large; Being a Compilation of All the Laws of Virginia*. 13 vols., (Richmond, New York, Philadelphia, 1800-1823), III. p. 87 [1691 law] *ibid.*, IV, p. 133-4 [1723 law]
2. Hening, *op. cit.* IV, pp. 133-134 [1723 loss of vote]; Donald R. Wright, *African Americans in the Colonial Period: From African Origins through the American Revolution* (Arlington Heights, Ill., 1990), p. 123 [Hugh Drysdale quote]
3. Edmund S. Morgan, *American Slavery, American Freedom: The Ordeal of Colonial Virginia* (New York, 1975) offers an excellent discussion of the American paradox and the evolution of slavery in colonial Virginia.
4. Hening, *op cit.*, II, p. 167 [1662 law—mother status of child]; *ibid.*, II, p. 267 [1668 law free black women to pay tax]
5. In later years, Milly is sometimes referred to as Mildred, but, early on and most often, she is called Milly. Her surname varies in spelling occasionally, sometimes spelled Pearce rather than Pierce.
6. Goochland County Deed Book (GDB) 19, pp. 365-6 [Milly's lease to Samuel Johnson]. Milly was apparently illiterate. She always signed with an "X." GDB 18, p. 679 ["reputed" husband owned by Brydin]; Goochland County Register of Free Negroes (GFN) # 128 John Pierce, Jr. registered in 1814 at 21.
7. Tucker Woodson was a descendant of John Woodson (died 1715) who, rather than being "a typical Friend farmer" was a large landowner in the Richmond area, including several thousand acres in what would become Goochland Jay Worrall, Jr., *The Friendly Virginians: America's First Quakers* (Athens, Ga., 1994), p. 85. Tucker Woodson may no longer have been a practicing Quaker. His son Samuel, forced to chose between his faith and fighting in the Revolution, chose the latter—Worral, *op. cit.*, p. 219, and in 1778 John Woodson (3) was a member of the vestry when Beaverdam Episcopal Church in Goochland was founded (Helene B. Agee, *Facets of Goochland County Historical Society Magazine* vol. 9, no. 2, pp. 32-35. GLT 1793 [Woodson 600 acres]; GDB 16, pp. 484-5 [Tucker Woodson's will]
8. Hening, *op. cit.*, IV p. 132 [1723 law revokes private manumission]; Worrall, *op. cit.*, pp. 225-7 [Quakers and the private manumission law of 1782]; Hening, *op. cit.*, VI, pp. 39-40 [Law of 1782—reinstates manumission]; GDB 13, p. 246 [Thomas Pleasants, Jr., deed of manumission]. Also manumitting their slaves that day were Mary Youngblood and Benjamin Watkins. The language of the deeds is identical suggesting its origin in the Quaker Meeting.
9. John H. Russell, *The Free Negro in Virginia 1619-1865* (Baltimore 1913), pp. 84-86 [Emancipation by will]
10. GDB 18, p. 679 [Payne to Pierce deed]

11. Goochland Land Tax (GLT), 1804. In this year, and others, the tax collector did not note which of the tax payers was a free black; but none of those listed can be identified as a free black, except Milly. Before 1804, only Roger Cooper and David Grantham can be identified as free black landowners.
12. GLT 1797 to 1860 [Free black female landowners]. Other women who owned land in Goochland prior to 1860 were Bridget Allen (inheritance), Sally Banks (inheritance), Martha Brooks (inheritance), Mary Cook (inheritance), Evelina Copland (inheritance), Louisa Copland (inheritance), Lydia Pierce Cousins (inheritance and purchase), Chloe Cousins (inheritance), Margaret Cousins, Polly, Cousins, Susanna Cousins (inheritance), Paulina Fox, Sally Fulcher, Polly Fulcher (inheritance), Elizabeth Grantham (inheritance), Milly James (owned jointly with Timothy Pleasants), Charlotte Lynch (inheritance), Salina Lynch, Jane Pierce (inheritance and purchase), Mary Pierce (inheritance and purchase), and Rissa (no surname). Lebsock, *op. cit.*, p. 164 [women and property]; GOB 19. P. 64 [David Grantham's Will] Grantham is also spelled Grantum in the Goochland records. The Mealys remain in Goochland today, owners of the Mealy Funeral Home and prominent members of the community.
13. GDB 19, pp. 365-6. [Pierce to Johnson lease]. Milly, apparently illiterate, signed with an "x."
14. GDB 19, pp. 70-71 [Tucker Woodson's agreement with Samuel Woodson]; GDB 20, p. 530 [Samuel Woodson's will identifies Lydia as his servant]
15. GDB 24, p. 355 and GDB 26, p. 168 [Deeds reference House of Entertainment]. The first deed is to John Pierce and the second to Milly Pierce. Both make reference to the prohibition against a House of Private Entertainment. Suzanne Lebsock, *The Free Women of Petersburg: Status and Culture in a Southern Town, 1784-1860* (New York, 1984) pp. 98, 147, 177-178 [Quote, p. 178] Lebsock's Chapter on Free Women of Color is an excellent discussion of Milly's situation in general, although with an urban slant.
16. GDB 18, p. 679 [Payne to Pierce, "reputed wife"]
17. Dr. Brydin never paid tax on more than one slave and that slave is first identified as John Pierce in Milly's 1803 deed. Goochland Order Book (GOB) 25, p. 376—A plat of the two acres condemned for the Courthouse in 1823 indicates "Brydin's old house" was very close to the southeast corner of the old Courthouse. United States Census 1810, Goochland County (USCG) indicates that Dr. Brydin had no family.
18. Brydin's suits for payment of his fees begin in 1797 with the suit against Peter Berry (GOB 20, p. 480). In the eight suits recorded through 1800, four of the defendants were deceased.
19. GOB 23, p. 547 [Trial of Leake's Jack]; GOB 24, p. 287 [Brydin paid from County Levy for attending castration]
20. Hening, *op. cit.*, II. P. 59 [1781 law forbidding slaves to earn wages]; Eugene D. Genovese, "the Slave States of North America," *Neither Slave Nor Free: The Freedmen of African Descent in the Slave Societies of the New World* (Baltimore, 1972), p. 267.

Milly Pierce

21. GOB 23, p. 622 (Payne and Smith paid for Pierce); GOB 25, p. 334 [The County Levy includes a payment of $22.68 to "John Pierce, Sr. jailor" [sic] for a claim in connection with criminal prosecutions "to be paid Wm Miller [clerk of Court] blk," this last referring to Pierce.
22. GOB 26, p. 82 [Pierce is paid $35 for keeping jail and stove, an amount he continued to receive annually until 1816 when it increased to $50. Also paid for glass.]; GOB 26, p. 546 [John paid for stove]
23. GOB 21, p. 33, p. 321; GOB 22, p. 107, p. 406; GOB 23, p. 27 [Samuel Woodson paid for "keeping the Courthouse"]
24. GOB 27, pp. 430-431 [Richard Layne charged with stealing corn]; GOB 28, p. 455 [Layne fails to appear]
25. GOB 28, p. 292 [Layne charged with stealing hog]; GOB 29, p. 450 [Layne nolleprosequey]
26. Goochland Court Minute Book 1811-16, p. 438 [Trial of Peyton]; GOB 28, pp. 264 and 287, GOB 30, p. 28 [Payments to John Pierce on account of Layne]
27. USCG 1810 [Layne family size]; GPPT and GLT, 1810 and 1820 [Layne owned no taxable property, employed in agriculture]; GOB 28, p. 622 [Sheriff to seize Layne chattels]; Legislative Manuscripts, Goochland ms. A7110 [Mayo petition: Layne children's education to be paid by county]; Layne's legal troubles did not end here. In 1830, he was tried and found not guilty of stealing "a parcel of undressed leather" (GOB 31, p. 506).
28. GOB 24, p. 205 [John Pierce bound to Samuel Johnson]; Hening, *op. cit.*, XII, pp. 27-28 [apprenticeships moved from wardens to overseers; requirements]; Samuel Shepherd, ed., *The Statutes at Large in Virginia*, 3 vols., (Richmond, 1835), vol. 2, p. 124 [education dropped]
29. Ira Berlin, *Slaves Without Masters: The Free Negro in the Antebellum South* (New York, 1974), pp. 226-7 [conditions of apprentices]; See p. xxx this ms regarding John's literacy and business skills.
30. GDB 19, p. 631 [Ann Johnson terminates Milly's lease]
31. Goochland Personal Property Tax (GPPT) 1809 Milly is listed here for the first time and paid tax on one horse or mule; USCG 1810 [Milly's household]; GPPT 1809-1851 Milly paid taxes on 1 to 4 slaves; John H. Russell, "Colored Freemen as Slave Owners in Virginia," *Journal of Negro History*, vol. 1, June 1916, no. 3, pp. 233-243; Philip J. Schwarz, "Emancipators, Protectors, and Anomalies: Free Black Slaveowners in Virginia." *The Virginia Magazine of History and Biography*, vol. 95, no. 3 (July 1987), pp. 317-338.
32. USCG 1810 and GPPT 1810 [households owning slaves. The two records do not entirely agree, the 12 slave-owners appear in one or the other and sometimes both]; Shepherd, *op. cit.*, vol. 3, p. 252 [1806 law]; for more about this law, see pp. xxx of this ms. Eventually, both Dean and Gwyn did emancipate their families and secured permission for them to remain in Goochland. USCG 1820 all members of the Gwynn, also spelled Guinn, household are free; USCG 1830 Philip Dean's wife is listed as free.

33. USCG 1810. All of the Cowpers (later Cooper) like Milly, had free black families. Miles and Edward Cooper owned one slave each; Jacob, two. Berlin, *op. cit.*, pp. 143-144 [quasi-free slaves]
34. Schwarz, *op. cit.*, p. 325 [free black slave owning]
35. GOB 28, p. 69 [John registers a boat]
36. Wayland Fuller Dunaway, *History of the James River and Kanawha Canal Company*, (New York, 1922), p. 87 [Canal to Maidens]; Anthony R.D. Perrins, "The James River and Kanawha Canal in Goochland," *Goochland County Historical Society Magazine*, vol. 13, 1981, p. 35 [description of bateaux]
37. Berlin, *op. cit.*, pp. 218-219 [free blacks and boat trade]; Perrins, *ibid.* [description of boatmen on the James]
38. Other free black boatmen found in the orders books, personal property records and census were: Peyton Cooper, John Coplan, Samuel Howell, Charles Gray, Caesar Giles, Philip Cousins (John's grandson), Samuel Cousins, James Frenti, IshamFuzmore, Jordan Giles, Henry Logan, Jeremiah Mayo, Peyton Mayo, Richard Morse (Moss), Henry Smith, Isaac Smith, Moses Brooks, James Cousins, Robert Crump, James Henley, William Howell, Henry Logan, John Logan, Robert J. Logan, John Lynch, Billy Martin, Thomas Moss, John Sims, John Snead, and Matthew Snead.
39. GDB 20, p. 530 [Samuel Woodson's will]; Worrall, *op. cit.*, p. 219 [Samuel served in Revolution]; GDB 20, p. 631 [Samuel Woodson's inventory]; Berlin, *op. cit.*, pp. 150-152 [selective emancipations]
40. Berlin, *op. cit.*, pp. 151-152 [women emancipated]
41. Berlin, *op. cit.*, pp. 56-57 and 150-152; E. Franklin Frazier, *The Negro Family in the United States* (New York, 1948), pp. 145-146 [mulatto's status]; John H. Russell, *The Free Negro in Virginia 1619-1865* (Baltimore, 1913), pp. 127-128 [mulattos]; Benjamin Quarles, *The Negro in the Making of America* (New York, 1987), p. 84; Berlin, *op. cit.*, p. 178 [1860 census figures]; Designations about skin color in the Goochland records are imprecise and inconsistent. Of the 42 free blacks who paid taxes on real estate in 1850, 8 were black; 6 were brown; 5 were "of colour;" 3 cannot be determined; and 20 were mulatto. All ten of those who owned 50 or more acres were mulatto. For more on this subject, see pp. xxx this ms.
42. Frazier, *op. cit.*, pp. 300-308 and Berlin, *op. cit.*, pp. 56, 57, 247 [Mulatto elite]; GMR, 1812, p. 353 [Lydia Pierce m. Henry Cousins]; USCG 1850 [Henry Cousins identified as cooper]; for more about the Cousins family see p. xxxx this ms.
43. GMR, *ibid.* [Chaudoin minister]; Cameron Allen, "Francis (Francois) Chaudoin," *The Virginia Genealogist*, vol. 40, no. 2, (April-June 1996), pp. 87-92 [Chaudoin family]; James B. Taylor, *Virginia Baptist Ministers*, (Philadelphia, 1859), series 2, pp. 219-21 [quote from Richmond Enquirer]
44. Garnett Ryland, *The Baptists of Virginia, 1699-1926* (Richmond 1955), pp. 150-55 [Baptists denounce slavery]; Russell, *Free Negro*, pp. 57-58 [Quakers and Methodists and free blacks]; Berlin, *op. cit.*, p. 66 [free blacks join

Milly Pierce

Baptists]; Robert B. Semple, *A History of Baptists in Virginia*, (Polyanthus, Inc., Cottonport, La., 1810, reprint 1970) p. 140 [Goochland revival]

45. GMR p. 353, Lucy Pierce m. Daniel Moss Oct. 23, 1812; p. 356, Susan Pierce m. Austin Isaacks Mar. 6, 1815; p. 361, Sally Pierce m. Reuben Dungee Jan. 21, 1819; p. 364, Phebe Pierce m. Page Carter Nov. 8 1820; p. 368, Martha Pierce m. Wilson Morris July 21, 1825. John Pierce is listed as the official witness for the weddings of Lydia, Phoebe and Martha.

46. The birth dates of Milly's children are approximate as the Goochland Register of Free Negroes indicates ages "about 21," and there are inconsistencies in the ages several of them gave in various censuses. Judith (Ude), Lucy, and Ledy (Lydia) are cited in Tucker Woodson's will. John (Jack) and Susan (Suky) are cited when the will was proven. Sally's wedding was witnessed by Milly's son-in-law Henry Cousins. Isaac Pierce cited his emancipation by Tucker Woodson's will when he registered as free black #241 in 1819 at age 21. Phebe's wedding was witnessed by John Pierce. Martha's wedding was witnessed by John Pierce. Thomas, Jane and Mary were cited by Milly as her three youngest children in her 1850 will. A Rebecca Pierce who registered as free Negro #303 in 1823 at age 16 might also have been Milly's daughter, although there is no more information about her. GPPT 1813 [John and Judy named]

47. _____. Acts of the General Assemby (Acts). 1812 (Richmond, 1813), p. 20

48. Russell, *Free Negro*, pp. 62-63, p. 170 [Self Purchase]: Hening, *op. cit.*, XI, 40 [working off taxes]

49. Hening, *ibid.*: _____ Acts (Richmond, 1814), p. 61 [free blacks hired out to pay taxes]; USC Virginia 1790 Free blacks numbered 12,866, whites 442,117, and slaves 292,627. In 1810, whites numbered 551,534 and slaves, 392,518; USCG 1790 Free blacks numbered 257, whites 4130 and slaves 4656; USCG 1810 Whites numbered 4240 and slaves 5454. All 1790 figures are estimates as the original census was burned during the War of 1812. Shepherd, *op. cit.*, vol. 1, p. 239 [1793 law forbade immigration]

50. GPPT 1813 [Milly's tax burden and tax rates]

51. GFN #54 Billy Perry registered at age 31 in 1808 citing his emancipation by Isaac W. Pleasants as the result of a court decree. For more about the court case, see pp. xx this ms; GOB 21, p. 669 [Tax delinquents for 1814]

52. GOB 22, pp. 72-73 [Tax delinquents for 1815]; _____ Acts (Richmond, 1815), p. 8; GDB 20, p. 10 [Anderson Royster's will]; GOB *ibid.*; GPPT 1816 [Lually listed with John Royster; others gone]; _____ Acts (Richmond, 1813), p. 20 [rate for working off taxes]

53. GOB 22, p. 190 [coroner's request]

54. GPPT 1815. In this year only, the tax collector includes cattle as another revenue generator; GDB 22, p. 51 [Deed from Benjamin Anderson]; 23 acres and 34.75 acres would add up to 57.75 acres. This discrepancy is, in part, explained in GDB 21, p. 682 which records Milly's trade of 2.20 acres to her neighbor William Miller for .90 acres from Miller, reducing her 23 acres to 21.70. This would make her total acreage 56.45, not 56.25. Discrepancies of

even an acre or so are not uncommon, however, in Goochland deeds and land taxes. GOB 29, pp. 293, 344, 347, 248. [Payments to John Pierce]; Lebsock, *op. cit.*, pp. 33-35 [19th c. marriages]
55. GDB 22, pp. 292-3 [John's deed of manumission]
56. GOB 29, p. 295 [evidence of Bydin's death; executor named]; GPPT 1815 [John Curd's slaves]; Hening, *op. cit.*, VI pp. 39-40 [1782 no slave dumping]
57. GOB 29, p. 295 Although the court appointed five men to "appraise the personal estate of Dr. James Brydin," no record of that appraisal can be found. The procedure was pro forma, and possibly there was no possessions to be reported. Brydin never paid personal property taxes on anything except one slave over the age of 16. He is never listed in the land records. GOB 29, p. 454 [John Curd, Sheriff, collector of levy]
58. GOB 29, p. 440 [Milly's suit against Brydin's estate]
59. Shepherd, *op. cit.*, vol. 3, p. 252 [1806 law]
60. Free blacks were never deprived of the right to seek redress in the courts for civil matters; see Russell, *Free Negro*, pp. 98-99 for a discussion of how this presumption of slavery developed in common law [presumed a slave]
61. Shepherd, *ibid.* [1806 law]
62. Berlin, *op. cit.*, p. 145-147 [manumitted remain illegally]; Russell, *Free Negro*, p. 76 [Some freed slaves would not leave home]
63. In 1800, North Carolina required free black immigrants to post a 200 pound bond. Kentucky outlawed free black immigration in 1807; Maryland in 1808; Delaware in 1810. (Berlin, *op. cit.*, p. 92); Quarles, *op. cit.*, p. 79 [Ohio open]
64. The Goochland Personal Property records list free black male titheables over 21 whether or not they owned personal property. Eight free black males listed first in 1806 do not reappear in the records, and seven first listed in 1807 also disappear; Berlin, *op. cit.*, p. 175 [aging of free black population]
65. Russell, *Free Negro*, p. 12 [St George Tucker's estimate]; USC Virginia 1790 and 1800
66. Shepherd, *ibid.* [Law of 1806] The law forbade anyone from bringing a slave into Virginia for more than a year; the penalty, forfeiture. Bringing slaves into to sell or hire out was prohibited; the penalty, $400 fines on both seller and buyer. The section regarding free blacks was actually a Senate amendment to a House bill regarding the incorporation of slaves.
67. *Richmond Argus*, Tuesday, Jan 17, 1805, pp. 2-3 [Debate on free black law]
68. Douglas R. Egerton, *Gabriel's Rebellion: The Virginia Slave Conspiracies of 1800 and 1802* (Chapel Hill, 1993); *Richmond Argus, ibid.*
69. GOB 29, p. 514 [Magistrate summoned for John]; GOB 29, p. 550 [John given permission to stay]
70. GOB 29, p. 454 [John's raise to $50]
71. Lebsock, *op. cit.*, p. 106 [quote], pp. 23, 103-111 [discussion of free black women's legal and economic status]
72. USCG 1820 free blacks numbered 685; in 1830, 795; in 1840, 653; in 1850, 649; in 1860, 691. The number of women is from the same source.
73. GDB 24. p. 355 [John's Deed from Benjamin Anderson]; GDB 25, p. 375 [For $1 Benjamin Anderson sells 2 acres to the county]

Milly Pierce

74. GDB 25, p. 161 [plat of Courthouse]; GDB 24, p. 355 [John's deed]
75. GDB 24, p. 355 [John's deed]
76. GOB 30, p. 213 [John's 1822 raise to $50]; Superior Court Orders 1809-1822, p. 530 [paid for John Pleasants]. In the course of John's 24 years as jailer, he received at least 13 payments specifically for criminal prosecutions.
77. GOB 30, p. 217 [Pleasants charged]; _____ Acts 1831-1832, p. 22 [no trial by jury]; Superior Court Orders 1809-1822, p. 510 [Pleasants found not guilty]
78. Agee, *op. cit.*, p. 23 [jail conditions]
79. _____. Acts 1822-1823, p. 56 [deportation for felony]; _____ Acts 1824, p. 36 [law extended to misdemeanor]; _____, Acts 1827, p. 29 [repeal of this law]; Russell, *Free Negro*, p. 106 [claims 35 persons deported]; _____, Acts of 1827-1828, p. 29 [new felon law]
80. USCG 1820 [Pierce household]; GDB 25, p. 144 [John's deed of trust on land]; GOB 30, p. 157 [John registers boat]
81. GDB 26, p. 168 [Milly's deed for 2 acres from Fleming] Although the deed clearly states 2 acres and Fleming's property is reduced from 381 to 379 acres, these 2 acres are never included in Milly's holdings and the Land Tax records continue to show John as owning 1 acre
82. GDB 26, p. 285 [Curd to Fleming]; GDB 25, p. 381 [Anderson deed of trust] John S. Fleming and Charles F. Pope authorized to sell Anderson's land to settle his debts; GDB 26, p. 282-283 [Anderson to Curd]
83. GDB 26, p. 168 [Milly's deed] Fleming's note about his conversation with John is entered immediately following the deed. For more about the transfer of this tract from Fleming to Thompson, see pp. xx this ms. Milly was still living on the Courthouse land at her death in 1850, and her daughters Mary and Jane continued there until 1855, the last year the acre is listed in John Pierce's name.
84. GLT 1825-1855 [John Pierce or "John Pierce dec'd." taxed on 1 acre]; GDB 26, p. 168 [note that deed delivered to Thomas Pierce]
85. Shepherd, *op. cit.,* vol. 1, p. 238 [1793 immigration and registration law]
86. The Goochland Register of Free Negroes was maintained from May 21, 1804 through November 23, 1864. Although the last numbered registration is 2046, the records were misnumbered in the original jumping from 1099 to 2000. The actual number of free blacks who registered was 1145.
87. Many of these registrations occur in clumps of family names on the same date. Of those who registered, 32% did so around age 21. GFN # 128 John Pierce, Jr. emancipated by the will of Tucker Woodson; GFN # 241 Isaac Pierce "of colour" emancipated by the will of Tucker Woodson.
88. 47% of those who registered were female. GFN #758 Clarissa Cowigg or Cowig was black and cited her emancipation in 1782 by Thomas Pleasants, Jr. (GDB 13, p. 246)
89. GFN # 249 Sally Dungee; # 265 Phebe Carter; #350 SukeyIsaacks; #352 Martha Morris; and #380 Lucy Moss. A Page Carter is listed in the Richmond Census. In the 1830 Richmond census, only a Phoebe Carter is listed as the

head of a household of eight containing no adult male. Presumably Page either left or died. Sally and Reuben Dungee disappear from the County records and the Virginia census following their marriage in 1819 and Sally's 1820 registration. Lucy and Daniel Moss remained in Goochland until around 1827 when they disappear from the Personal Property records and Lucy registered. They do not appear in the 1830 or 1840 Virginia census. Austin and Susan Isaacks were still in Goochland in 1826 when Austin sued John Martin (GOB 21, p. 50). In 1827, however, in another hearing regarding this suit he is described as "a non-resident of the Commonwealth" (GOB 31, p. 131). GMR, p. 368-Martha Pierce m. Wilson Morris, 21 July 1825. A Wilson Morris appears in the 1830, 1840 and 1850 Richmond census, but his wife's name is Nancy. A cooper, he was John Pierce Jr.'s partner in a land deal in Richmond in 1849. When the property was sold in 1851, he and Nancy had moved to Philadelphia (Hustings (Richmond) Deed Book (RDB) 66, p. 305). Possibly he was Martha's widower?

90. USCG 1830 Judith Pierce's and Lydia Pierce Cousins' households: GPPT 1821, Isaac is listed as living as a free male over 21 in John Pierce, Jr.'s household and appears to still be there in 1830; USCG 1830 John Pierce, Jr. household: "John Pierce...lived between the Courthouse and BollingHall, east of Little and Cheney Creeks." (William Bolling, "The Diary of Colonel William Bolling May 1836," *The Goochland County Historical Society Magazine*, vol. 9, no. 2, p. 31)

91. USCG 1830 [composition of Pierce household]; Thomas, Mary and Jane were still living with Milly when she died in 1850. Their ages are based on the registrations as free blacks. GFN # 532 1835 Thomas about 24; GFN # 812 1843 Mary about 28; and GFN #625 1840, Jane about 23. The only information about Rebecca Pierce is her registration as # 303 in 1823 at age 16 in which she is described as "of colour" and born free in Goochland. Madison Pierce registered as #514 in 1833 and was described as about 21, light yellow and born free in Goochland. William Henry Pierce registered in 1840 as #626 and was about 22, bright yellow and born free in Goochland. They were not Milly's as she clearly identified Thomas, Mary and Jane as her three youngest children in her will. Based on their ages, both Madison and William could have been John Pierce, Jr.'s sons. The suspicion about their relationship to John is also raised by the fact that both are listed in the personal property records with John, Jr. in 1855 and 1858, and Madison, at least, was living with John Jr.'s son John Pierce. John Pierce, Jr. m. Eliza Ligon Dec. 8, 1820 in Chesterfield County, Va. (County Marriage Register, p. 160).

92. GLT 1826 Milly's land holdings were reduced to 21 acres in the tax records with a note that 34 ¾ acres had been sold to John S. Fleming, but no deed can be found. Hereafter, she paid tax only on the 21 acres. GPPT 1826 Milly taxed on only 1 slave and 1 horse. GOB 31, p. 58 [John's 1826 salary], p. 84 [$65.50 for "attending...prosecutions"]; GOB 31, p. 245 [John registers second boat.]

Milly Pierce

93. GDB 30, p. 165 [Copland, Howell, and Grey register boats]; GMR, p. 366 Ridley Cousins married ~~married~~ John Copland in 1824. The only Samuel Howells in the Goochland records are free blacks who appear in the Marriage Register, personal property and census records, but none of the right age registered. The free black Howell family was large and moderately successful, owning some property. Charles Gray registered as # 161 in 1815 at age 31 and cited his emancipation by Isaac W. Pleasants.
94. Dunaway, *op. cit.*, p. 87 [canal improvements]
95. *Ibid.*, p. 168 [Canal tonnage and revenues]; Agee, *op. cit.*, pp. 74-76 [end of canal]
96. GOB 31, p. 254 [John omitted from Levy] John served as jailer from 1803 through 1827.
97. GOB 31, p. 254 [Milly in county levy; Sheriff paid as jailer]
98. Lebsock, *op. cit.*, p. 147 [women's work]
99. GOBs 1828-1841 each year Milly was paid $70; Agee, *op. cit.*, p. 49 [new courthouse]; Circuit Superior Court of Law and Chancery Order Book 1837-1846 and 1847-1863. Milly was paid twice a year in the spring and fall in amounts from $4 to $8 per session; GOB 32, p. 470 [Milly paid $75]; GOB 1836-44 (not numbered), p. 83 [Milly's job affirmed]
100. GOB 32, p. 160 [Thomas becomes jailer]; *ibid.*, p. 272 [Thomas cares for Underwood]; *ibid.*, p. 501 [Thomas paid for two lunatics in jail]; *ibid.*, p. 226 [Thomas paid $15 for whitewashing]; *ibid.*, p. 406 [Thomas paid for repairing rail]; GOB 1838-1843, p. 156 [Judith paid for straightjacket]; *ibid.*, p. 264 [Henry Cousins paid for ford]
101. GOB 1838-1843, p. 403 [Milly paid for Sims coffin]; Elisha Sims is occasionally referred to as Elijah and his last name sometimes spelled "Syms." All information on Sims is from the GPPT records. 1788 through 1837 and the USCG 1810, 1820 and 1830. He is presumed to have been alone and possibly a resident of the Poor House because there are no Sims at all in the 1840 Goochland census.
102. GOB 1844-1852, p. 416 [John Pierce paid for coffin]; Circuit Court Common Law Order Book 5 1863-1883, pp. 149, 184, 272, 318 [William Pierce paid for guarding jail]; GOB 1862-1871, p. 455 [Martha Jane Cousins paid for feeding jurors in Commonwealth versus Mat Jasper]; *ibid.*, p. 565 [Philip Cousins Overseer of Poor]; Hening, *op. cit.*, XII, pp. 27-28 [Overseer's duties]. Although the circumstantial evidence indicates that Philip Cousins was a son of Milly's daughter Lydia, there is some question about this.
103. GOB 1844-1852, p. 131 [Franklin paid $5 allowance]
104. _____ Acts 1847-1848, pp. 119, 120. The law forbade blacks to assemble and forbade a slave to remain on anyone's property for more than four hours without his master's permission. For good discussions of the relationships between free blacks and slaves, see Russell, *Free Negro*, pp. 130-137 and Berlin, *op. cit.*, pp. 269-70.
105. GDB 36, p. 222 [Milly's will]; GOB 1852-1862, p. 46 [Franklin allowed to register]; GFN # 957 Franklin registered in 1853.

106. Circuit Superior Court of Law and Chancery Order Book 1847-1863, p. 110 Milly paid in April and p. 198, Franklin paid in September; GOB 1844-1852, p. 521 [Franklin's pay]
107. Frazier, *op. cit.*, pp. 192-205, 300-313; Berlin, *op. cit*, pp. 57, 247 [privileged position of mulattos]. The Goochland tax records are inconsistent throughout in the designations of individuals as free Negroes or mulattos, but at various points both John and Milly are described as mulatto; GFN #128 John Pierce, Jr., 1814; *ibid.*, # 662 Judith Pierce, 1842; *ibid.*, # 683 Mary Pierce, 1843; *ibid.*, # 957 Franklin French, 1853.
108. Thomas Jefferson, *Writings: Notes on Virginia* (The Library of America, New York, 1984), p. 270 [racial mixture]
109. For discussions of white preference for mulattos, see Berlin, *op. cit.*, p. 151 and Frazier, *op. cit.*, pp. 145-146; Morgan, *op. cit.*, p. 314 [brutish sort]
110. Paul Finkelman, *Slavery and the Founders: Race and Liberty in the Age of Jefferson* (Armonk, N.Y., 1996) pp. 129, 142-143. [Jefferson's slaves]
111. _____. Legislative Petitions, Goochland, MS. A7095-1831 [petition for removal of free blacks]
112. *Ibid.*
113. *Ibid.* Harris, Morris and Fleming each owned land that according to the land tax records adjoined Milly's at one time or another.
114. Examples of increased legislative pressure on free blacks: _____, Acts 1819, p. 22-23. Overseers to check every three months for free Negro self-sufficiency, if not, declared vagrants. Not allowed to deal with slaves without consent of master; if do so, declared vagrant; Acts, 1822, p. 35. Instead of punishment in penitentiary for two or more years, stripes and banishment; Acts, 1824, p. 37. Punishment for grand larceny to value of $10 or more punishable with stripes, sale and banishment.
115. Berlin, *op. cit.*, pp. 136, 397, 399 [Virginia population figures]; USCG 1820 and 1830 [Goochland population figures]
116. Kenneth S. Greenburg, *The Confessions of Nat Turner and Related Documents* (Bedford Books of St. Martins Press, Boston, 1996), pp. 21, 22 [Nat Turner Rebellion]
117. *Ibid.*
118. _____. Documents of the Virginia General Assembly, House of Delegates 1832, Document 1, p. 1 [Governor Floyd's remarks]; Goochland County Minute Book 1811-1818, pp. 440-441 [George, Grandison and Plato ordered to be hanged between 11 am and 3 pm, June 5, 1818]; *ibid.*, p. 439 [John Binns charged and acquitted]
119. John Binns [Bins] was the son of Gabriel and Sally Binns. Gabe Binns registered in 1814 as GFN #150 and cited his emancipation by Thomas Pleasants, Jr. His wife was named in the 1813 GPPT; John Binns never registered; Goochland County Minute Book 1811-1818, pp. 440-443 [Testimony in the trial of George, Grandison and Plato]
120. GFN # 138 Royal Cowig registered at 21 in 1814. GFN # 758 Clarissa Cowig or Cowigg registered in 1847 and cited her emancipation by Thomas

Milly Pierce

Pleasants, Jr.; Goochland County Minute Book 1811-1818, p. 441 [Testimony Binns and Cowigg]
121. Goochland County Minute Book 1811-1818, pp. 439-440 [Sentencing of slaves]; _____, Acts of 1817 (Richmond, 1818), p. 5 [Appropriation for executed slaves]
122. GPPT 1817 John Binns owned 1 horse or mule and 1 slave over 16 years; After 1817, John Binns disappears from this and all Goochland records.
123. _____, Documents of the Virginia General Assembly, House of Delegates, Document 1, p. 2. [Governor Floyd's remarks]
124. *Ibid.*
125. Jefferson, *op. cit.*, p. 264-270 [deportation]
126. GOB, p. 216 [Sheriff to interview free blacks]; _____, Acts 1855-1856, p. 37 [right to be a slave]
127. Jefferson, *op. cit.*, p. 264 [Deep rooted prejudices]
128. Worrall, *op. cit.*, pp. 290-291 [Quaker interest in colonization]
129. Agee, *op. cit.*, p. 170. James Pleasants was born at "Green Level" (later called "Contention") at Crozier, Va. In 1769 and died there in 1836.
130. *Ibid.*, pp. 179-180 [Pleasants' career]; *The Annual Reports of the American Society for Colonizing the Free People of Color of the United States*, Volumes 1-10, 1818-1827 (Negro Universities Press, NY, 1969) Seventh Annual Report, p. 169, 1824 and following. [James Pleasants involvement]
131. Worrall, *op. cit.*, p. 291 [Quaker disillusion]
132. _____, Acts of 1831-1832, pp. 20-24 [act for reducing into one...]; _____. Journal of the Senate of Virginia, 1832, Bill no. 6
133. _____, Acts 1831-1832, p. 20 [no preaching or assembly]
134. *Ibid.*, p. 21 [certification of agricultural products]; United States Agricultural Census, Goochland County, 1850. Only this census which lists her real estate as 23 acres suggests that Milly still held the 2 acres at the Courthouse, although it was listed as the property of John Pierce deceased through 1855.
135. *Ibid.*, p. 22 [trades]; Russell, *Free Negro*, 151 [barbers]; Berlin *op. cit.*, pp. 235-236 [barbers]
136. *Ibid.*, p. 24 [no trial by jury]; Russell, *Free Negro*, 104-106 [trial and punishment of free blacks after 1832]
137. *Ibid.*, p. 21 [no firearms]; GOB 29, p. 449 [Austin Isaacks to keep a gun]; GOB 32, p. 80 [search for guns]; _____, Acts 1839, p. 24 [firearms search]
138. _____, Acts 1833, p. 51 [mixed blood exception]
139. _____, Acts 1832, p. 21 [slave ownership]
140. USCG 1810. Milly owned two slaves; GPPT 1810 through 1860. Pierce, Cousins, Isaacks, and Moss slave ownership. Milly owned 3 slaves in 1812 through 1814 and 4 in 1815. Austin Isaacks paid taxes on three slaves in 1818. Daniel Moss paid tax on three slaves in 1819. GOB 30, p. 165 [Austin Isaacks collateral]
141. USCG 1840, [Judith's household]; USCG 1830 [Judith's household]
142. Russell, *Free Negro*, p. 77, p. 170 [Free blacks owning their spouses]
143. GPPT 1832 [John Pierce, Jr.'s slaves]

144. Hening, *op. cit.*, IV, p. 133 [1723 disenfranchisement]; Hening, *op. cit.*, VI, pp. 39-40 [1782 law]; _____ Acts 1849-1850, p. 7 [penalty on taxes]
145. *Ibid.* [$1 poll tax]; GDB 38, p. 494 [Moses Mayo dead]
146. United States Social Census Goochland 1850 [Goochland wages]; Russell, *Free Negro,* p. 147 and Berlin, *op. cit.,* p. 229 [free blacks work for less]; Luther Porter Jackson, "The Virginia Free Negro Farmer and Property Owner 1830-1860," *Journal of Negro History,* 24 (1939), pp. 394-395 [value to small farmer]
147. GDB 36, p. 222 [Milly's will]; GLT 1851 [Value of Milly's farm]; GDB 36, p. 311 [Inventory of Milly's estate]
148. GDB 20, p. 530 [Samuel Woodson's will]; GMR, 1812, p. 353 [Pierce m. Cousins]; USCG 1850 Henry Cousins gave his profession as cooper. His father Francis was also a cooper. Henry Cousins first appears in the Goochland records when he is listed in the column for "white male titheables" in the personal property ledger for 1809. The tax collector's assumption that all free taxpayers must be white gives some small indication of how oxymoronic "free black" was to the white mind. To designate those taxpayers who were not white, "free Negroe" or "f.n." was noted next to the appropriate names. GLT 1811 [location of Lydia's ½ acre]; The deed to this ½ acre and to 134 acres purchased 1841 are in Lydia's name only and both were carried in the land tax ledger in her name only.
149. Lebsock, *op. cit.,* pp. 17-18 [19th century marriage]; USCG 1820 Cousins household; two sons, two daughters; USCG 1830 Cousins household: four sons, four daughters
150. GFN # 000 1823 Henry Cousins registered at age 31 and cited the Pleasants' wills as his source of freedom. The lack of a number suggests there may have been some question about his registration, although it seems to have caused him no problems. He registered again in 1852 as # 868 at age 65. Francis Cousins registered as "Frank" # 290 at age 66 in 1822 and cited the Pleasants' wills.
151. Stephen B. Weeks, *Southern Quakers and Slavery* (Baltimore, 1896), pp. 213-215 [Pleasants prominence]; Daniel Call, *Reports of Cases Argued and Adjudged in the Court of Appeals of Virginia* [Richmond, Michie Co., 1900], vol. 2, p. 329 John Pleasants' will
152. Call, *op. cit.,* p. 330 [Jonathan Pleasants' will]
153. Worrall, *op. cit.,* pp. 225-226 [Robert Pleasants and law of 1782]
154. Call, *op. cit.,* p. 31 [property versus liberty]; Berlin, *op. cit.,* p. 101 [changing attitudes to manumissions]
155. Call, *op. cit.,* pp. 329-341 [arguments in the Pleasants case]
156. *Ibid.,* p. 333 [Marshall quote]
157. GFN Only those who were born prior to 1800 and cited the Pleasants' wills when they registered are included in these figures
158. GMR p. 78 [Francis m. Chloe Cousins]; GPPT 1801 Both Francis Cousins and Edward Fuzmore are listed as planters on Robert Pleasants' land. Luther Porter Jackson, *Virginia Negro Soldiers and Seamen in the Revolutionary*

Milly Pierce

War, (Guide Quality Press, Norfolk, Va. 1944), p. 33. He is listed as Francis Cozens in *Virginia Soldiers of the American Revolution*, compiled by Hamilton J. Eckenrode (Virginia State Library, Richmond, 1989), p. 116 and in the NARS Revolutionary War Service Index, Reel 12, General Index Card 2273. For a thorough history of free blacks in the Revolution see Benjamin Quarles, *The Negro in the American Revolution* (University of North Carolina Press, Chapel Hill, 1961).

159. Quarles, *Revolution*, p. 183 [legislature forces masters to free slave soldiers]; *ibid.*, p. 8 [free Negroes in militia]; *ibid.*, pp. 80, 108-110 [bounties]; Berlin, *op. cit.*, p. 19 [best be spared]

160. Jackson, *Virginia Negro Soldiers*, p. 33 [Francis enlists]; Hening, *op. cit.*, IX, p. 280 [Certificate of Freedom required]; Russell, *Free Negro*, p. 110 and Jackson, *Virginia Negro Soldiers*, p. vi [Negro roles in army]; Jackson, *op. cit.*, p. 1 [Banks]; Jackson, *ibid.*, and "Virginia Negro Soldiers and Seamen in the American Revolution," *Journal of Negro History*, vol. XXVII, no. 3 (July, 1842), pp. 247-287 [other Goochland free blacks in Revolution]; Margaret Walker, "Goochland's Post-Revolutionary Militia," *Goochland County Historical Society Magazine*, vol. 4, no. 2, p. 14 [Mealys served]. John Banks, born free in Goochland in 1749, served for two years 1779-1781 in TheoderickBland's regiment and was awarded an annual pension of $90 per year in 1818. His brother Jacob served as a wagoneer in the service of supply. Others from Goochland who served were George Tyler, Isaac Howell, James Johns, James Cooper, John Cowigg, and James Mealy.

161. PPT 1815 [Francis last on R. Pleasants dec'd. land]; USCG 1810 Cousins household; GPPT 1805 Francis a cooper; GPPT 1811 Francis a planter or farmer; GPPT 1804 Francis owns first horse; GDB 21, p. 137 [Page to Cousins]; GDB 22, p. 191 [Francis emancipates Ridley]; GFN # 238 Ridley registered in 1822 at 30 citing the court decree and her ownership by Charles Logan. GMR, p. 366 [Ridley Cousins m. John Copland]; GFN # 231 registered in 1819 at 30 as former property of Charles Logan's estate. Copland is also spelled Coupland and Copeland. Why Ridley, alone, of Francis Cousins' children remained in bondage in 1816 is unclear. Henry is listed in the 1809 GPPT as a free male and was only in his early twenties in 1812 when he married Lydia Pierce, yet, although he was not yet 30, both are evidence that he enjoyed the privileges of a free black. Conceivably, Robert Pleasants had given all of Francis's family in his possession their freedom once the court case was settled, but Ridley, owned by Charles and Mary Logan, had remained under their control awaiting the outcome of a few relatively minor legal questions referred back to the lower court by the Court of Appeals. Mary Logan had opposed the emancipations, pleading that "her husband had died indebted to several persons," those debts secured by the slaves in dispute (Call, *op. cit.*, p. 330).

162. USCG 1830 Cousins household; GPPT 1818 Cousins' slaves; there were two sons between the ages of 10 and 24 in the Cousins' household; USCG 1840 Henry Cousins household included one female slave 10-24 years of age.

163. GFN # 637 Lydia Cousins and # 636 Elizabeth, "about 21 and yellow."

164. GDB 36, p. 305 David Royster to Lydia Cousins, GLT 1841 23 free black landowners. The women were: Lydia Cousins, 134 ½ acres; Polly Cousins (no relation), 2 ½ acres; Milly James, 9 ¼ acres (jointly with Timothy Pleasants); Charlotte Lynch, 1 acre: Milly Pierce, 21 acres; and Rissa, 1 acre.
165. There is no record of agricultural production in either Lydia or Henry's name in either 1850 or 1860 (US Agricultural Census Goochland), and in his 1869 suit to settle Henry Cousins estate, Lydia's son John described this 134 acres as "poor land" (Chancery Cases, File 6).
166. GOB 1844-52, p. 35 [Francis Cousins will proved November, 1844]; GDB 34, p. 41 [Francis Cousins' will]; GLT 1844, Francis Cousins taxed on 4 tracts west of the Courthouse totaling 236 1/6 acres; GDB 34, p. 89 [Francis Cousins' inventory]
167. GDB 34, p. 41 [Francis Cousins' will]
168. Russell, *Free Negro*, p. 88 [property rights]; GLT 1792-1860 [free black landowners]; twenty of these relatively rare propertied free blacks were members of the Pierce-Cousins clan, both blood relatives and relatives by marriage.
169. GOB 1844-1852, p. 42 [Walter Cousins appointed executor]; GDB 37, p. 380. This deed of May, 1848 refers to Samuel and his wife Frances as living in Ohio and Frederick and his wife Phebe in Fluvanna; GOB 1844-1852, p. 115. Walter's accounts were audited by Walter Coles, Thomas B. Gay, Esq., and James B. Ferguson, Esq.
170. GOB 1844-1852, p. 114 [Walter sues Henry Lynch]; *ibid.*, p. 163 [Walter fails to appear; judgment against him]; *ibid.*, p. 211 [Thomas James qualifies as Chloe's administrator]; *ibid.*, p. 214 [Walter protests]
171. GOB 1844-1852, p. 230 [Coplands sue]; GDB 35, p. 172 [Francis Cousins to John Copland]; GOB Book 1844-1852, p. 269 [Cousins to Copland]; *ibid.*, p. 273 [Copland suit dismissed]
172. GLT 1850 Francis's land listed as sold for taxes; GLT 1852 taxes paid, and Francis's land stricken from sold for taxes list. Chancery Suits File 6, Goochland Courthouse [Philip Cousins v. Cousins heirs]
173. GMR p. 332 [Philip Cousins m. Lucy Ann Lynch June 22, 1846]; GDB 37, p. 380 [39 ¾ acres to Philip Cousins, May 1848]; GDB 37, p. 436 [Agreement between Henry and Philip for 30 acres also adjoining the property of his aunt Charlotte and her husband Henry Lynch]; Goochland Record Order Books 1852-1862 p. 270 [Henry sues for his ½ of 100 acres]; *ibid.*, p. 330 [Henry awarded his 50 acres]; *ibid.*, p. 349 [Henry and Lydia Cousins acknowledge deed of Jan. 19, 1858 to Philip for 50 acres]
174. GOB 1852-1862, p. 373 [Henry qualifies as executor]; *ibid.*, p. 437 [Philip appointed committee for Milley; James Copland his security]; *ibid.*, p. 610 [Henry moves to Philip's removal]; *ibid.*, p. 671 [Evelina moves to remove Philip]; USCG 1850 and 1860. In 1850, Milley is listed as age 66 and "insane." She does not appear in the 1860 census.
175. GOB Book 1844-1854, p. 208 [Kinney versus Cousins]; GOB 32, p. 125 [1832 order to bind out]

176. GOB 24, p. 205 [John Pierce, Jr. bound to Samuel Johnson]; GOB 31, p. 449 [Powder versus Cousins]; USCG 1850 [Henry Cousins household includes Kinneys]
177. Goochland Chancery Order Book 1871-1873, p. 10 [Cousins versus Pierce]
178. USCG 1860 Margaret Cousins, 40, living with Cragwall and an infant Henry Cousins; USCG 1870 Henry Cousins, now John J. Cousins, 10; Goochland Circuit Court Common Law Order Book 6 1883-1916, p. 88 John J. Cragwall, administrator, sues for Margaret Cousins' estate. In USCG 1850, the only member of Cragwall's household was Edward Cooper, an 84 year old farmhand.
179. Hening, *op. cit.*, III, pp. 86-87 [1691 law regarding white/black relationships]; USCG 1840, 1850, 1860: Five white men can be identified as co-habiting with a free black woman when there is no other adult female in the household: Jack Ragland, M.F. Anderson and E. Johns in 1840. George W. Cox with Evy Gray and Elijah Cragwall with Betsy Randolph in 1850; and John J. Cragwall with Margaret Cousins in 1860. One white woman Anna Thurston, age 65, lived with John Jenkins, 65, a free black male in 1860.
180. Legislative Petitions, Goochland, 1850 ms. (no number) divorce petition of Mary J. Terry.
181. USCG 1850 and 1860 Elijah R. Cragwall household
182. Legislative Petitions, Goochland, 1831, ms. 7095 [John J. Cragwall, a signer]; Agee, *op. cit.*, p. 135. John and Elijah Cragwall's father, Samuel N. Cragwall, and his wife Nancy donated the land on which Bethel Methodist Church was built in 1834.
183. USCG 1870 [John Cragwall age]; USCG 1860 [Margaret identified as a seamstress]; Lebsock, *op. cit.*, pp. 97-99 [seamstresses]; GDB 40, p. 466 [Cragwall to Cousins]; USCG 1870 [all property in Margaret's name and values]
184. GOB 1852-1862, p. 97, [Peyton charged]; Hening, *op. cit.*, III, p. 102 and IV, p. 127 [Courts of Oyer and Terminer-slave trials]; _____, Acts 1832, p. 24 [free blacks denied trial by jury]; GOB 1852-1862, p. 99 [Peyton's trial]
185. GOB 1872-1873, p. 10 [Cousins versus Pierce]; GDB 38, p. 715 [Mary and Jane Pierce deed for Cedar Point]; Goochland Chancery Order Book 1874-1785, p. 45 [Mary Pierce's land divided]; *ibid.*, p. 207 [Margaret's case as creditor dismissed]; Goochland Circuit Court Common Law Order Book 6 1883-1916, p. 88 [Cousins versus Cocke]
186. GOB 1862-1871, p. 3 [Cousins versus Cousins]. Details of the case are in File 6, Goochland Chancery cases. Lebsock, *op. cit.*, pp. 100-111 [Independence of free black women]
187. Lebsock, *op. cit.*, p. 136 [quote] and p. 142 [concern for female heirs]; United States Social Census, Goochland 1860 [Lydia's death]; GDB 39, p. 295 [Lydia's will]; USCG 1860 Philip identified as propertied boatman; GMR, p. 332 Philip Cousins m. Lucy Ann Lynch, June 22, 1846, James Copland and Walter Cousins, witnesses. Lucy Ann was the daughter of Henry Cousins'

sister Charlotte Lynch; GFN # 866 Fields Cousins registered; GFN # 654 John Cousins registered and disappears from Goochland records; GFN # 995 Henry Cousins registered; USCG 1860 Henry Cousins household.
188. Lebsock, *op. cit.*, p. 103-111 [Non-marriage among free black women]
189. GFN # 707 Philip Cousins registered at 21; in his 1878 lawsuit (Chancery Case File 6), Philip Cousins lists his wife as Lucy Ann, the daughter of his paternal aunt Charlotte Lynch. Mary Cousins does not appear in the marriage register, but Lydia refers to her in the will as Mary Francis; Margaret Cousins in her 1872 suit names her as the wife of Robert Francis; and she registered in 1863 as Mary Ann Francis, formerly Cousins, GFN # 2033, age 37, and "bright yellow." According to the marriage register, an Elizabeth Cousins married James S. Woodson in 1853 (p. 390), but Lydia's daughter Elizabeth was still at home in 1860, and it appears that she died prior to 1871 when her executor sued her aunt Evelina Lynch over rents which may have been owed to her father's estate (OB 1862-71, p. 526). Margaret Cousins was living with John Cragwall when Lydia died.
190. Goochland Chancery Cases, File 6. In his statement to the court, John Cousins states that Henry died in 1868, intestate.
191. GOB 1862-1871, p. 359 [John Cousins sues other heirs]; details of the case are in File 6, Goochland Chancery cases. The case was not settled until 1876.
192. USCG 1870 [Martha Jane Cousins household and assets]; Common Law Order Book 1870, p. 294, Martha Jane and partners sued over the purchase of the Courthouse property and prevail. No deed could be found. GOB 1862-1872, p. 455 [Martha Jane paid for jurors' meals]
193. Berlin, *op. cit.*, p. 279 [quote]
194. GPPT 1817, 1820, 1822, 1826, 1829, and 1832. [John Pierce's slaves]
195. GPPT 1832-1858 [evidence of John Pierce's slave trading]. The tolerance of Goochland's officials towards free blacks is evident not only in the lax enforcement of some free black laws but also by the fact that the county had the second largest population of free blacks of any of the Piedmont counties in 1860. One of every nine blacks in Goochland was free; one of six in Loudon County (Russell, *Free Negro*, p. 15).
196. William Bolling, "The Diary of Col. William Bolling of Bolling Hall (1836-1839)," Part II, *Goochland County Historical Society Magazine*, vol. 9, no. 2 (Autumn, 1977), p. 23 [flood and John Pierce's boat]; *ibid.*, Part V, vol. 11, no. 1 (Spring, 1979), pp. 36-37 [ships tobacco with John Pierce]; *ibid.*, Part VII, vol. 13, 1981, p. 64 [pays for shipping wheat].
197. GPPT 1822 [John Pierce's holdings]; GDB 25, p. 144 [loan to father]
198. USCG 1830 [John Pierce's slaves]; Luther Porter Jackson, *Free Negro Labor and Property Holding in Virginia* (New York, 1942), pp. 210-211 [practices of slave owners]
199. Schwarz, *op. cit.*, p. 393 [boatmen and others owned slaves]; GOB 32, p. 95 [Court ordered Pierce's hands to work road]. Eight of Stanard's hands to work on one road, and John Pierce's hands to work on another.
200. William Bolling, *op. cit.*, vol. 11, no 1, p. 36 [John Pierce's hands working the canal]; Bolling, *ibid.* [dines at John Pierce's]

Milly Pierce

201. Bolling, *op. cit.*, vol. 11, no. 2, p. 83 [Tom Pierce fiddler]; *ibid.*, vol. 15, p. 66 [Madison Pierce builds pillars]
202. Bolling, *op. cit.*, vol. 11, no. 1, p. 41 [sits on riverbank with John Pierce]; in 1847, Pierce bought 451 acres owned by Shelton (GDB 35, p. 67).
203. Jackson, *Free Negro Labor*, p. 211 and 211n [John Pierce commercial slaveowner]
204. Schwarz, *op. cit.*, p. 319 [Number of free black slaveowners]; _____, Acts 1832, p. 21 [slave owning restricted]. Both John Pierce's family and his wife's family were free; there appear to have been no enslaved family members.
205. USCG 1850 [Philip and Sam Cousins, boatmen]; USCG 1860 [James Cousins, boatman]
206. Russel, *Free Negro*, pp. 130-137 and Berlin, *op. cit.*, pp. 57, 269-273 offer good discussions of the relationships between free blacks and slaves.
207. Gaillard Hunt, ed., *The Writings of James Madison*, (New York, 1900-1910). 9 vol., vol. 1, p. 107 [James Madison on free blacks. Letter to Joseph Jones, Nov. 28, 1780]. Berlin, *op. cit.*, pp. 271-277 [attitudes of upwardly mobile free blacks]
208. John Pierce, Jr. appears in neither the Goochland nor the Richmond census for 1840. In 1841, he appears in the Richmond Personal Property taxes, paying tax on 2 slaves, 1 horse or mule and a carry-all (vehicle). He reappears in the Goochland personal property taxes in 1846 with a note that he was a resident of Richmond and paid taxes on 3 slaves and 3 horses/mules. Berlin, *op. cit.*, p. 175 [statistics re: urbanization]
209. GFN # 662 Judith registered in 1842 at age 50; RDB 69A, p. 94 [Judith purchased Lot 12 on west side of Third St. from David Judah]; USCR 1820 [Page Carter is listed as a resident]; USCR 1830 [Phoebe Carter is listed as a resident]. An 1852 deed of gift (GDB 37, p. 101) refers to Thomas as "now residing in Danville." He appears in the Personal Property taxes in Goochland through 1849. RDB 56, p. 635 [William Henry Pierce buys Duval Street Lot from David Judah]; RDB 56, p. 636 [William Henry Pierce "of Goochland" sells Duval Street lot]; RDB 72B, p. 24 [James Madison Pierce's property]; Goochland Chancery Order Book 1871-1873, p. 4 [Cherry St. property sold to settle Henry Cousins' estate. Chancery Cases, File 6 describes property. Could not find deed.]
210. Russell, *Free Negro*, p. 150 and Berlin, *op. cit.*, 273-274 [lure of the city]; Russell, *Free Negro*, pp. 150-151, Lebsock, *op. cit.*, 97-99, and Berlin, *op. cit.*, p. 218, 234-238 [Free black occupations]
211. USCG 1830 Number of black slaveowners and John Pierce's and John Lynch's households
212. GDB 32, p. 33 [John Lynch's will]; GDB 31, p. 368 [Poor to Lynch-John's farm]
213. GDB 32, p. 320 [John Lynch's estate]; Polly Lynch is identified as a spinner living on Sarah Bowles land in the GPPT in 1804 and after. John and Billy (William) are listed with her.

214. GDB 32, p. 474 [Wm. Lynch pays for clothes, gives cash]; GDB 32, p. 475 [James Poor pays Chaudoin, buys corn]; GDB 33, p. 211 [Poor collects debts]; GDB 35, p. 408 [Poor collects rents]
215. GOB 1836-1844, p. 209 [executors request hearing 1839]; GOB 1836-1844, p. 232 [second request]; GPPT 1840 to 1850 [John Lynch's estate taxed]; USCG 1840 [Lynches listed as free blacks]
216. GOB 1844-1852, p. 487 [hearing]; GDB 37, p. 206 [Poor paid Rutherford and court costs]. For more about Rutherfoord's beliefs, see p. xx this ms.
217. GDB 36, p. 196 [Poor and Lynch to Bibb-1853]; GFN 1853 # 894 James Lynch, # 896 Sally Ann Lynch, # 897 Mahala Ann Lynch and # 898 Alley [sic] Lynch. All cited John Lynch's will as the source of their freedom; GFN 1853 # 957 Franklin French registered.
218. GPPT 1846 [John Pierce, Jr. resident of Richmond]; RDB 41, p. 182 [Abbott to Pierce]; Richmond Land Tax (RLT) 1841 [Description as Southgate Garden]; RLT 1850 [value of property]; RDB 59, p. 153 [Pierce to Sterns]. Although Navy Hill was just east of Jackson Ward, a hub of the free black community, there does not appear to have been a concentration of blacks on the Pierce property. Housing in Richmond was not segregated at this time, although there were pockets of primarily black households (Elsa Barkley Brown and Gregg D. Kimbell, "Mapping the Terrain of Black Richmond," *The Journal of Urban History*, vol. 21, no. 3 [March, 1995], pp. 296-346).
219. GDB 34, p. 481 [Pope trustees to Pierce]; GLT 1846 [Holdings of Pierce and Sampson]
220. GDB 35, p. 67 [Miller (Shelton's trustee) to Pierce]; GLT 1847 Free black landowners
221. William S. Wight, *The Story of Goochland* (Richmond, 1935), pp. 20-23; Agee, *op. cit.*, pp. 94-99, 167-168 [Morsons and Seddons]
222. CeCe Bullard, *Goochland: Yesterday and Today, A Pictorial History*, (Donning, 1994), p. 12. Wight, *op. cit.*
223. GOB 34, pp. 237-238 [Indictment of Mims]
224. GOB 34, p. 237 [testimony in Mims hearing]
225. *Ibid.*
226. Goochland Superior Court Order Book 4, p. 56 [Trial of David Mims]
227. GOB 34, p. 237 [Pollard and Agee testimony]
228. GLT 1848 and GPPT 1848 [Property of Pierce, Mims and jury]. Richmond Personal Property Tax (RPPT) 1848 [Pierce property]. The only wealthy juror was John Michie who owned 804 acres and 22 slaves.
229. Both the Pope and Shelton properties had been sold because the owners were unable to meet the terms of their deeds of trust (mortgages); GOB 20, p. 468 [Pierce versus Gay]; Circuit Superior Court of Law and Chancery Order Book, Goochland, 1837-1842, p. 358 [Pierce versus Robert R. Watkins] and p. 384 [Pierce versus Robert and John Watkins]; Superior Court Orders 1831-1855, p. 356, and Chancery Cases File 20 [Pierce versus Pope].
230. GPPT 1838 [Pierce paid tax on barouche; other vehicle owners]
231. Berlin, *op. cit.*, p. 89 [quote]
232. United States Agricultural Census, Goochland 1850 [Mims' real estate]

Milly Pierce

233. USCG 1840 slaves owned by David Mims. There were also 7 free blacks on his property. USCG 1860 Mims household
234. GDB 35, p. 600 [Mims emancipates Matilda]; GMR, p. 334 Matilda Mims m. Tarlton Tyler. GFN # 1083 Tarlton Tyler registered in 1860 at age 33; GFN # 159 George Tyler registered at age 60 in 1814; Jackson, *Free Negro Soldiers*, p. 45 [George Tyler in Revolution]; Margaret Walker, *op. cit.* p. 14 [George Tyler in militia]; GDB 36, p. 323 [Mims emancipates Judy and children]
235. GDB 1862-1871, p. 111 [Mims' will]
236. *Ibid.*
237. Agee, *op. cit.*, pp. 99-101 [Martin Robinson]
238. GDB 1862-1871, p. 111 [Mims' will]; Samuel Mims, *Leaves from the Mims Family Tree: A Genealogic History* (Minden, La., 1961) [Family names]
239. GOB 32, p. 57 [Mims and Copland sued by Cousins]; GOB 36, p. 221 [Mims security for Philip Cousins]
240. Agee, *op. cit.*, p. 174 [Rutherfoords and Rock Castle]
241. _____, Journal of the House of Delegates, 1853 (Richmond, 1853); John C. Rutherfoord, *Speech of John C. Rutherfoord of Goochland in the House of Delegates of Virginia, on the Removal from the Commonwealth of the Free Colored Population, Delivered February 18, 1853* (Ritchie and Dunnavant, Richmond, 1853).
242. *Ibid.*, p. 4 [idle, ignorant]; pp. 6-7 [crime figures]; Russell, *Free Negro*, p. 165 [remarks of Gov. William B. Giles]
243. Rutherfoord, *op. cit.*, p. 8 [burden to slaves]; USCG 1850 Residents of Poor House
244. *Ibid.*, p. 5 [threat to peace and happiness etc]
245. *Ibid.*, pp. 13-14 [horrors of free Negro life]
246. *Ibid.*, p. 9 [life in Liberia]; *ibid.*, p. 20 [agents of providence]
247. Berlin, *op. cit.*, p. 104 [pathetic hope]
248. _____, Documents of the Virginia General Assembly 1854 (William F. Ritichie, 1853-40), Document 1, p. 15 [Governor's remarks]
249. Rutherfoord, *op. cit.*, p. 20 [secret sympathies]
250. Mary and Jane Pierce apparently lived in the Courthouse house until 1855, the last year it is listed as the property of John Pierce deceased, when they moved to Cedar Point [GDB 38, p. 715 Cedar Point purchase]
251. Berlin, *op. cit.*, pp. 270-271 and Genovese, *op. cit.*, 273-275 [Discussion of free blacks and slaves]
252. USCG 1860 [Henley household]; Helene B. Agee, "Dover Baptist Church, Manakin, Virginia," *Goochland County Historical Society Magazine*, vol. 21, 1989, pp. 37-38, 39 [the plot]
253. Agee, *Dover*, pp. 37-38, 39 [Consequences of DuVal plot]; Mrs. Bernard Henley who died at 100 in 1996 told the author she remembered seeing Caroline arrive at Dover.
254. Hustings Court Minutes Richmond (RCM), 23, p. 12 [William Cousins to work off jail debt]; *ibid.*, p. 129 [William again in jail]

255. John managed to elude the census taker entirely in 1840. He appears in the Richmond Personal Property records only sporadically. RCM 26, p. 102 [John and Eliza register]
256. Chesterfield County Marriage Register, p. 163 [John Pierce m. Eliza Liggon (sic)]; RCM 26, p. 102 [Pierce children]; GPPT from 1853 on, John Pierce (3) and Madison Pierce are listed together right after John Pierce, Jr. USCG 1860 John Pierce, a 28 year old mulatto was living with James Madison Pierce, a 44 year old mulatto, and William Henry Pierce, a 42 year old mulatto is listed in the household of John Thompson, Jr., hotel keeper. The most logical explanation of Madison and William's parentage is that they were John Pierce, Jr.'s children. They were not Milly's, and based on the ages and marriages of Milly's other children, they could not have belonged to any of them.
257. Chesterfield County Deed Book 21, p. 273 [WinnyLigon buys lot in Manakintown]
258. United States Agricultural Census Goochland 1850 [Pierce versus Sampson]; GPPT 1850-60 [John Pierce's slaves] and RPPT 1850-60. John never kept more than three slaves in Richmond. Presumably, they were personal and house servants.
259. RDB 56, p. 343 [Mayo executors to Pierce]; RDB 59, p. 233 [Two lots on Concord Street]; RDB 60, p. 521 [Sells one of Concord St. lots to John Dwyer]; RDB 59, p. 266 [Goddin to Pierce 100 sq. feet at Marshall and 15th for $900]; RDB 59, p. 267 [Green to Pierce 65 x 100 ft. at Marshall and 15th for $1200. Land was east of 15th and north of Marshall]; Brown and Kimbell, *op. cit.*, p. 301 [Shockoe Valley]
260. RDB 66, 305 [Rutherfoord to Pierce, Pierce to Rutherfoord recorded at same time]
261. GDB 34, p. 481 [Harris security for Pope purchase]; GDB 35, p. 67 [Harris and Morris securities for Shelton purchase]
262. Berlin, *op. cit.*, pp. 339-340 [Alliances with whites]
263. GPPT 1838 [Thompson merchants license]; GDBs 32-37 are littered with deeds of trust to John Thompson, Jr. GDB 34, p. 461 [Thompson acquires lease of ½ of Ben Dover]; GDB 37, p. 415 [Slaves as collateral]
264. GDB 32, p. 1 [John Thompson security for Fleming]; GDB Book 33, p. 276 [John Thompson, Jr. deed of trust on Courthouse tract. Cannot find actual deed. This deed of trust June 19, 1843. The land is first listed in Thompson's name in the land tax in 1842.]
265. GPPT, 1841 John Thompson, Jr. and John T.A. Martin paid tax on 4 slaves over 16. In 1842, Thompson only paid tax on 5 mature slaves and 6 horses and mules. Over the next 8 years the number of slaves varies from 0 to 19, the number of horses or mules from 2 to 18, both with fluctuations in between. Circuit Superior Court of Law and Chancery Order Book 1837-1847, p. 378 [David R. Shelton sues Pierce and Thompson for debt]
266. GDB 35, pp. 426-427 [Pierce to Thompson]; GFB 35, p. 67 [Pierce buys Shelton land]; GDB, pp. 422-423 [Pierce to Miller]; 1851GLT 1851 [value of Pierce property]

267. GDB 38, p. 503 [new deed of trust on Shelton property]; GDB 38, p. 327 [new deed of trust on Pope property]
268. RDB 70A, p. 77 [Deed of trust on his residence]; RDB 60, p. 521; RDB 63, p. 610; RDB 64, p. 331; RDB 66, p. 320; RDB 69A, p. 264; and RDB 71A, p. 238; [Pierce sales of Richmond property]; RDB 64, p. 331 [Sale to Central Virginia Railroad]
269. Details of these suits are covered in John Pierce versus James Madison Pierce, this ms.: GDB 38, p. 715 [Pierce to Jane and Mary Pierce]; GDB 38, p. 620 [Pierce to Haden]; GDB Book, 39, pp. 316-317 [Pierces and Haden satisfy lien]; GDB 38, p. 691 [Deed of release on Pope property]; GDB 38, p. 707 [Pierce to Barret]; GLT 1860 [value of Barret land]
270. USCG 1860 [Jacob Sampson worth]; GFN 1820 Jacob Sampson registered as #242 at age 25 and a second time as #2002 at age 69 in 1862; United States Agricultural Census, Goochland, 1860 [Sampson farm production]
271. GDB 20, p. 621 [Thomas Taurman's will]; GDB 21, p. 17 [Taurman's inventory]; GLT 1810 [Taurman owned 83 acres]
272. GFN 1820 #242 Sampson; GOB 30, p. 81 [permission to stay in Goochland]; GLT 1835 Sampson actually acquired these two tracts in 1830; Jackson, *The Free Negro Farmer*, p. 241 [Number of free black farm owners]; GPPT 1835 [Sampson's slaves, horses and gig]
273. GLT 1841 Sampson adds land from Taurman and Anderson; GLT 1843 adds land from Nuckols and Ware; USCG 1850 ages of Sampson children; Slave Schedule Goochland 1860 Sampson slaves; USCG 1860 Sampson household
274. GPPT 1830 [Sampson first pays license fee]; GOB 1836-1844, p. 44 [qualifications for ordinary owner]
275. GOB, 1836-1844, p. 5 [Sampson paid fee and granted license]; GOB 1836-1844, p. 8 [Fleming motion to revoke; court splits]; GOB 1836-1844, p. 13 [license revoked]
276. _____, Journal of the General Assembly 1844/1845, p. 36 [petition rejected]; GPPT 1848-1853 [Sampson renews license]; in 1851, 1853 and later years, the General Assembly stiffened the laws regarding slaves, free blacks and alcohol. _____, Acts of the General Assembly, 1851, pp. 51-52 [restrictions on buying a drink]
277. USCG 1870 [Sampson household]; Jacob's age is given as 84 although, based on his registrations, he may have been about 75. GLT 1870 [transfer of land from Jacob to Moses and Lewis; also, Moses' land holdings]
278. Goochland Chancery Cases, File 20. All of the information on Pierce versus Pierce is based on the original documents in this file.
279. *Ibid.*
280. *Ibid.*
281. GOB 35, p. 287 [First suit against Pierce, Pierce and Thompson]. Other suits: GOB 35 p. 315, p. 351, p. 381, p. 434, p. 480 and GOB 1852-1862, p. 287, p. 434 and p. 480. United States Agricultural Census Goochland 1860 Thompson's land was valued at $12000 and his livestock at $2500. In 1852, Thompson made an agreement with the James River and Kanawha Canal Company to build a commercial warehouse for wheat and tobacco next to the

canal on his land at Cedar Point 9GDB 37, p. 862). He also was a partner with Mark Aldridge and D.W.K. Bowles in the Gilmer Mining Company, a gold mining enterprise in Goochland (GDB 37, p. 900)
282. Chancery Court Cases, File 20. John's statement is written and signed in his own hand. Madison's is written as if narrated by a second party and is certified as his statement.
283. Russell, *Free Negro*, pp. 137-141 [Education of free blacks]
284. GFN # 514 Madison, "light yellow"; _____ Acts of the General Assembly, 1830, p. 107 [education denied free blacks]
285. Berlin, *op. cit.*, p. 237 [few free black bricklayers]; Chancery Cases, File 20 [Madison's statement]
286. Chancery Cases, File 20
287. *Ibid.*
288. *Ibid.*
289. *Ibid.*
290. Chancery Cases, File 20; 1853, 1 slave leased for $97 from N.B. Vaughan; 3 slaves at $100 each from Mrs. Ann L. Miller at different periods in 1854 and 1855; 1 slave from A.J. Mills. In 1853, John paid personal property taxes on 12 slaves in Goochland. In 1854, 12 slaves in Goochland; in 1855, 12 slaves in Goochland and 2 in Richmond.
291. Chancery Cases, File 20, GPPT and GLT 1860 Madison owned nothing
292. Chancery Cases, File 20
293. *Ibid.* [Turner quote]
294. GDB 40, p. 65 [Haden to J.M. Pierce]. At this date, $5 was the customary good faith money to make a deal legal; Chancery Cases, File 20 [obligation to A.J. Mills]
295. USCG 1870 [Madison's household and William's location in Lickinghole district]; Goochland Chancery Order Book 1871-1873, p. 10 [Margaret Cousins versus Madison Pierce et al.]
296. GDB 37, p. 101 [Deed of gift from Thomas to Mary and Jane Pierce]; GDB 38, p. 48 [Mary and Jane Pierce to Harris]; GOB 35, p. 22 [Thomas Pierce to Harris. Deed ordered recorded, but cannot find actual deed]; GDB 38, p. 715 [John Pierce, Jr. to Mary and Jane Pierce]
297. Chancery Cases, File 20 [plaintiff deceased]; Circuit Court Common Law Order Book 5, p. 73 [Thomas W. Pierce versus John Pierce abated]. No will for John Pierce, Jr. could be found in either the Richmond or Goochland records.
298. RCM 26, p. 102 [John Pierce indicted]. There were two John Pierces in Richmond at this time. The second was a white constable which suggests that this refers to the free black John Pierce.
299. USCR 1860 John Pierce household; his household also included a Margaret Pierce, 53, and Judy Payne, aged 60. Eliza was still alive in 1859 when she acknowledged her agreement to the sale of the Pope property to a Richmond notary (GDB 38, p. 707), but is missing from the 1860 census. USCG 1860 [John Pierce (3) living with Madison]; United States Social Census, Henrico County, Richmond Ward 1, 1870 [Deaths of Isaac Pierce and William Pierce,

Milly Pierce

identified as mulatto barbers]; Russell, *Free Negro*, p. 151 and Berlin, *op. cit.*, p. 235 [Free Black barbers]

300. Virginius Dabney, *Richmond: the Story of a City* (New York, 1976), p. 163 [quote] and pp. 163-186 [Richmond in early 1860s]. General George McClellen was positioned just southeast of the city, and Richmond was in a frenzy of preparation for an invasion that never came. John Pierce last appears in the RPPT in 1862, suggesting that he died that year.

301. Circuit Court Common Law Order Book 5, p. 747 [Isaac Finney versus J.M. Pierce's executor]

302. Randall Robinson, *Defending the Spirit: A Black Life in America* (New York, 1998), p. 265 [Vernon Jordan disease] and p. 270 [goes along]

303. The Associated Press, "Black's Rising Suicide Rate, Middle-Class Ties Linked," *Richmond Times-Dispatch,* March 20, 1998, p. A6 [Quote from Carl Bell]

Selected Bibliography

Manuscripts

Goochland County, Virginia Clerk's Office
    Goochland Chancery Court Case Files
    Goochland County Order Books
    Goochland Court Minute Books
    Goochland Deed Books
    Goochland Superior Court of Law and Chancery Order Books

Library of Virginia
    Chesterfield County Deed Books (microfilm)
    Chesterfield County Land Taxes (microfilm)
    Goochland County Land Taxes (microfilm)
    Goochland County Legislative Petitions
    Goochland County Marriage Register (microfilm)
    Goochland County Personal Property Taxes (microfilm and ms.)
    Goochland County Register of Free Negroes
    Henrico County Register of Free Negroes
    Richmond Hustings Court Minutes (microfilm)
    Richmond Hustings Deed Books (microfilm)
    Richmond Personal Property Taxes (microfilm)
    Richmond Land Taxes (microfilm)
    United States Census 1790 – 1880 (microfilm)
    United States Agricultural Census 1850 and 1860 (microfilm)
    United States Bureau of the Census, Slave Schedules 1850 and 1860 (microfilm)
    United States Social Census 1850 and 1860 (microfilm)

Newspapers
Richmond Argus (microfilm)
Richmond Enquirer (microfilm)
Richmond Times-Dispatch

Books

    _____. Acts of the General Assembly (Virginia) 1790-1865
    _____. The Annual Reports of the American Society of Colonizing the Free People of
        Color of the United States, Vols. 1-10, New York, 1969.
    _____. Journals of the General Assembly (Virginia)
    _____. Documents of the General Assembly (Virginia)

_____. *The Negro in Virginia*, compiled by Writers of the Works Project
Administration in the State of Virginia, Winston-Salem, N.C., 1994.

Agee, Helene Barret. *Facets of Goochland County (Virginia) History*. Richmond, 1962.

Berlin, Ira et al. td. *Free At Last: A Documentary History of Slavery, Freedom and the Civil War*. New York, 1992.

_____. and Ronald Huffman, eds. *Slavery and Freedom in the Age of the American Revolution*. Charlottesville, Va., 1983.

_____. *Slaves Without Masters: The Free Negro in the Antebellum South*. New York, 1974.

Bogger, Tommy L. *Free Blacks in Norfolk, Virginia, 1790-1860: The Darker Side of Freedom*. Charlottesville, Va., 1997.

Bracey, John H., Jr. et. al., ed. *Free Blacks in America 1800-1860*. Belmont, Ca., 1971.

Bullard, CeCe. *Goochland: Yesterday and Today, A Pictorial History*. Virginia Beach, Va., 1994.

Call, Daniel. *Reports of Cases Argued and Adjudged in the Court of Appeals of Virginia*, Richmond, 1900.

Dabney, Virginius. *Richmond: The Story of a City*. New York, 1976.

Dunaway, Wayland Fuller. *History of the James River and Kanawha Canal Company*. New York, 1922.

Eckenrode, Hamilton J. *Virginia Soldiers of the American Revolution*. Richmond, 1989.

Egerton, Douglas R. *Gabriel's Rebellion: The Virginia Slave Conspiracies of 1800 and 1802*. Chapel Hill, 1993.

Finkelman, Paul, ed. *Free Blacks in a Slave Society*. New York, 1989.

_____. *Slavery and the Founders: Race and Liberty in the Age of Jefferson*. New York, 1996.

Franklin, John Jope. *From Slavery to Freedom: A History of Negro America*. 6th ed. New York, 1987.

Frazier, E. Franklin. *The Negro Family in the United States.* New York, 1948.

Genovese, Eugene D. *Roll Jordan Roll: The World the Slaves Made.* New York, 1948.

Greenburg, Kenneth S. *The Confessions of Nat Turner and Related Documents.* Boston, 1996.

Gutman, Herbert G. *The Black Family in Slavery and Freedom, 1750-1925.* New York, 1977.

Hening, William Waller, ed. *The Statues at Large, Being a Collection of All the Laws of Virginia.* 13 vols. Richmond, New York, Philadelphia, 1810-1823.

Hunt, Gaillard, ed. *The Writings of James Madison.* 9 vols. New York, 1900-1910.

Jackson, Luther Porter. *Free Negro Labor and Property Holding in Virginia.* New York, 1942.

_____. *Virginia Negro Soldiers and Seamen in the Revolutionary War.* Norfolk, 1944.

Jefferson, Thomas. *Writings: Notes on Virginia.* New York, 1984.

Lebsock, Suzanne. *The Free Women of Petersburg, Status and Culture in a Southern Town, 1784-1860.*

Mims, Samuel. *Leaves from the Mims Family Tree: A Genealogic History.* Minden, La., 1961.

Morgan, Edmund S. *American Slavery, American Freedom.* New York, 1975.

Munford, George W., ed. *The Code of Virginia.* 2nd ed. 1860.

Olmstead, Frederick Law. *A Journey in the Seaboard Slave States.* 2 vols. New York, 1904.

Quarles, Benjamin H. *The Negro in the Making of America.* New York, 1987.

_____. *The Negro in the American Revolution.* Chapel Hill, 1961.

Robinson, Randall. *Defending the Spirit: A Black Life in America.* New York, 1998.

Russell, John H. *The Free Negro in Virginia 1619-1865.* Baltimore, 1913.

Rutherfoord, John C. *Speech of John C. Rutherfoord of Goochland in the House of Delegates of Virginia, on the Removal from the Commonwealth of the Free Colored Population, Delivered February 18, 1853.* Richmond, 1853.

Ryland, Garnett. *The Baptists of Virginia 1699-1926.* Richmond, 1955.

Schwarz, Philip J. *Slaves and the Criminal Laws of Virginia, 1705-1865.* Baton Rouge, La., 1988.

Semple, Robert B. *A History of Baptists in Virginia.* Cottonport, La., 1810, reprint 1970.

Shepherd, Samuel, ed. *The Statutes At Large of Virginia.* 3 vols. Richmond, 1835.

Snavely, Tipton Ray. *The Taxation of Negroes in Virginia.* Charlottesville, Va., 1916.

Taylor, James B. *Virginia Baptist Ministers.* Series 2. Philadelphia, 1859.

Weeks, Stephen B. *Southern Quakers.* Baltimore, 1896.

Wight, William S. *The Story of Goochland.* Richmond, 1935.

EDITOR'S NOTE: The author died before she was able to put the final finishes on this manuscript, and therefore some of the footnotes are incomplete. We regret the inconvenience.

CeCe Bullard, a columnist for the Richmond (VA) *Times Dispatch* and the Richmond *Style Weekly,* edited the *Goochland County Historical Society Magazine* in which some of the Milly Pierce material originally appeared. She also taught at Virginia Commonwealth University and J. Sargeant Reynolds Community College. She was the author of *Goochland: Yesterday and Today, A Pictorial History* (1994). She earned a BA and MA from George Washington University in Washington DC. Ms. Bullard died in 1999.

Miniver Press is a publisher of lively and informative non-fiction books, specializing in history, sports, movies, biographies, music, and culture. For more information, see miniverpress.com or contact us at editor@miniverpress.com

Miniver Press would like to thank Kristie Miller and Julia Riesenberg for their help in making it possible to publish this book, and the Library of Congress for its photo archive of former enslaved persons, which inspired the cover illustration.

Made in the USA
Middletown, DE
20 June 2020